# COMMUNAL INTIMACY AND THE VIOLENCE OF POLITICS

# COMMUNAL INTIMACY AND THE VIOLENCE OF POLITICS

Understanding the War on Drugs in Bagong Silang, Philippines

**Steffen Bo Jensen and Karl Hapal**

Foreword By Vicente L. Rafael

SOUTHEAST ASIA PROGRAM PUBLICATIONS

AN IMPRINT OF CORNELL UNIVERSITY PRESS   ITHACA AND LONDON

First published 2022 by Cornell University Press

Library of Congress Cataloging-in-Publication Data

Names: Jensen, Steffen, author. | Hapal, Karl, 1987– author.
Title: Communal intimacy and the violence of politics : understanding the war on drugs in Bagong Silang, Philippines / Steffen Bo Jensen and Karl Hapal ; foreword by Vicente L. Rafael.
Description: Ithaca [New York] : Southeast Asia Program Publications, an imprint of Cornell University Press, 2022. | Includes bibliographical references and index.
Identifiers: LCCN 2021036524 (print) | LCCN 2021036525 (ebook) | ISBN 9781501762765 (hardcover) | ISBN 9781501762772 (paperback) | ISBN 9781501762789 (epub) | ISBN 9781501762796 (pdf)
Subjects: LCSH: Violence—Social aspects—Philippines—Manila Metropolitan Area. | Violence—Political aspects—Philippines—Manila Metropolitan Area. | Drug control—Political aspects—Philippines—Manila Metropolitan Area. | Law enforcement—Political aspects—Philippines—Manila Metropolitan Area. | Police-community relations—Philippines—Manila Metropolitan Area. | Poor—Philippines—Manila Metropolitan Area— Social conditions. | Social conflict—Philippines—Manila Metropolitan Area. | Manila Metropolitan Area (Philippines)—Social conditions. | Philippines— Politics and government—21st century.
Classification: LCC HN720.M36 J46 2022  (print) | LCC HN720.M36  (ebook) | DDC 303.609599/16—dc23/eng/20211115
LC record available at https://lccn.loc.gov/2021036524
LC ebook record available at https://lccn.loc.gov/2021036525

# Contents

# Foreword

*Vicente L. Rafael*

Set in the sprawling barangay of Bagong Silang in Metro Manila, Steffen Jensen and Karl Hapal's research for their book began several years ago, prior to the onset of the COVID-19 pandemic and the rise of Duterte's catastrophic drug war. What is remarkable is how little has changed through the years of their longitudinal ethnography. The staggering number of deaths from extrajudicial killings continues to rise. Policing practices built on a history of counterinsurgency are pervasive, along with the systematic violation of human rights. Reports of the sharp economic contraction brought on by the virus along with reports of massive corruption fill the news. Meanwhile, the government has effectively surrendered its maritime sovereignty to the Chinese. A different government would have sunk under all these pressures, but not Duterte's, whose popularity has been barely dented. Recent surveys continue to place the president's approval ratings at stratospheric levels. His popularity seems to be predicated on his ability to govern by fear and produce a sense of security. Understanding how and why fear has become the organizing principle for ordering urban space and governing people's lives is one of the more important tasks that Jensen and Hapal's book undertakes.

Along the way, the authors raise a number of questions. How is it that a mass murderer registers such highly positive ratings, however skeptical one might be about the methods used in these surveys? Why does Duterte's murderous rhetoric and governance by fear meet with widespread approval? And why do the sources of opposition to his authoritarian rule remain remarkably weak and largely ineffective? What can we learn from looking at the largely impoverished communities like Bagong Silang, which have experienced the most devastating effects of the drug war, yet where expressions of confidence in Duterte remain high? Indeed, is there something about the construction of community that preceded and will continue beyond Duterte's regime—something about the logic and logistics of living together—that also creates the conditions for cultivating violence and spreading death?

Jensen and Hapal approach these questions by focusing on the production of a sense of order and security through the dis-ordering force of violence. We see this, for example, in one of their accounts that show how community and violence, appear to be co-constitutive to residents of the barangay:

Kuya Jerry had been killed in a drug bust. He was the cousin of an old informant. Ten police officers had chased him. In the end, he tried to escape by climbing a light pole to get across a wall. He had been shot in the leg in the process before being killed. The police claimed it was self-defense but a neighbor, also an old informant, had seen the incident. "In the leg . . . from below . . . ?" he asked rhetorically. However, everyone knew that Kuya Jerry was on drugs and sometimes sold smaller quantities to support his habit. Asked about the incident, his sister told us, "No, we know who it was and why. We are no longer afraid. We consider it a closed deal." In this way, the family told us that violence had been predictable. They obviously did not agree with the methods, however, ". . . it was no surprise that Jerry died," as the mother continued with grief in her voice.

Here, Jerry's execution under the usual pretext that he fought back (*nanlaban*) is met with a mixture of skepticism and resignation. Recognizing the excessive violence of the police, Jerry's relatives and neighbors nonetheless cling to a narrative that sees his death as necessary and unavoidable. He was a drug user and he knew the risks he faced, and so his death was simply a matter of time. "We consider it a closed deal," his sister says, and in so doing reframes his death as the price for restoring order in the community. Fear thus emerges as the condition of possibility for living together in a time of war.

Seen from the ground up, extrajudicial killings are regarded by residents as disconcerting yet reassuring. They have the effect of cleansing the community of *adiks*, who are seen as the sources of disorder and fear. There is then something clarifying about the violence of the war insofar as it seeks to separate the deserving population from those who are undeserving, making the former's life dependent on the latter's death. It thus seeks to re-create a sense of community predicated on the exclusion of the accursed other, whose disposability defines the limits of one's security. How so? Is the dialectic of fear and security an effect of the drug war or is it that which the drug war builds upon? How does violence come to structure, though not wholly determine, the making of community? What does it take to live in close proximity and comity with one's neighbors? And do the practices of making community also bring with them the very means for its undoing?

In his classic work on nationalism, Benedict Anderson remarked on the paradoxical nature of the nation as an "imagined community," at once limited and sovereign. It is built on the circulation of novels and newspapers as well as legal fictions of equality and inclusion that transcend local identifications, yet held together by contested symbols that seek to suppress and manage social differences.

In this sense, we can think of the nationalist imaginary as constitutive of a community amid anonymity. Members of the nation will never meet each other face to face, Anderson says, but through language, print media and various other institutions, come to share a confidence in their existence within a common polity moving inexorably toward an open-ended future (Anderson 2006). Or do they?

The recent global rise of authoritarianism seems to suggest otherwise. Nationalist discourses have been used to create seemingly unbridgeable divisions, sharpening differences within the nation. The authoritarian imaginary instead views the nation as a site of perpetual struggles between the forces of good and evil understood as those who are insiders versus outsiders, lawful and deserving citizens versus poor, racialized criminals, between those who are gendered and sexualized as "normal" and those who are perverse and therefore "abnormal." For this reason, the authoritarian vision of the nation sees it as a site of unfinished civil wars. It deploys violence in all its forms as a way of governing an irreducibly pluralized population. In the case of Duterte, the figure of the "drug personality" sums up all that threatens the integrity of the nation requiring the exercise of extreme measures. Under Duterte, death becomes a means of governing life. But how is this possible? How do people come to accept the grim terms of this authoritarian imaginary? To answer this, we need to turn to the material and symbolic conditions for making community especially in places where the drug war has been most intensely waged.

As Jensen and Hapal point out, in impoverished barangays, living spaces are organized into highly compact and crowded residences—slums that warehouse people into a surplus and highly disposable population. From the outside, slums are usually seen by the respectable middle and upper classes as sites of disorder, places that are *magulo*, or dangerous, and thus in need of policing. As products of the violence inherent in the history of displacement and the conditions of precarity, slums exist as kinds of penal colonies, constraining residents to forge bonds of protection and mutual aid. The spatial and economic realities of the barangay require the formation of what they have termed a "community of intimacy." Given the flimsy housing materials and the tight pathways that serve as the only public spaces in Bagong Silang, residents are forced to live in close proximity, within the hearing and seeing of everything that happens to their neighbors. Privacy is at a premium, so everything is exposed to public knowledge. Additionally, gossip, or *tsismis* and rumor pass as information to fill in the gaps of knowledge about others and to keep everyone on guard about what others think of them. Under these conditions, as the authors point out, intimacy is both "compelled and compelling." According to one of their informants, "We have no choice. We live here and they [our neighbors] live here as well. We just need to get along with them."

The practice of "getting along" is commonly referred to in Tagalog as *pakiki-sama*, from the root word *sama*, "together." As Jensen and Hapal explain, it is a form of "affective relationality" that entails generosity, friendliness, and hospitality, sustained by networks of reciprocal obligations. *Pakiskisama* is thus less a "value" than it is a highly contingent and shifting set of practices that allow people to seek companionship and protection while enjoining mutual aid under conditions of scarcity and the constant threat of displacement. For this reason, *pakikisama* as a cultural practice essential for settling remains unsettled and unsettling. It must always be performed through such acts as ritual drinking and gambling—especially among men—sharing labor and resources, extending loans, and contributing emotional and material support to important events such as illnesses, weddings, births, and funerals among other things. The obligation to make *pakikisama*, however, requires that one be in a position to do so. Those with more resources usually have small businesses, both legal and illegal. They also enjoy the patronage of local politicians and the police by serving in the local barangay justice system as *tanods*, or security agents. Most of these are older men and some women, that is, age thirty-five and above in a population where the majority of are between the ages of eighteen and twenty-five. Their ability to make *pakikisama* is a function of their ability to engage in *diskarte*, the highly admired skill of improvising and making do that allows one to find the resources with which to help out those in need, pay off loans, bribe the police, and provide for one's family and friends, thereby enlarging one's influence and garnering respect from others.

The intimacy of community thus creates inequality and hierarchy. It privileges those who are adept at performing *pakikisama* and making *diskarte*. These are predominantly older men who have managed to accumulate resources and cultivate the skills needed for forging connections and patronage among those in authority. For this reason, as Jensen and Hapal point out, intimacy is predicated on a patriarchal gerontocracy. As exemplars of *pakikisama* and *diskarte*, older men, by virtue of their membership in the barangay justice system, also feel entitled to enforce order, disciplining younger men and "uppity" women, whom they see as falling short of the demands of intimacy. Discipline in this case includes violent measures to keep those below in line and contain their potential for disrupting community. Generosity and mutual aid come with the violent imperative to secure the boundaries of intimacy exercised by a "patriarchy of the street." Such violence also serves to divide the spaces of community between those who belong and those who do not by virtue of their failure to participate in *pakikisama*. The violence of intimacy constitutes a policing power that secures the line between those who are part of and those who are apart from community, between those who contribute to the bonds of friendship and hospitality and those who are potential threats to their functioning.

The fact that intimacy faces two ways is not surprising. It holds the private up for public regard even as it demarcates an inside that must be kept safe from the outside. It is sustained by amity that is grounded on hostility and fosters conditional hospitality that sets rules and relies on the enforcement of the inhospitable. The drug war is built precisely on the contradictory structures of the community of intimacy, which exposes its doubleness, the authors point out, as both a "resource and a risk." Beginning with compiling the illegal drug lists required to conduct police operations, intimate knowledge of one's neighbors along with the workings of gossip and rumor allow for the targeting of suspects by the police. The collaboration of mostly older male barangay officials with the police and vigilantes weaponizes community into the site for counterinsurgency as suspected enemies—those who are disruptive and fail to perform *pakikisama*—are identified for execution. The drug war thus did not determine the violence inherent in community; but it amplified and transformed it by exploiting existing hierarchies and inequalities. It generated a fear beyond the everyday fear of living precariously under the threat of constant displacement. It presented this other fear as a kind of regenerative violence necessary for the removal of the undeserving who endanger community. In other words, the drug war is a violent event that intensified the violence already inherent in the structuring of the community of intimacy. It exposed something about the material and symbolic constitution of community itself: its autoimmunity.

Autoimmunity is usually defined in biological terms as the condition of becoming immune to one's own self, as if one harbored foreign bodies that threatened one's health. In response, the "immune system that is meant to protect the body's organs produces antibodies that attack normal body tissues. Autoimmune is when your body attacks itself. It sees part of your body as a disease and tries to combat it" (American Academy of Allergy, Asthma, and Immunology 2020).

If we think of the community as a living body, we see in our examples above how its existence is dependent on the very things that endanger it: the acts of conviviality, reciprocity, conditional generosity—in a word, intimacy (Derrida 2003). "Compelled and compelling," as Jensen and Hapal put it in their text, intimacy is the condition of possibility for life under conditions of neoliberal precarity. Yet, as we saw, it also opens life to the risk of exclusion, displacement, and death. It immunizes individuals from the ever-present threats of abandonment and alienation precisely by exposing them to the quotidian violence of gendered and class hierarchies. The autoimmune community thus creates the criminal and therefore disposable other in the very process of guarding its boundaries. Thus do intimacy and impunity go together. Extrajudicial killings from this perspective is less about a violation of human rights as the affirmation of a moral calculus. It confirms that the targeted victim does not belong here, that it is not me, and its death means it no longer poses a threat to my safety. The autoimmunity of community thereby echoes Duterte's genocidal logic. During a briefing on the spread of COVID-19, for example, the president circles back to his usual obsession:

> "If you die, that's because I am angry with drugs. That's what I am saying. If you bring me to court or send me to jail, fine, I have no problem. If I serve my country by going to jail, gladly."
>
> While he is open to facing charges, Duterte said he should not be accused of committing "crimes against humanity." *Kailan pa naging humanity itong p\*\*\*\*\* i\*\* mga drug na ito* (Since when did these sons of b\*\*\*\*\*s become part of humanity)?" the President said.
>
> "And how much has been reduced in the use of shabu? I really do not know until now. But we are still in the thick of the fight against shabu," Duterte said.
>
> The President again justified his controversial war on drugs, saying the health and the welfare of the people are "really the paramount concern." He advised parents to supervise and check on their children so they would not be addicted to drugs. (Romero 2020)

To save the nation, it is necessary to kill its enemies, those bodies rendered inhuman and foreign within the body politic. Duterte thus folds the discourse of the imagined community built on notions of sacrifice and mutual caring into the vernacular language of intimacy, promising unremitting vengeance on those antibodies that menace the community. Small wonder then that despite mixed feelings regarding the killings, the drug war as such continues to enjoy widespread approval especially among the poor. If the drug war is a war against the poor, as many of its critics have insisted, "it is a war," as Jensen and Hapal point out, "where the poor, willingly or unwillingly, have been made complicit. While the onslaught may have emerged from the outside, it reverberated through the resettlement site, widening and recasting existing conflictual fault lines in devastating ways."

Securing life by exposing one to death, the autoimmune community thus has the ironic effect of immunizing Duterte and those who support him from the critics of the drug war. The thousands of deaths and their traumatizing effects can be rationalized as the price one pays for securing security. The terms of intimacy, *pakikisama*, and the means with which to practice it, the skills of *diskarte*, are plunged into crisis by the drug war. Mutual trust is replaced by suspicion while the predictability of violence is supplanted by its sudden, arbitrary explosions. But from the perspective of those who suffer its effects, such violence has a clear source and can be traced back to a singular father-sovereign.

Delusional, menacing, and vulgar, he speaks in the familiar accent of intimacy, reveling in the obscenity of death as the transformative cure for what sickens society. In this way, the authoritarian imaginary infects as much as it is infected by the practices of making community.

Seen from below, authoritarianism is woven into, even as it is profoundly disruptive of, intimacy. Is there some way of opposing it and offering a nonauthoritarian alternative? There have been all sorts of speculation from critics of Duterte about who or what might replace him. But without a social movement or political machinery to back them up, many of these oppositional figures have few prospects for challenging his rule and possible successors. Meanwhile, the patriarchal gerontocracy of the Communist Party of the Philippines, who at one point supported Duterte continues to hold on to its Stalinist policies and wage what has been a futile "protracted peoples' war" for well over half a century. It remains doubtful that they can provide alternatives in the near or even far future, even as the military pursues its brutal counterinsurgency war against communist-tagged sympathizers such as peasant organizers, labor union leaders, human rights lawyers, and the like. Human rights advocates continue to call attention to the killings but these have had little effect on the administration and now barely register on the world stage. The Catholic Church, meanwhile, has vigorously opposed the drug war but finds itself outflanked by Duterte's attacks on clerical immorality and corruption. Within Congress and the Senate, there have been a handful of principled voices that have steadfastly criticized Duterte's policies but they, too, have been overwhelmed by the majority's unstinting support of his rule. Indeed, his fiercest critics on and off social media admit that the sources of opposition, while determined, remain fairly weak.

Their weakness, I suspect, stems from the fact that they are unable to account for, much less challenge, the autoimmune construction of community on which authoritarianism flourishes. Some even contribute unwittingly to its propagation by seeking to return to conventional notions of morality, decency, and patronage. Others invoke liberal democratic notions such as human rights and the rule of law without any sense of the vast cognitive and linguistic distance that separates such concepts from the practices of communities of intimacy. The paradox, which is also the tragedy, of the imagined community of the nation is that it is predicated on colonial legacies of policing as counterinsurgency; on class, gender, and sexual hierarchies as a precondition for comradeship and solidarity; on socioeconomic inequality to underwrite order but also to spur disorder that then calls for discipline; and on violence, both institutional and extrajudicial, as ways of regulating and enforcing a social order that is always in the process of being undone. The drug war is but one event in a series of other wars that is both symptom of and a spur to the illnesses that bedevil even as they constitute the nation.

With Duterte's scheduled exit in 2022, the drug war and its authoritarian appeal will not end, but most likely continue by other means and through other figures given the immunizing effects of the autoimmune community.

Within this troubling landscape, *Communal Intimacy and the Violence of Politics* provides us with resources for mapping the autoimmune structure of community and the history of the current sociopolitical moment from which it unfolds. It offers us rich materials for thinking through possibilities yet unthought of and perhaps unexpected for the future. For this reason, it deserves to be seriously considered and closely read by anyone concerned not only with the Philippines but also with other global sites of authoritarian violence.

# Acknowledgments

This book represents nearly a decade of work in Bagong Silang. It would not be possible if not for all the people who have blessed us with their graciousness, welcomed us in their homes, and shared their stories. To the community activists, purok leaders, tanods, community leaders, fraternity members, and our friends who have accompanied us on this journey, we are eternally grateful. We would also like to thank the people from Balay Rehabilitation Center, Kaloy, kuya Louis, Joy, and Juancho, whose insights provided us with guidance as we navigated the field. The work of Balay in trying to keep residents in Bagong Silang safe without judgment has been a constant inspiration to us. We also need to thank Anna Warburg, who traveled along and discussed with us in our attempt at understanding the war on drugs as well as Vince Rafael, Sheila Coronel, and Neferti Tadiar, who prompted us and without whom this book would not have come to fruition. Nina Thrige Andersen, Lotte Buch Segal, Toby Kelly, Sif Lehman, Brigitte Dragsted and Anja Kublitz read and commented on earlier drafts and helped us sharpen our arguments. We are also grateful for the comments and suggestions from the two anonymous reviewers. Finally, we would like to thank the people from DIGNITY: the Danish Institute against Torture, specifically, Andrew Jefferson, Mette Møhl, Erik Wendt, and Jens Modvig, for their invaluable support. DIGNITY has also financially supported the research for and publication of the book.

Steffen Jensen personally extends his thanks to his family, Birthe, Amalie, and Jonathan, who trailed along to Manila and who have been some of the most constant commentators on the arguments in the book. He also would like to thank Kuya Jack, Aldin, Janet, Lita, Eric, and Marilou in Bagong Silang for being so nice to and patient with the white guy and his horrible Tagalog and his lack of knowledge of even the simplest notions of how to behave. He just hopes he got better. The University of the Philippines College for Social Works and Community Development, notably Nilan Yu, Tess Tungpalan, Silvia Claudio, Mo Pagaduan, and Amar Torres, as well as Mary Racelis from Anthropology, who welcomed Steffen and gave him an academic home for a period of time and offered critical reflections on the work as well as being patient with a newcomer to Philippine studies. Elmer Malibiran needs a specific and particularly warm-felt thanks. Steffen would have understood very little had it not been for Elmer's amazing knowledge, camaraderie, and solidarity in the little house in Bagong Silang. Finally, thanks go to my coauthor, Karl Hapal, who has grown to become quite the formidable field worker and writer over the past twelve years and without whose friendship and collaboration this book would not have been possible.

Karl Hapal would like to thank his mother, Amy; brother, Fidel; aunt, Grace; and deceased father, Jesus. Thanks also go to Neca Reyes, for her enduring partnership and love; the faculty members of the Department of Community Development; and Kaloy Anasarias, Joy Lascano, JP, and Van Nuguit, my mentors and colleagues from Balay Rehabilitation Center. His thanks also go to Steffen Jensen for his mentorship and the opportunities he provided to collaborate in various projects, including this book. And to the people of Bagong Silang, your stories deeply inspired me to write this book—*tuloy ang laban*. I am deeply grateful.

# Abbreviations

| | |
|---|---|
| Balay | Balay Rehabilitation Center, Inc. |
| CAFGU | Citizens Armed Forces Geographical Unit |
| CIS | Community Investigative Services |
| CPP | Communist Party of the Philippines |
| CVO | Civilian Volunteer Organizations |
| DA | disciplinary action |
| DIGNITY | Danish Institute against Torture |
| DILG | Department of the Interior and Local Government |
| DPA | deep penetration agent |
| HVT | high-value target |
| INC | Iglesia ni Cristo |
| KPML | Kongreso ng Pagagkakaisa ng Maralitang Lungsod (trans., Congress of the Solidarity of the Urban Poor) |
| KPMP | Kalipunang Pambansa ng mga Magsasaka sa Pilipinas (trans., Association of Peasants of the Philippines) |
| Lupon | Lupon Tagapamayapa (trans., pacification committee) |
| MASA-MASID | Mamamayang Ayaw sa Anomalya, Mamayang Ayaw sa Iligal na Droga (trans., Citizen Watch against Corruption and Illegal Drugs) |
| NAMRIA | National Mapping and Resource Information Authority |
| NHA | National Housing Authority |
| NPA | New People's Army |
| OFW | overseas Filipino worker |
| OIC | officer-in-charge |
| PAMALU | Pagkakaisa ng Maralitang Lungsod (trans., Unity of the Urban Poor) |
| PKP | Partido Komunista ng Pilipinas (trans., Communist Party of the Philippines, 1930) |
| PNP | Philippine National Police |
| PO | police officer |
| SCAN | Special Community Action Network |
| SOBA | State of the Barangay Address |
| SPO | senior police officer |

| | |
|---|---|
| Tokhang | Operation Plan Tuktok Hangyo (trans., Operation Plan Knock and Plead) |
| trapo | traditional politician |
| TYM | Triskelion Youth Movement |
| UDHA | Urban Development and Housing Act of 1992 |
| UP | University of the Philippines |
| WCD | Women and Children's Desk |
| ZOTO | Zone One Tondo Organization |

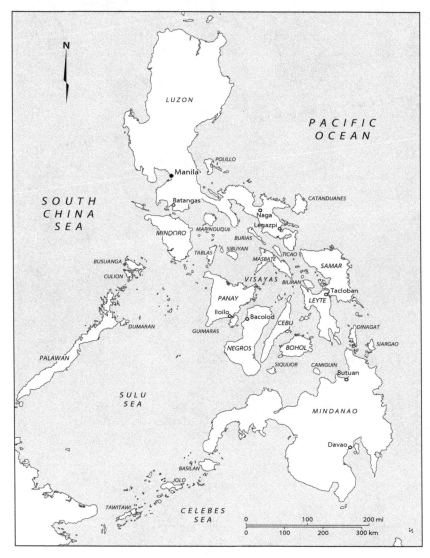

**FIGURE 1.** The Philippines

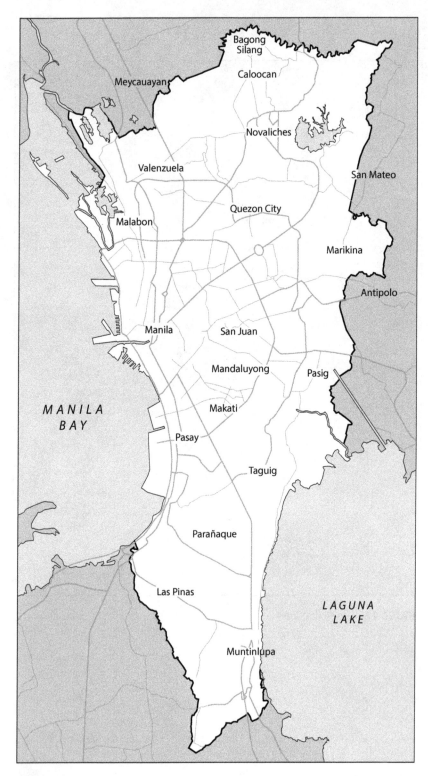

**FIGURE 2.** Metro Manila

# COMMUNAL INTIMACY AND THE VIOLENCE OF POLITICS

# INTRODUCING INTIMACY, VIOLENCE, AND SUBALTERN POLITICS

About one year into the Philippine war on drugs August 2017, we received the following Facebook post from Maria, a longtime friend. It had been posted by the children of her deceased neighbors:

> To my parents, rest in peace. Thank you for everything that you have done to raise us. I am sorry I was not able to do anything when you were targeted. The people in the adjacent house were the target. It is very painful especially when I heard my parents screaming as they were shot. The police did not stop there; they also threw a grenade on them. My parents were good people; they did not cross anyone. Why did you have to kill them even if they were not your targets?! What you did was unbelievable. You even told the media that my parents transacted with you [the police] at around 2 a.m. Are you stupid? You broke into our house, destroyed our gate. And the grenade, you sons of bitches, you ran away before you threw it and you did not let us out of the room. You also did not allow the media to talk to our neighbors so that they will not tell about the crimes you have committed. Justice please! (Facebook post translated by Karl Hapal, August 18, 2017)

This was not the first post Maria shared with us from our field site in Bagong Silang, a huge urban area in the northern part of Metro Manila. Areas such as this had become the epicenters of the war. The social media update alludes to many of the war's hallmarks: accusations of drug dealing and overwhelming violence and assertions of police acting in self-defense when arresting people to avoid discussions of responsibility. In the following days, residents of the community shared pictures of the deceased victims and discussions ensued as to the legitimacy of the killings. While many focused on the brutality and on the innocence and virtue of the victims, others commented that the family was indeed involved through two children who sold drugs (not the adjacent family mentioned in the post). Maria embodied these torturous discussions. She was horrified about the brutality while at the same time noting that the police had targeted the wrong people and, by implication, that killing the child drug-dealers would somehow have been legitimate. Scenes like this became a staple of media reports across the Philippines as thousands lost their lives, resulting in haunting discussions of the legitimacy of the war, who should live, and the impact of the war on social relations from the national to the local level.

The war on drugs and the ensuing violence began as Rodrigo Duterte assumed the presidency of the Philippines after a comfortable victory in June 2016. Duterte had won the elections on a promise to conduct a war on drugs and so-called drug personalities—dealers and addicts—who were said to undermine and destroy Philippine society. This book sets out to explore three interrelated questions: How did violent conflict over drugs become so omnipresent? How will the drug war end and with what consequences? Why was it exactly that poor, urban areas in the Manila area like Bagong Silang came to dominate in the numbers of dead? In regard to the first question, many observers agree that it was the election of Duterte that enabled a rise in drug-related violence and killings by police.[1] This image has been reproduced in much of the documentation from human rights organizations that aim to place a smoking gun in the hands of the president (Amnesty International 2017; Human Rights Watch 2017). However, while we certainly concur that Duterte has been important in establishing the conditions necessary for the large-scale slaughter, what happens in places like Bagong Silang relates to wider sociopolitical histories rather than a singular moment resulting from Duterte's election. In this way, the ultimate aim of the book is to explore what happens to a place and its people during extraordinary times.

The name Bagong Silang literally translates as "new birth." It was the brainchild of a dying dictatorship, and especially of Imelda Marcos, who had been charged with the responsibility for urban development in Manila in order to realize the dream of Bagong Lipunan, Marcos's "New Society." For years it was referred to as La Kubeta ("The Toilet"). It is easy to imagine how it could be construed as populated by what Balibar (2001) calls human garbage flushed out of the expanding metropolis. However, the name supposedly was coined by a journalist who was given a tour of the enormous site from the air and saw the endless rows of toilet fixtures that marked each 90-square-meter plot. These plots extended for miles. Residents were supposed to build their houses around the toilet fixtures. This marked Bagong Silang off as a resettlement site. When it was built, it was some 20 kilometers outside the city, far away from most economic activity. In this way, it became the quintessential place for surplus people, with above-average unemployment and poverty rates. Rather than being the embodiment of productive informality, those who ended up in Bagong Silang had lost the battle for the right to stay in the city.

Bagong Silang was also born amid conflict and violent politics. Located as it was at the frontier of the metropolitan area, it constituted the frontline between the Maoist insurgency of the New People's Army (NPA) and the government. According to our older informants, NPA soldiers, known as *taong labas* (outside people), regularly came into Bagong Silang. Partly as a consequence of this incursion, the military had a large presence in the area. Furthermore, residents of particularly rebellious parts of Manila were evicted and relocated to Bagong Silang. This was the case with what was known as the Diliman commune, a settlement based on an alliance between students from the University of the Philippines and urban informal settlers, as well as well-organized settlers from the old harbor district of Tondo, who formed the iconic organization ZOTO (Zone One Tondo Organization) for poor urban settlers (Karaos 1993). Moreover, it had a reputation for crime and drug dealing as well as gang violence. After the first years of unrest and instability, the area gradually settled into what it is today. Nonetheless, Bagong Silang has maintained its reputation of being a place rife with criminality and violence.

In this way, Bagong Silang had long been a killing zone, but it had also been an exclusion zone, a surplus people zone, and a relocation zone. This is illustrative of the bifurcation of Philippine society, in which some people are worth less than others in ways that give them an uncanny resemblance to colonial, racialized others (Stoler 2016). Therefore, to explain the violence in Bagong Silang and answer our other questions, we need to turn to an examination of Philippine politics beyond dominant perspectives on Duterte and the elite. The drug war and its consequences cannot be reduced to violent and sovereign practices of disposing of unwanted populations. Neither can an understanding of what happens in Bagong Silang be solely based on elite politics and a focus on big men, patronage, elite culture, and populism, factors that have dominated the analysis of Philippine politics for decades. Instead, we propose to explore communal intimate politics. This requires a serious examination of intricate webs of relationships, forms of violence, and exchange relations both animated by and animating the war on drugs.

This book aims to make two overarching contributions, one that is empirical, or historically specific, and a second that is conceptual, or theoretical. First, in empirical terms, the book offers a reading of the historical specificities of the

drug war as it occurred in one place in Manila. We aim to explore the consequences of the war in places like Bagong Silang rather than exploring the drug
war in its own right. We contend that an understanding of the war on drugs and
its consequences can only be achieved by examining what preceded it and the
conditions that made it possible in specific places. This compels us to explore
how violence and conflict animated communal life before the war, how local politics was carried out, and how the state, notably the police, conducted themselves. This perspective treats the drug war as a product of what Neferti Tadiar
(2009, 9) calls historical experience. Tadiar explores how domination and power
animate, without fully colonizing, revolutionary, gendered, or urban subaltern
subjectivity in the Philippines.[2] In her analysis, previous experiences and ways
of surviving a crisis are ingrained parts of experiencing and dealing with the
present crisis. The historical continuities of violent tendencies of the state are
readily apparent if we draw from the Bagong Silang experience. Acts of violence
by the police, even killings, were already frequent, even though they were not as
rampant as during the drug war. Without this longitudinal view, we risk describing the war as a fleeting moment of violence.

Second, conceptually, we aim to contribute to the understanding of local politics, especially in relation to violence in the Philippines, within Southeast
Asian studies. Our approach draws on feminist and anthropological studies of
politics and violence, a literature to which the discussion of the war situated in
Manila can also respond. However, the main aim is to contribute to Philippine
and Southeast Asian studies of violence and intimate politics. To a significant
extent, Philippine historiography and studies have been preoccupied with understanding politics and violence from the top down. The top-down approach
has produced substantial and important insights that have animated our analysis.[3] However, to echo, for instance, Wataru Kusaka (2017b) as well as earlier critics, we stress the need to take seriously what we could call politics from below,
or subaltern approaches.[4] We home in on communal forms of affective relationality as they are informed and animated—but not determined—by structural
forms of oppression and violence. Our data provides important insights into how
people deal with police violence through a combination of both vertical and horizontal social relations, money, and what is referred to as *diskarte*, that is, the ability to deal with and survive ongoing crisis-like situations (Jensen and Hapal 2018,
45). Our data illustrates how policing regimes are maintained, justified, or regulated based on the interactions among and between various communal actors.
While forms of dealing with violence have been reconfigured as a result of the
drug war, our analysis shows that they continue to affect how people respond,
serving as models for action that are slightly out of sync. We suggest that we
should understand local politics as more than functions of or reactions to elite

political culture or a bifurcated space pitting the poor against the elite. Instead, we propose to focus as well on the intricate horizontal and vertical relations and how they are entangled with relations to and exchanges with authority—state or nonstate—locally. As we show, there is a perpetual conflict, which is often violent, between aspirations of equality and social hierarchies, which is folded into intimate relations at the local level. It is this configuration that we attempt to capture through the concepts of communal intimacy and the violence of politics.

Based on these remarks, the remainder of this introduction is intended to accomplish four things. In the first two sections, we address and elaborate on the empirical and conceptual contributions of the book. First, we briefly introduce the war on drugs, asking what kind of event it was. In the second section, we unpack the conceptual lens suggested earlier by situating it within politics in Bagong Silang as well as thematic, and especially anthropological, studies on intimacy, violence, and conflict in the Philippines. In the third section, we situate our research methodologically in Bagong Silang as a social space in the broader national and metropolitan economy and in its history of violence, dispossession, and displacement. In the final section, we introduce the different chapters that make up this book and explain how each contributes to the overall narrative of the book.

## The War on Drugs

Much has already been written about the war on drugs and it makes little sense to rehearse all these discussions.[5] However, in order to explain our arguments, a few remarks are necessary. The war on drugs began quite literally in late June 2016, when President Duterte took over the reins of government. Duterte's war on drugs was based on his conviction that illegal drugs were destroying the Philippines. In his election campaign, he managed to convince the public of a drug crisis in the Philippines and called for immediate action. Calling the Philippines a "narco-state," in which drugs had become a threat to national security and the integrity of the nation, Duterte claimed that the number of drug users had reached a high of four million. He built the campaign on the back of his reputation from the southern city of Davao, where he and his family had been running local politics for decades. As he became known for his crackdown on crime in Davao, which earned him the nickname of "the Punisher," Duterte gained momentum. His strong message of law and order resonated with voters, and he ultimately won the election in a comfortable victory in May 2016. While the actual extent of the drug problem is a matter of debate, Duterte activated fear and anxiety among the population—Curato (2016) referred to this as a "latent anxiety"—through which he successfully inscribed a narrative about a drug crisis by highlighting drugs as the single most serious threat to society (Quimpo 2017).[6]

Immediately after Duterte assumed office, the chief of police signed a plan that put into action the war on drugs. The action plan was dubbed the "Double Barrel"; the first barrel was aimed at the high-level drug dealers and merchants and the second barrel was aimed at identifying and reforming drug addicts. This second barrel became known as Oplan Tokhang (literally, Operation Knock and Plead). In this effort, the police would make rounds in the communities to convince drug personalities to desist from drug use and reform through offers of rehabilitation. The police acted based on so-called watch lists, compiled by local authorities, information from the public, or drug addicts turning themselves in. While the lists formed part of a potentially benevolent and supportive intervention, the watch lists often turned into kill lists. Officially, the police and the government vehemently denied this. However, local policing agents were quite open about the connection between the lists and the killings. One asserted, "The really bad people here, the most bad ones [sic], they hurt people. I give the name to the police, then after a while, maybe two days . . . [they are] gone" (quoted in Warburg and Jensen 2020a, 10). He made a gesture with his hand across his throat, leaving little doubt as to what he meant. In the early phases of the war, many drug addicts turned themselves in, but as this came to be known locally as a "passport to death," fewer risked following the advice of the police.

It has been notoriously difficult to establish the death toll in relation to the war on drugs. According to official statistics, the Philippine National Police recorded 27,928 killings between July 1, 2016, and July 31, 2018. Of these, 4,410 deaths occurred in "legitimate antidrug operations," in which police shot people as they were resisting arrest or in self-defense. "Homicide cases under investigation" accounted for the remaining 23,518 deaths (Philippine National Police [PNP] 2018; Santos 2018). Few of our informants in Bagong Silang, at least, harbored any doubts about the involvement of the police and collaboration with vigilantes in some of the killings. Elsewhere (Warburg and Jensen 2020a), drawing on Erwin Goffman, we suggest that the police and the government made use of a representational front in which they acted inside the parameters of the law, not killing anyone without due process except for a few rogue elements and in cases of self-defense. A practical backstage in which the police acted with impunity complemented this representational front stage. The effect has not been to obscure the violent practices but rather to allow Duterte to escape legal responsibility while consolidating political power and support through his role as the "Punisher," who single-handedly rid the Philippines of the drug scourge. Duterte and his chief of police had successfully employed the same strategy of oscillating between the front- and backstage in Davao when they claimed credit for more than a thousand deaths (on the backstage) while avoiding any legal responsibility (Altez and Caday 2017).

Besides the thousands of killings, the war has had dramatic effects on society, many of which we will explore through the focus on Bagong Silang in this book. For instance, the war has led to massively overcrowded detention facilities to the point where Philippine prisons in 2018 were the second most overcrowded prisons in the world, at 436 percent of capacity (McCarthy 2018). The justice system has been even more stretched as the number of prisoners awaiting trial increased twenty-two percent in the first year of Duterte's government (VOA News 2017). Opportunities for corruption within the police have also accompanied the many killings and turned the war into a "murder enterprise" (Coronel 2017). Finally, the war has radically reconfigured relations between state officials and residents and between residents in Bagong Silang as well as in the rest of the country (Warburg and Jensen 2020a). Despite these consequences, Filipinos have largely supported the war on drugs, also in places like Bagong Silang. While there have been incidents of overt resistance also in Bagong Silang (Palatino 2019), outright opposition has frequently been the domain of human rights organizations, the Catholic church, and some NGOs, along with parts of the media. However, support has always been ambivalent. For instance, the Social Weather Stations documented that widespread support of the war (up to 80 percent) was equaled by similar levels of fear that respondents or their families might become victims of the war (Social Weather Stations 2017). In this book, we also trace other forms of implicit or ambivalent engagement with the war on drugs in, for instance, echoes of revolutionary demands for equality, religious sentiments, and fear for the family and other kin.

While the war was clearly the result of Duterte's policies, our data from Bagong Silang suggests that the police killed people in ways that resembled the killings before the war began (Jensen and Hapal 2015; Coronel 2017; McCoy 2009). In 2009, for instance, we documented and pursued the case of Aris's killing (see the photo that follows). Aris was found dead in the neighboring province across the Marilao River. Shortly thereafter, stories began to circulate that a law enforcement unit had detained him immediately before his disappearance. In the months following the incident, banners showing Aris's mutilated body and demanding justice were exhibited in a central part of Bagong Silang. A police officer we interviewed, who was unrelated to the murder of Aris, suggested that the law enforcement agency had picked up Aris so many times before but had had to release him again because he was under age. This time, he guessed, they wanted to teach him a lesson, which resulted in his death.

This raises questions about what kind of event the introduction of the war on drugs was. Was it indeed the doings of Duterte, maybe even reducible to him? While few would maintain such a simple view, there has been a strong emphasis on explaining the war by explaining Duterte. Rather than discussing this as a purely empirical question, it might be useful to distinguish conceptually between notions of radical transformation, critical events, and escalations. As should be evident from the previous discussion, we do not subscribe to the idea that the ascension of Duterte and the launch of his war on drugs were entirely a rupture from the past. Instead, we may think of the drug war as what Bruce Kapferer (2010) refers to as a "critical event . . . conceived as a particular plateau of intensity that has immanent within it a potential that effectively becomes knowable through the actualization or realization of the event itself" (15). The critical event is both transformational and a revelation of structures that became knowable through the drug war. While this is certainly true, there is also something quite dramatic about the drug war such that the notion of "critical events" does not suffice. Lars Højer and colleagues (2018) instead suggest the term "escalation" to capture how quantitative shifts in, for instance, killings may have lasting qualitative effects, what they call a "change of change," at the same time as these shifts must be rendered legible by being "culturally measured" (52). Understanding the war on drugs as a critical event as well as an escalation allows us to explore how sudden change seldom happens out of nowhere and is made legible through the past and can have lasting effects.

It is also useful to widen the scope beyond the Philippines. The drug war is and has been analyzed primarily as a Philippine event—not least because of the focus on Duterte. However, the war actualizes the broader comparative perspectives on "wars on . . . ," that is, situations in which someone in power has been able, correctly or not, to frame a particular situation as an emergency that threatens the life of the polity. When framed as securitization (Buzan, Wæver, and de Wilde 1998) or antipolitics (Walters 2008), a war on gangs, crime, drugs, terror, or even poverty gives those in control extraordinary powers to block a development, such as a putative drug crisis run amok.[7] To take but one example, in our own work in South Africa (Jensen 2010), we have explored how a war on gangs, carried out as counterinsurgency, reconfigured national and local politics. Counterinsurgency wars in Guatemala (Schirmer 1998) and the war on terror after 9/11 (Amoore and de Goede 2008) provide other examples where power protects a polity through dispensing life. In this way, understanding the Philippine war on drugs offers us new insights into a range of other potential murderous politics around the globe, and the global view allows us to understand the drug war as a patterned process beyond Duterte and even the Philippines.[8]

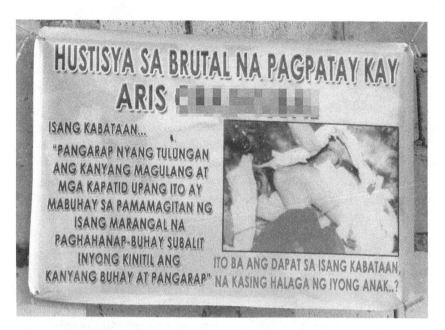

**FIGURE 3.** A banner clamoring for justice for the violent murder of Aris. Photo by Steffen Jensen.

**FIGURE 4.** Family members mourn the death of a child killed amid the crossfire of vigilante killings. From *Bagong Silang*, directed by Jayneca Reyes, 2016. Courtesy of Jayneca Reyes.

# Toward Communal Intimacy and the Violence of Politics

Conceptually, the book places itself within what can be referred to as subaltern politics (Tadiar 2009; Spivak 1988; Mbembe 2001). We understand subaltern politics as the attempt to understand local politics on its own terms as well as the political practices of people who are often invisible. This moves attention away from, for instance, motivations for the war on drugs to how different groups in Bagong Silang—potential victims, the people who carry out the killings, and those who watch, bear witness, and sometimes collaborate with the state—live, understand, and engage with the war. In recent years, subaltern studies have gained traction in the Philippines.[9] Some of the best of these studies are by Chuan Yean Soon (2012) and by Wataru Kusaka (2017a, 2017b). These studies explore what the authors call voices from below or subaltern politics. Taking his cue from James Scott (1985) and his notion of "hidden transcripts," Soon excavates the hidden logics and perceptions in his informants' understanding of politics. He identifies the concept of *tulong*, or "help," as a meaningful way to understand how people talk about and perceive the morality of politics. Parallel to this in our work in Bagong Silang, *tulong* emerges as a central concept, even in relation to monetary exchanges with officialdom, which might otherwise be construed as corruption. It is important that when done in the right fashion, that is, when they are transformed into *tulong*, Soon argues, these monetary exchanges build safety and provide both sides with important means of survival (see also Hapal and Jensen 2017).

In parallel with the work of Soon, that of Kusaka (2017b) focuses on the morality of local politics from below. Based on long-term fieldwork in an informal settlement in Manila, Kusaka identifies what he calls a "dual public sphere," comprising both a civic sphere and a mass sphere where the civic sphere comprises formal, associational politics, often conducted in English whereas the mass sphere is animated by a different set of political motivations emerging from poor communities mostly conducted in Tagalog. He employs the spheres as heuristic categories for understanding politics in a different way than from above. Using this heuristic device, Kusaka produces an exemplary analysis of a bifurcated society. He shows how class divides are reinforced by language, whereby all that matters to the elite—the economy, the legal system, the important part of the media, education and politics—is conducted in English, a language that few within the mass sphere really master. The sensibilities and moralities are often at odds such that those in the civic sphere frequently feel contempt toward the mass sphere. To some extent, this is reciprocated within the mass sphere, as Michael Pinches's 1991 analysis of perceptions of the middle class in a poor urban neighborhood also illustrates. One of Kusaka's (2017b) important contributions is that he empirically substantiates the divide by combining statistics with a qualitative analysis of data from both the mass and civic spheres that provides the reader with an understanding of how these spheres are both discursive realms and concrete life worlds. A second, possibly more important, contribution is his explicating, in positive ways and with much empathy, of the life worlds of his poor informants in the informal settlement. From his account, we are able to see the contours of a subaltern politics—or in the words of Achille Mbembe (2001), in his exploration of postcolonial African subjectivities, how they "exercise their existence" (9).

The concept of the dual public sphere allows Kusaka to explore class divides and moral politics in insightful ways, including how the mass sphere engages with politics. However, the juxtaposition of the two spheres arguably takes on a life of its own, with the potential implication that they become monolithic entities pitted against each other. Yet our data from Bagong Silang suggests that it is difficult to think of residents there as part of a homogenous group. In an article published in 2016 as part of a collection attempting to understand the war on drugs, Kusaka develops the argument and identifies internal divisions within the settlement of the urban poor to illustrate the conviction that some people were deemed beyond repair and hence killable by their neighbors, and indeed even by themselves. This analysis resonates with Nicole Curato's insightful 2016 contribution on what she calls "latent anxieties" about drugs, which become translated into anxiety about the potential, violent acts of neighbors in urban, poor communities.

We propose the overarching concept of communal intimacy to develop the understanding of this form of politics. The concern with intimacy emerged for us long before Duterte's drug war, when we did field- and survey work in Bagong Silang around 2010 as an intuitive way to understand a range of empirical incidents revolving around and given force by the density of communal relations.[10] The concept of communal intimacy has important scalar dimensions in our attempt to understand what happens at a communal level between the household and, for instance, electoral politics. Typical of other poor neighborhoods in the Global South, residents live close together and have quite an extensive, if sometimes slightly distorted, knowledge of each other that needs to be managed carefully. Life is lived within so-called path walks, that is, narrow streets lined with attached houses. Little more than the thickness of a concrete wall or zinc roof separates what goes on in these path walks. This includes happy moments as well as desperate times; periods of abundance and love and stints of hunger, violence, and neglect. Intimacy—intimate knowledge—is unavoidable. As Lauren Berlant suggests (1998, 281), it is both intimated and explicated. Furthermore, most residents have stayed in the same place for years, producing temporally and spatially dense, sometimes claustrophobic, communities. In that sense, intimacy is imposed on people; it is inescapable in terms of bodily and sensorial presence (Böhme 2016). One sign, photographed by Karl, captures both the spatial and temporal dimensions of sensorial cohabitation when it informs potential culprits not to "throw dead mice here; we know who you are." In another example from a survey, we asked if people trusted their neighbors, to which a staggering 95 percent responded in the affirmative. When quizzed further, one informant responded, "Yes, because I don't give them any chance to cheat me." Communal intimacy can also be managed by forms of silencing of, for instance, domestic violence or by engaging in commentary via what is known as *tsismis* (gossip) or *sabi-sabi* (hearsay). In both cases, there is an ongoing oscillation between knowing, not knowing, and pretending that others do not know in ways that make particular events public. In one case, for instance, our friend Ken was known to have frequent violent rows with his wife that people would ignore and pretend not to hear, even when we were around. However, one day she yelled at him that he had been lying about his credentials to his neighbors—and suddenly the row made it across the zinc wall and became public, with severe consequences for Ken.[11]

While intimate, communal, and interpersonal dynamics contribute to intricate webs of relationships in Bagong Silang, they also animate local and national politics and state formation. For example, families and family relations are absolutely central for almost all communal relations, as both our interlocutors and the literature testify (McCoy 1994; Roces 2000). Finally, the drug war is also steeped in issues concerning communal intimacy. Take, for example, the so-called watch lists of suspected or known drug personalities. As we show in chapter 2, local leaders with intimate knowledge of families and households compile the lists, which are also based on reports from neighbors through the MASA-MASID program (Mamayang Ayaw sa Anomalya, Mamayang Ayaw sa Iligal na Droga, which roughly translates to Citizen Watch against Corruption and Illegal Drugs). Indispensable, life-saving forms of relationality and intimate knowledge became dangerous and unknowable—who said what to whom? Intimate knowledge and affective relationality are what help people survive crises, but during the drug war, they are also what put them at risk.

In studies of the Philippines, violence is often explored as a function of electoral or elite politics (Anderson 1998; Sidel 1999), whereas the concept of intimacy has been used to understand domestic and gendered power dynamics (Cannell 1999).[12] In our adaptation of communal intimacy, we aim to combine these discussions by invoking three distinct theoretical movements within anthropology and gender studies on intimacy, exchange relations, violence, and

**FIGURE 5.** A resident posts a stern warning to their neighbors not to throw dead mice near their house. Photo by Karl Hapal.

**FIGURE 6.** A path walk in Bagong Silang. From *Bagong Silang*, directed by Jayneca Reyes, 2016. Courtesy of Jayneca Reyes.

power that link the communal sphere to larger political processes. These concern the public nature of intimacy, the governance of intimacy, and unequal, affective exchange relations. The three movements can be seen as dimensions of communal intimacy, of which some will be more relevant at certain moments.

In the first movement, on the public nature of intimacy, Lauren Berlant (1998) asserts that while intimacy is set "within zones of familiarity and comfort, . . . the inwardness of the intimate is met by a corresponding publicness" (281). To Berlant, the intimate needs to be public as well. For Bagong Silang we may say that the intimate always, or at least very often, has to be public, as the fate of Ken suggests. In his 2014 book *Cultural Intimacy*, Michael Herzfeld expands the intimate beyond the domestic by suggesting that in any given polity (in his case, the nation), there are intimate ways of knowing each other; of realizing implicit embarrassments as shared, as expressed through little ironies and winking eyes. "Cultural intimacy," he states, "is the space of all such self-recognition" (8). Based on our material, we may say that the way people have coped with each other and with authority has been based on shared cultural intimacy; on knowing when and how to bribe a police officer and on seeing—and not seeing—the violence or drug abuse next door, for instance. However due to the "change of change" (Højer et al. 2018, 36) instituted by the war on drugs, communal intimacy has been radically reconfigured. The question we need to ask in this regard is how communal intimacy has been reconfigured and, in particular, what people in Bagong Silang can do about it.

As for the second theoretical movement, Herzfeld's analysis also points to how states appropriate intimacy and kin relations, for instance, in notions of the mother or father of the nation; this is prolific in the Philippines (Rafael 2000). To explore this dynamic is beyond the scope of this study, which is concerned with communal politics. More to the point, however, intimacy is also an indispensable part of biopolitics, or what Natalie Oswin (2010) calls the governing of intimacy. Goodfellow and Mulla, in their 2008 article on "compelling intimacies," suggest, "Domestic relations are enmeshed within the formidable and subtle regulatory processes of such things as the law, institutional ethical discourses, moral economies, therapeutic practices, and such things as the sense of taboo that infuses intimacy and other forms of affiliation found in household relations" (259). In this way, to quote Ann Laura Stoler, "To study the intimate is not to turn away from structures of dominance but to relocate their conditions of possibility and relations and forces of production" (in Oswin 2010, 62). In our work in Bagong Silang, we are not concerned directly with the domestic sphere, although we do explore gendered and generational conflicts both during the drug war and before. Rather, we use this mode of thinking as a way to understand how communal intimacy is drawn into political and regulatory processes as well as how these processes are only made possible (as in the case with the watch lists) by tapping into and preying on intimate and affectionate relationality. We can look at it in reverse and suggest that state violence, for instance the war on drugs, folds itself into and reconfigures communal and family intimate relations, as Javier

Auyero and Fernanda Berti argue in their 2016 study of violence in Buenos Aires.[13] This means that the parameters of intimacy shift along with shifts in politics. In his analysis of what he calls agonistic intimacy, Bhrigupati Singh (2011) suggests similar relations as he explores how intimate relations between neighbors in a diverse Indian community with Muslim and Hindu residents are ever shifting, agonizing terrains of conflict and cohabitation. How violent or how intimate they are, he suggests, depends on matters of politics produced beyond the local, intimate relations. We may say that the parameters of agonizing terrains shift when the parameters of politics change, as they did with the war on drugs. Suddenly neighbors are transformed from "people like us" to dangerous outsiders in need of violent disciplining (Kusaka 2017a).

One way of understanding how intimacy is infused with societal and communal power is to take seriously the relationality of intimacy. To understand this kind of politics, and with the addition of the third theoretical movement, concerning unequal, affective exchange relations, we adopt the conceptual language introduced by feminist economic anthropology, in which exchange and gift relations are inherently unequal (Weiner 1992). Many traditional analyses of gift relations took place in relatively stable and putatively equal contexts—gift relations involved reproducing structure and long-term relations that were frequently part of the patriarchy. However, as Marilyn Strathern (1992) argues, exchange relations do not have to be equal or harmonious. In fact, gift exchanges are often compelled in which the recipient is able to elicit an object from a future donor through coercion. The exchange is then based on the "successful persuasion" of the donor that he or she is, in fact, able to part with something (Strathern 1988, 178), such as money, a house, or even the donor's life. Furthermore, the focus on hierarchy and coercion in exchange relations allows us to explore the entangled relations with authority (for instance, the police). While when analyzing the drug war, most of the focus has been on the killings, the war has also allowed for an expansion of a corrupt economy of survival. This even has a name: Tokhang (Knock and Plead) for Ransom. Following Sheila Coronel, in her 2017 analysis of the drug war as a murderous enterprise, we may say that survival has also become an enterprise. Moreover, all accounts suggest that during the war on drugs, the price of a life has gone up (Jensen and Hapal 2018, 58). This price is not only exerted through direct payments between drug personalities and police but also involves preying on intimate relations with kin and neighbors to bail out the suspect.

Hence, rather than focusing only on the drug war as a sovereign act of necropolitics (Mbembe and Libby 2003; Reyes 2016), we must also focus on exchange relations that are both compelling and compelled. Economic anthropologist Janet Roitman (2004, 194) suggests that we must look at the relationship produced by state regulation—of, in our case, criminal justice, prisons, the drug war, and anti-corruption drives—rather than state regulation as such. It is the relationships that are produced rather than regulation per se that are central for how people engage with the system. If that is the case, it is crucial to understand what relationships are produced by prison conditions—for instance, the need to get out of prison and the implication of families in survival. These relationships and the negotiations they lead to were incredibly complex even before the war. But there was predictability to them—not always leading to good results but at least with a promise of resolution. It was the parameters of these social exchange relations that the war reconfigured, not the need to engage in exchange relations with authority. If anything, exchange relations became even more important as they became destabilized and fragmented.

It might be useful to introduce the life trajectory of Maricel, one of our key informants in Bagong Silang for over a decade, to situate communal intimacy within these theoretical movements and empirically within the violent politics right up to the war on drugs. When we first met Maricel, she was a *tanod*, or community guard, nominated by Garcia, the *purok*, or area leader, in the area in which we lived during fieldwork in 2009 and 2010. Maricel promised to take us around the area "to keep us safe," as she dramatically put it. While she was a peace officer, she had a tolerant view of much crime—including abortion and drug dealing—and focused more on the social relations that both abortionists and drug dealers engaged in for the community. She was also a known supporter and organizer of Oca Malapitan, who was then a member of Congress and who she desperately hoped would run for mayor in 2010 against the then mayor, Recom Echiverri. That would have secured Maricel income and opportunities. He failed to run, however, and Maricel had to contend with the less remunerative role as a community guard and local political operator. She was friendly and high-spirited with her neighbors and known to be really good at *pakikisama*, that is, good at engaging with neighbors. The term *pakikisama* has often been invoked as central in understanding communal relations in the Philippines more broadly.[14] We shall return to this in detail later in the chapter. For now, suffice it to say that discussions have been somewhat essentializing when trying to agree on what Filipinos are really like. What does remain clear is that *pakikisama*, as an emic concept, is embedded in contestations about its true meaning.[15] Hence, that Maricel was good at *pakikisama* also indicates that others were not, as was the case with another friend, Inday, who was seen as arrogant and aloof even when she engaged in communal activities. Inday was adamant that rather than spending your time in the path walk, you must take care of your family. The friction between Maricel and Inday informed communal activities for much of the extended period of time for we stayed in this section of Bagong Silang.

Maricel was a wonderful interlocutor. During several hour-long interviews, we discussed emic concepts such as *pakikisama* and *utang na loob* (inner debt or debt of gratitude), as well as *diskarte* (the ability to stay afloat during times of crisis through cunning and street wisdom) and *hiya* (shame). What characterizes all these concepts is that they all, in different ways, map out a relational, affective economy structured by horizontal and vertical ties as well as notions of subjectivity. In relation to her political patron, Oca Malapitan, for example, Maricel was adamant that theirs was a purely transactional relationship. She did not feel any debt to Oca. At other times, she had incurred emotional debts to people who "had" been there for her. This suggests that people constantly negotiate these emic concepts. As one of our friends, Eric, advised, as Steffen asked him whether Aldin was indebted to him after he had assisted with medical expenditures for Aldin's child, "It's up to you." Apart from the infuriatingly vague answer, it revealed a deeper truth: choice, relationship, and even practices enter into and are negotiated and contested through an interpretative scheme of affective relationality. The objective situation—that thing that happened—did not determine the outcome—a debt was incurred. It was up to protagonists as well in the intimate space made up of the path walk.

In their analysis of civility, Sharika Thiranagama, Toby Kelly, and Carlos Forment (2018) suggest that this is exactly what civility is about—finding arrangements that allow people to share the same public space. Contrary to normative celebrations of civility, they insist that civility is not the opposite of violence. There are dominant ways of being civil; manners that cannot be negotiated. This is so for the very local, intimate politics in the pathway. It is equally so for the relation between authority (state or nonstate) and residents, whereby particular forms of civility are allowed and sanctioned. Drawing on Norbert Elias's 1994 analysis, they assert: "Civility is reproduced in a context where violence has been radically reorganized, monopolized by the state and placed quite literally out of sight. But at the same time, it is important to remember that the military can be sent back onto the street at any moment. Civility does not see the eradication of violence, but its reorganization, with the state playing a crucially important role" (Thiranagama, Kelly, and Forment 2018, 162).

This is what happened in a radical sense with the war on drugs. The police were sent back in. Sanctioned forms of civility as a type of state coercion have always been entangled with intimate relations in Bagong Silang. Again, Maricel's fate is illustrative. While she was known as an effective political operator and skilled in social exchange relations, she was also known as someone who had had serious problems with drugs. In 2016, this came back to haunt her as Duterte initiated his war on drugs. She was one of the first to be included on the watch lists of the drug war. After months of anxiety, she finally escaped Bagong

Silang to another part of Metro Manila. She could not escape or hide from the intimate relations that before the war had maintained her and given her a position in the path walk, but that after the war made her vulnerable to state-sanctioned forms of civility. State-sanctioned civility is, predictably, often at odds with local forms of civility, but as the war on drugs shows, this difference is then dealt with through violent politics.

To sum up briefly, the way we employ the concept of communal intimacy allows us to explore, simultaneously, how intimate affective relationality is, and has been, central to how people in Bagong Silang are able to survive at the same time as it is inescapable due to the space in which they are confined. This has led to the production of particular forms of cultural intimacy whereby people know, sometimes in distorted ways, a lot about their neighbors and the state. A certain style of coping and morality had developed in which people knew how to engage with each other and with the state through particular forms of exchange relations. However, this intimacy—or the intimate knowledge people have of each other—also forms the very backbone of the drug war, in both its lethal and extortionist forms. Hence, the intimate affectionate relationality that keeps people alive is also what puts them at risk. While the war on drugs has often legitimately been cast as the ultimate sovereign act of creating disposable bodies (Reyes 2016; Quimpo 2017), our work in Bagong Silang also suggests that the war itself as carried out on the ground relied on intimate relations and in turn reconfigured and disfigured the very same intimate relations between residents of the path walk and between state authorities and residents (Warburg and Jensen 2020a). In this way, the Philippine war on drugs highlights the need for anthropological analyses of intimacy, violence, and local politics to pay acute attention to how the local—Bagong Silang—is reconfigured, structured, or animated by larger societal and historical processes at both the metropolitan and the national levels. As Loïc Wacquant (2008b, 9–11) stresses, we cannot understand the fate of ghetto dwellers (his object of analysis) from the ghetto alone or from a specific point in time. Rather, we must trace the historical trajectories of, for instance, killability, as well as how certain spaces take up certain roles in the larger metropolitan and national economy. While violence and the war on drugs are not their primary concern, this is also the urban economy that Marco Garrido (2019) and Arnisson Ortega (2016) map out in their discussions of urban transformations in Manila. Hence, in this book we aim to explore how these forms of affective and intimate relationality were disseminated in urban space, what kind of violent politics emerged before and developed during the war on drugs, and how the drug war has reconfigured urban space and the possibility for survival for the residents of Bagong Silang.

# Studying Bagong Silang

The book builds on a decade of engagement with Bagong Silang and its people. Our engagement began in 2008, when our partner organization and future employer, Balay Rehabilitation Center, initiated a community-led intervention project concerning state violence in one section of Bagong Silang. Steffen Jensen was employed as a senior researcher in the Danish organization DIGNITY—Danish Institute against Torture (then the Rehabilitation and Research Center for Torture Victims), which funded Balay and its engagement in Bagong Silang. Fresh out of university at twenty-three, Karl Hapal had just been employed as a researcher by Balay and was assigned to work with Steffen on the implementation of different knowledge and intervention projects. Our positionalities in relation to Bagong Silang were very different. Steffen came to Bagong Silang as a white, middle-aged, middle-class, male academic, who was recognized in some circles as a competent scholar of gangs, violence, and politics in South Africa. Traveling with an expansive theoretical and empirical baggage, he engaged in constant comparisons—some fruitful and some not. On touching ground in Bagong Silang, friends and colleagues constantly reminded him about the dangers of the place and how disorderly (*magulo*) it was. Having stayed in South African townships, however, left him with the impression that Bagong Silang was much less violent than what he had experienced in South Africa. While drugs were clearly prevalent, for instance, they did not have the same visceral presence. Furthermore, in relation to gangs, while there were peer groups, which often engaged in violence, he was not left with the sense that gangs ran the place. Hence, he had no misgivings or fears when he moved to Bagong Silang with Elmer Malibiran, a research assistant–cum-teacher, to begin fieldwork on fraternities, violence, and local politics. Steffen lived in Bagong Silang for six months between late 2009 and mid-2010. Alternating between language courses in Tagalog and fieldwork on the streets and somewhat hampered by theoretical and empirical baggage, he only slowly gained his footing. He needed a completely new conceptual language concerning topics such as exchange relations and intimacy to understand what went on around him as well as having to accustom himself to a rich, new regional literature. He also suffered everyday humiliations. For months, he was certain that his next-door neighbor hated him. Every morning, as he sat smoking his cigarette outside the house in the path walk, the neighbor would go to great lengths to ignore him. Only when he realized that an almost invisible raising of the eyebrow to recognize the neighbor but without really looking at him was enough, he began to understand that this was indeed a very sensible way to manage the density of social relations. The same happened in relation to debt relations and social hierarchies. Many of these cultural lessons took place in the path walk in conversations about his cultural mishaps with Emilio, Maricel, Inday and her son Eric, and the Flores family, the ethnographic focuses of this book. Steffen forged another set of relations with members of three community fraternity chapters in other parts of Bagong Silang, including Aldin, Mariza, and Ken, all of whom we will meet later in this book. Through the years, Steffen visited regularly and engaged in projects in Bagong Silang with Balay, and in 2017, he went back to stay with his old networks in the path walk and the fraternity to enquire about the effects of the war on drugs and try to understand how this war was different from similar wars elsewhere, notably in South Africa.

Like Steffen, Karl was warned that he had to be very careful. His colleagues in Balay told horror stories about Bagong Silang; how taxi drivers would refuse passengers visiting or passing through Bagong Silang and various incidents of torture and extrajudicial killings. In line with the horror stories, his colleagues advised him to leave Bagong Silang before it got dark. His access into Bagong Silang was facilitated by his employment in Balay, which had initiated human rights interventions in two of the poorer areas, known as Phases 7 and 8. As part of this work, Karl visited every single (village) official in Phases 7 and 8, engaged with hundreds of young people and community activists, and also carried out interviews with local officials and police officers. Karl came from a left-wing, middle-class family in Quezon City, and Bagong Silang proved to be an unfamiliar place, where he, like Steffen, had to learn about cultural codes, although from a very different vantage point.[16] He spent time passing through or hanging out (*tumatambay*) in path walks lined with rows of bungalow houses, some subdivided and populated by two or three households. He observed people hanging out, some of whom were merrily drinking, and heard people singing on top of their lungs along with their blasting karaoke machines. He encountered children playing along the alleyways, young men playing basketball in makeshift basketball courts, and women selling various types of foodstuffs. He was often accompanied on these walks by Betty, a young female resident and partner in the Balay Center's work. Betty taught him about the hidden alleyways where police had dumped bodies, about navigating communal conflicts, and about how to stay safe in Bagong Silang. When Karl left Balay to pursue an academic career, it was these same networks, developed over years of working at Balay, that allowed him to carry out fieldwork among activists of all ages.

These different positionalities and networks combine to animate the content of this book as well as our decade-long engagement with Bagong Silang. They allow us to write a story that spans more than ten years before and during the war on drugs and to understand how the war has affected people in Bagong Si-

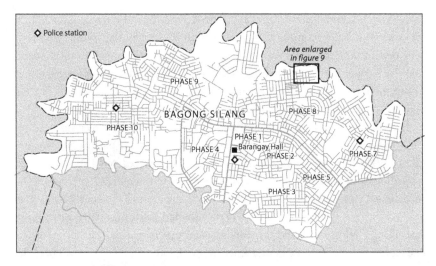

**FIGURE 7.** Bagong Silang

lang. In 2009, through our work with Balay (with whom Steffen still works), we began studying the police and violence before it became imperative to do so. As part of Balay's intervention, we conducted a victimization survey in 2010 (Jensen, Hapal, and Modvig 2013). The survey assessed the levels of risk, perceptions of violence, and remedial action after experiences of violence. The survey gave us a rare insight into social capital, trust, and violence in Bagong Silang.[17] We explored a collection of blotter reports from all 115 *purok* (area) leaders constituting almost sixteen thousand reports. Blotter reports constitute a first step in local dispute mediation. Covering a period of two years (2008 and 2009), these reports represent a unique view into local conflicts and their resolution.

Parallel to the survey, Steffen also embarked on ethnographic fieldwork with fraternities in Bagong Silang. In the mid-2000s, fraternities, especially the university-based Tau Gamma Phi, had begun to spread rapidly through poor, urban neighborhoods outside the universities. As part of a global project of exploring organized violence and militant mobilization (Jensen and Vigh 2018), we engaged with several fraternity chapters in Bagong Silang to understand violence, ritual, and the production of what we call a "world of significance" (Jensen 2018). Several of our informants in the fraternities became victims in the drug war, although we were unaware of this at the time of the fieldwork. After the survey and ethnographic fieldwork were completed, we continued to monitor the situation in Bagong Silang through local contacts and as part of our work with Balay Rehabilitation Center. In 2014, we conducted interviews with police officers in Bagong Silang to explore the relationship between torture and corruption. Accounts from police officers suggested an informal moral code justifying and regulating the use of violence and bribes (Hapal and Jensen 2017). In 2015, Karl conducted interviews with senior community organizers in Bagong Silang. These interviews served to outline the history of Bagong Silang as a relocation zone and a site of popular struggle and resistance against state coercion. The interviews offered us a glimpse of local politics from the perspective of the *masa* (masses) and Bagong Silang's reconfiguration due to sociopolitical developments (Hapal 2017).

In both the qualitative and quantitative data, state violence emerged as a constant theme long before the onset of the war on drugs. As part of our engagement with the Balay Rehabilitation Center, we carried out interviews and workshops with local law enforcement personnel in the national police and the so-called *Barangay* Justice System concerning their use of violence.[18] Balay also worked with cases of torture. Several of these ended in death—which was termed "salvaging." Both police and inhabitants used this term as a description of police violence. As a term, salvaging emerged during the martial law era where the act of killing of communists and criminals was equated to saving the nation from peril. While the police were clearly engaged in violent practices, there was a sense in the Philippines that human rights had been disseminated and remained strong as a method and a language of opposing police brutality. However, this was all to end in June 2016, when Rodrigo Duterte assumed the presidency. Human rights became almost as suspect as being associated with drugs—in fact, as human rights were seen to prevent the war, human rights organizations were indeed associated with drugs. This antagonism was not only prevalent within the government. Many ordinary residents in Bagong Silang shared the misgivings about human rights and the fear of drug dealers (Curato 2016; Kusaka 2017a). Hostility against human rights organizations, local as well as international, also appeared to have been fueled by Duterte's anti-imperialist agenda, which saw human rights as a way to further entrench colonial and imperial rule. It was in this hostile climate that the Balay Center's documentation practices had to be turned toward accounting for and counting the killings along with finding ways of addressing the murderous onslaught.[19]

To understand the implications of the war on drugs, we also carried out fieldwork in two periods in 2017—in January and February and in April and May. During these fieldwork periods, we tried to assess the perception of the war on drugs by law enforcement agencies, the social implications of the war for relationships between residents and between residents and the state, and how the police made money from the war on drugs. A graduate student, Anna Warburg, who was affiliated with DIGNITY and Balay, carried out the first period of fieldwork (Warburg 2017). Anna's work revealed the extent and kind of support the war enjoyed at that time among police and local officials as well as the kinds of antagonisms that the war had produced. The second stint of fieldwork that Steffen carried out tapped into networks created over the years of engagement with residents in Bagong Silang to understand how the war had transformed social relations and the role of money in the war.[20]

## Organization of the Argument

What kind of book has this long-term engagement with Bagong Silang allowed us to write? The short answer is that the book explores a place, Bagong Silang, at a time of great distress and extraordinary transformation. The book is clearly not a book about the war on drugs alone, nor is it a book only about Bagong Silang. When we first discussed writing a book about Bagong Silang in 2015, before the war on drugs, Karl asked why? That question was answered a year later, when the war on drugs began affecting Bagong Silang. To write a book about a place in extraordinary times instead of about the war on drugs itself also shifts the focus slightly to include much more about the place, at the expense, for instance, of a detailed analysis of the war and its rationalities. Similarly, a book about Bagong Silang would pay more attention to topics such as structures of governance or economic livelihoods. However, Bagong Silang is central for our account. We do believe that writing a book about a place is necessary for understanding the extraordinary times in the context of everyday life. Hence, we refuse to explore the war or Duterte outside the context of Bagong Silang. Some of these analyses can be found in different forms in previous publications. However, the book draws together and reinterprets the analyses we have done before in ways that allow the reader—and we ourselves, as we wrote the book—to understand, in a more coherent way than articles and book chapters frequently allow, the extent to which communal intimacy and violent politics are animated by the drug war and how state violence folds itself into intimate communal relationality. Furthermore, while we invoke the concepts of communal intimacy and the violence of politics, our aim is primarily to use these concepts as ways to understand how the drug war took root in Bagong Silang, not to exemplify concepts through Bagong Silang. We hope that some of our analysis may resonate in other places where these wars on drugs, crime, terror or gangs distort social relations. We return to this point in the last chapter of the book.

Following this introduction, we have organized the book in five empirical chapters. All chapters have the same, basic longitudinal structure, whereby we move from the time before the war on drugs into an account of how the specific issue either structured or was structured by the drug war. We do this to explore the drug war in the larger structures of Bagong Silang and Philippine violent politics beyond the present moment. The second organizing principle is to start with an analysis of policing in chapters 2 and 3, as policing most directly relates to the war on drugs. We then explore three issues in chapters 4, 5, and 6 that are important for an understanding of the drug war: displacement and the production of local moralities, communal and activist politics, and the masculine peer groups from which many of the victims in the drug war came. These three chapters tell different stories and are relevant in different ways. One way of situating the three chapters is that they explore how structures of domination and violence were created and maintained at the metropolitan and local levels, how residents and activists tried to intervene and change these same structures but became marginalized, and how a particular group of young men then came to be caught as helpless victims in these structures of domination as the war started. A second way of positioning the three chapters is to note that they all fundamentally describe a cry for equality and dignity from the margins and the extent to which the elite and the government have denied those people that equality and dignity. We explore this in calls for moral communities of equals, revolutionary equality, or recognition as part of a national fraternity. The three chapters explore how state violence folded itself into intimate communal relations in (sometimes uncanny, sometimes straightforward) violent ways before the war as well. In this way, they help us understand the continuities in communal intimacy and violent politics that we explored in chapters 2 and 3 directly in relation to policing. We conclude the book with a short chapter that summarizes some of the important and rather tragic insights concerning Bagong Silang and beyond by situating the war on drugs in relation to other wars in the Philippines and the world at large.

In chapters 2 and 3, we explore different aspects of policing before the war on drugs to understand how these aspects developed during the war. While the two chapters do explore the war on drugs, they do so from the perspective of the people in Bagong Silang—as fraught relations to neighbors and local state officials and increasingly extortionist practices by the police. In chapter 2, we explore the relationship between order making, politics, and intimacy, whereas in chapter 3 we focus on exchange relations, money, and survival. Chapter 2 traces policing practices as inextricably linked to local politics. The chapter explores the emergence and practices of machine politics, that is, the transformation of electoral politics into politics of specific (personalized) interests, as well as how intimate communal relations inform the practices of policing. With the war on drugs, policing acquired an even more important role. Increasingly, policing the war on drugs began to work on and transform the very societal relations in which it was practiced. This led to a fundamental reconfiguration and destabilization of culturally intimate state-resident relations as well as relations between residents and neighbors.

Chapter 3 continues this line of inquiry but shifts the focus slightly. While we examine police violence prior to and during the drug war, as in the previous chapter, here we focus on the moral justifications regulating police violence and illustrate how people managed their relationship with the police through interpersonal networks, cunning, and money before the onset of the war. In the second part of the chapter, we turn to the drug war. This section describes its impact on Bagong Silang and how exchange relationships between the police and the policed have been reconfigured, not least in relation to what has been known as Tokhang for Ransom, that is, how police have been cashing in on the war on drugs. By focusing on corruption and violence, we understand how the war on drugs cannot be reduced to sovereign acts of violence but must be understood also as part of old, ingrained structures of exchange and entanglement between authority and population.

In the following three chapters, we explore the different conditions that allowed the war on drugs to take the specific form it took, as well as to understand the political culture, which in some ways resisted, but also allowed, the war on drugs. These struggles took place in a constant tension between calls for equality and social structures that constantly reproduced social hierarchies. Chapter 4 explores the production of Bagong Silang as a marginal space on the edge of the urban political economy where particular forms of social, gendered, and generational moralities emerged. In outlining the history of Bagong Silang, we relate it to the continuing displacement of the urban poor in the light of the creeping encroachment of the "new" city. We show the extent to which violence and violent dislocation as critical events (Kapferer 2010) have always been at the center of politics. The war on drugs—as a specific critical event in a violent history—is but one instantiation of a long history of violence in which polite society has waged something akin to war on the unwanted, the surplus people, of the Philippines. Central to the chapter is also the analysis of ongoing differentiation in terms of intersecting class, gender and generational structures. This intersectional analysis (Crenshaw 1990) illustrates how displacement was central in producing a gendered and generational underclass of people in need of discipline. Focusing on the path walk, the narrow paths that organize communal life in Bagong Silang, we show that levels of trust are high—but only because people are always wary of each other (Carey 2017; Mayblin 2019). In these path walks, conflicts abound. When analyzing data from thousands of blotter reports to the state-appointed area leaders, an image of negotiated conflicts emerges that is often organized along lines of gender and generation. To say it bluntly, and counter to the dominant belief, it is older men who perpetrate violence against the young, not the other way around. This, of course, is just the prequel to the war on drugs, in which older men and women, on behalf of and in the employ of the state, targeted the young by drafting lists of those to be killed, which illustrates the degree to which patriarchy works to legitimate violence. The chapter then moves on to discuss concepts, such as *utang na loob, pakikisama,* and *diskarte,* that we found to animate communal life. These concepts are not objective categories that describe vertical and horizontal relations as well as cunning and ability; rather, they should be understood as ever-negotiated concepts at the frontline of survival and well-being. The chapter ends by illustrating that it was these horizontal relations concerning notions of equality that were renegotiated and reconfigured violently by the war on drugs.

In chapter 5, we shift focus to describe the evolution of the popular struggle in Bagong Silang prior to, during, and after the establishment of Bagong Silang through the history of community activists. In examining the struggle, we illustrate the change from militant action to its erosion, and in some instances, co-optation. Moreover, this illustration provides key insights regarding relationships that inform local politics. The chapter illustrates that while patron-client relationships persist, there is a constant echo of other, more egalitarian ways to imagine society. These other ways, however, always seem to be perilously close to being marginalized in professionalized or relentlessly hierarchical forms of politics. Community activism was caught between the revolution and patron-client relations, which both shaped and were transformed by the drug war. The chapter introduces and explores the life worlds of a series of central characters in Bagong Silang and in our work, like Emilio, Lita, and Arnel. In various forms, they have embodied the struggles and paradoxes of life in Bagong Silang for decades and continue to do so as they try to position themselves in Duterte's and the Philippine elite's drug war.

In chapter 6, we home in on one of the central masculine youth peer groups in 2009 and 2010, the members of Tau Gamma Phi. We describe their internal dynamics and engagements with local politics to be included as equal and dignified people despite the seemingly impenetrable glass ceilings of Philippine society. We locate their attempts of inclusion in a hundred-year-long struggle for equality that resonates strangely with the aspiration of the activists described in chapter 5 and communal politics described in chapter 4. Through an analysis of ritualized violence, we argue that they aspire to a transcendental world of significance beyond the spatial and temporal confinement of the relocation site. While young men were drawn to Tau Gamma Phi in their thousands in 2010 and chapters existed in almost every area, it had already begun to weaken. It was thus no surprise that by 2017, the fraternity's power and influence had considerably waned. However, what was even more chilling is that these were exactly the young men who suffered the hardest when the war hit Bagong Silang. Hence, by looking at the fraternities, we are offered privileged insights into the practices and imaginaries of those who would become the victims of the war and their craving for equality and inclusion. While their practices were sometimes violent and often counterproductive, the fraternities were, for lack of a better word, patriotic and keenly interested in contributing to society. Ironically, many of their practices also echoed the underlying notions of the war on drugs—that many young men were *magulo* (disorderly), uninformed, and in serious need of discipline that had to be installed through violent rituals (Kusaka 2017a). What the war on drugs illustrated was that the state agreed and the young people had failed to convince polite society that they had reformed. It became a case of fraternity denied.

Finally, in chapter 7, we aim to accomplish two things as a way of leaving Bagong Silang: we revisit our argument and we draw out comparative aspects in order to understand the war on drugs as more than a contemporary, Philippine tragedy. Summarizing the argument, the war struck Bagong Silang in ways that fundamentally reconfigured sociality and were animated by historical structures of displacement and violence. Communal intimacy had been central for survival, but the war could only work because it folded itself into these intimate forms of affective relationality. Furthermore, the war also worked on and reproduced intersecting differentiations of class, gender, and generation. While the war enjoyed what seemed to us to be puzzlingly high levels of support in Bagong Silang, these supporters were always ambivalent. Their support was mixed with fear that the war would put them or their families at risk as well as a sense that the war, yet again, reproduced structures of inequality and indignity that people had been fighting against in communal relations, in activist politics, and in the production of moral communities of significance. The second part of the chapter takes its point of departure in the fact that while much of what we write happened in Bagong Silang, it could happen and, arguably, has happened in many similar places around the globe. Based on this insight, we look at earlier forms of state violence in the form of counterinsurgency in the Philippines as well as drawing parallels to other wars on drugs in South Africa and the Americas. We explore the war as a global phenomenon, the kind of politics the war on drugs constituted, and how those politics privileged particular forms of policing. In this way, we hope, though possibly in vain, to contribute to a different form of politics beyond the violence of politics that does not take hostage forms of communal intimacy, through which people should be able to live, not to die.

# INTIMACY, POLICING, AND VIOLENT POLITICS IN BAGONG SILANG

Maria, a long-term friend, and Steffen were sitting in the rain under a tree in May 2017 in one of the thousands of path walks with a former member of the fraternity, Kenny, and his father, discussing the killings in the area. Kenny's father told us about a killing he had witnessed across the road in which ten police had shot and killed a local drug pusher. "He was trying to escape by climbing one of the poles," he told us. "The police said he was resisting arrest. I guess he was, but he was not posing a threat. They just killed him." Purok Tan, a local *barangay* official, had put the drug pusher on the list. The pusher was far from the only person that the official had put on the list. This is when a young man who had joined us muttered that maybe this could cause the violent demise of Tan: "Maybe Purok Tan will not survive for so long . . ." Kenny's father, who worked under Tan as a community guard, concurred hesitantly, caught as he was between the young man and the local leader.

This little vignette suggests at least two issues that we will explore in this chapter—the deeply fraught question of the legitimacy of the drug war locally (Kusaka 2017a; Curato 2017b) and how and the extent to which policing is embedded in communal life in Bagong Silang.[1] As we shall see, while this is not new, the ascension of Duterte to the presidency increased the mandate for police and policing incursion into everyday life. Except for a very few academic works (Austin 1999; Varona 2010; Gutang 1991; de Campos 1983; McCoy 2009; Jensen and Hapal 2015), the police and policing had not been the subject of any real critical scrutiny in and of themselves in the Philippines. Mostly, observers explored policing and the police, if at all, as institutions caught in elite politics

(Sidel 1999). We attempt to address this lacuna in this chapter and the next. Each of the two chapters follows the same template of analyzing policing before the onset of the war on drugs and into and through the critical event of the war to understand how the war transformed or reconfigured sociality, policing, and order making in Bagong Silang. We illustrate how policing before the war was also central in the ways in which intimate and effective relationality with the state produced and maintained particular forms of life and set the parameters for survival in Bagong Silang. In the second half of chapters 2 and 3, we then explore how the critical event and the escalation of state violence reconfigured those parameters for life and, increasingly, death. The two chapters differ on two accounts. First, whereas this chapter primarily focuses on what we could call the intimate politics of policing, the next chapter will focus on the affective exchange relations between the residents and the police before and after the onset of the war on drugs. Second, and related to this, this chapter primarily focuses on communal relations between residents and the state and especially the role of what is called the Barangay Justice System (Katarungang Pambarangay), whereas the next chapter will pay much more attention to the Philippine National Police. There are empirical reasons for this. The Barangay Justice System simply plays a more important role in the intimate politics of Bagong Silang, and most of the violent exchange relations between citizens and policing structures involve the Philippine National Police. This was so before the war and after its onset.

After this brief caveat, let us return to the analysis of how policing practices animate and are animated by intimate, effective relationality in Bagong Silang. Despite the lack of explicit interest in policing, seeing it primarily as an expression and instrument of elite politics, it is clear that policing has always been intimately related to political processes and family relations in the Philippines. Its lack of capacity—for that was how it was most often talked about—was seen as part of what we may call the weak states paradigm, whereby accountability is lacking and private interests dominate (Abinales 2005). While this may also be true, the fragile states approach offers a diminished insight into the politics and practices of policing in Bagong Silang. We cannot reduce policing to looking at the practices of the formal police or at formal mandates. Instead, we need to explore how the policing structures are embedded in, formed, and performed through local practices and imaginations, along with who actually performs authority and with which legitimacy it is exercised (Lund 2006; Albrecht and Kyed 2015).[2] We need to focus on how order making is part and parcel of local politics and how local politics impact what we elsewhere have called everyday policing (Buur and Jensen 2004), that is, the actual forms of policing and order making that take place on the ground. Our analysis indicates that while policing is subsumed under local, electoral politics and family and community relations, these relations are inherently complex and can only be fully grasped if we pay close attention to relations between order making, policing, and politics. This has, of course, only become more pertinent with the advent of the war on drugs.

The Philippine National Police has been the lead agency in the war on drugs and is responsible for many of the killings. However, the war on drugs has implicated local government structures, especially the Barangay Justice System, in important ways, as is evident in the case of Purok Tan. Oplan Tokhang, literally Operation Knock and Plead, involves police officers going around to suspected drug personalities (especially small-time drug dealers and drug addicts), warning them about the consequences and trying to get them to mend their ways. The visits are based on watch lists frequently drawn up by people involved in the Barangay Justice System. While ordinary residents can and do report neighbors and families to the police, it has mainly been the task of the barangay officials like Tan to ensure that the lists are available. This puts the Barangay officials at the center of the war on drugs. Also, before the onset of the war on drugs, the Barangay Justice System was central to policing because this system represented the most accessible and widely used order-making mechanism in everyday policing. Hence, while we do explore the Philippine National Police (PNP) in this chapter, we primarily focus on the Barangay Justice System and its relationship to residents of Bagong Silang. This system was first introduced in 1978 during the Marcos regime and further developed by the Local Government Code in 1991 after the fall of Marcos's dictatorship and with the new government's attempt to decentralize and demilitarize the police. It aimed to unclog the formal court system and to introduce a locally sensitive arbitration system (Asian Development Bank 2009). The system has been quite successful in generating trust and ensuring locally sensitive forms of arbitration. Furthermore, it operated as a central institution in upholding what we could call the patriarchy on the streets. It was therefore almost inevitable that the system and its many local representatives would play a crucial part in the war on drugs.

We organize the chapter in four sections. The first section describes in some detail the Barangay Justice System and its relation to larger policing structures. The following two sections focus on the period before the onset of the war between 2009 and 2013. We explore policing as intimate practices informed by family and communal relations and show that it is not analytically possible to separate policing practices from intimate communal relationality. This argument is further developed in the second section, where we analyze how formal politics and policing are entangled practices. We show this in case studies focusing on electoral politics, political transitions, and policing. We follow the representatives of the Barangay Justice System as they engage in conflict resolution; are caught in community and family conflicts, including their own; and are expected to play a central role in electoral politics by those political masters that pay and/ or recognize them. The terrain set out by these political masters was highly uncertain, temporary, and fraught with dilemmas. For some of the purok leaders, the political masters represented their best chance to access networks and resources to realize their political ambitions, while for others they incarnated dangers of disenfranchisement, marginalization, and potential violence. The last, long section before the concluding remarks is set in the time after the introduction of the war on drugs. Here we explore and try to explain the radical unpredictability of violence locally that the war produced. It is this in unstable terrain that we return to the Barangay Justice System. Some purok leaders endorsed and supported the war on drugs whole-heartedly while others were much more reticent and even tried to resist their enrollment in the war, as was the case with Tan and Kenny's father. Whatever the case, the war radically reconfigured their relationship to both the state and the citizens as well as their sense of community. To follow and understand the purok leaders and *tanods* (guards) is to be at the frontline of the war on drugs and the transformation of intimate and effective relations central to both survival and risk in the poor and urban margins of Philippine society.

## The Barangay Justice System

Bagong Silang has always been a complex place to police. Between 1985 and 1990 up to 250,000 people were displaced from some of the poorest, most overcrowded areas of Manila: Tondo, Valenzuela, Divisoria, Commonwealth, and Payatas. These areas were all perceived as inherently violent places, a reputation that Bagong Silang inherited. Apart from a reputation of gang- and drug-related violence, Bagong Silang also constituted the frontier between the New People's Army (NPA) and Metro Manila. A large part of the responsibility for policing fell to the Barangay Justice System (Katarungang Pambarangay). Introduced during a period of martial law, the Local Government Code further developed the system in 1991, after the fall of Marcos's dictatorship, in the new government's attempt to decentralize and demilitarize the police. The same legislative process relocated the Philippine National Police to the Department of the Interior and Local Government (Gutang 1991). This move clearly annoyed and vexed the police as they found it humiliating. That experience partly explains the police's excitement and endorsement of the war on drugs after the 2016 election. There will be more about that in the next chapter.

The concept of the barangay emanates from a precolonial past, when it designated the crew and population of a boat (Scott 1994). As such, the design is premised on small, intimate groups of people. In many parts of the Philippines, this is still the case and a barangay might comprise a few hundred or maybe a thousand people. However, with urbanization, some of the barangays have become sizable administrative entities often the size of municipalities. Of all the Barangays, Bagong Silang is the largest, with about 250,000 inhabitants. Apart from being an important administrative unit, it is also a very large voting block and the politician who commands the votes of Bagong Silang has come far in relation to controlling the municipality of Caloocan. Bagong Silang has been divided up into nine phases. Each phase is again divided up into packages that in Tagalog are called "purok," which again are divided into blocks. On these scalar levels, different political, administrative and order-making tasks are addressed.

A package typically covers between three hundred and six hundred houses, with up to twenty-five hundred residents. In Bagong Silang, there are 115 packages, each with a purok leader appointed by the head of the barangay. Each purok leader nominates a number of tanods. In 2010, this number was 10, making the total number of tanods 1,150. On an everyday level, the purok leaders and the tanods are charged with maintaining the peace and solving local, neighborhood disputes. These conflicts may be about debt, public misbehaving, neighborhood disagreements and conflicts, marital problems, problems with drinking and with the youth, swearing, and so forth (see chapter 4). If the purok leader and his or her tanods are not able to solve the conflict or if the parties are not willing to let them mediate, the case is transferred to the next level of the Barangay Justice System, the Lupong Tagapamayapa (Lupon), which is a barangay-wide mediation council or directly translated the pacification committee. Together, the purok leaders, tanods, and Lupon constitute the first step in the criminal justice system in the Philippines (Asian Development Bank 2009). The Barangay Justice System has jurisdiction in less serious criminal cases—those carrying a penalty of less than one year of imprisonment or a fine of less than PHP5,000.[3] Cases that involve children, land, and real estate conflicts; corruption cases; and cases involving people from different local government structures are also dealt with by other legal entities, like the police and the Barangay Council for the Protection of Children.

Between 2008 and 2010 more than twenty thousand cases were heard by the Bagong Silang Barangay Justice System. Most of the cases were dealt with at the lowest level of the system, that is, the purok. In 2008 and 2009, about three thousand cases (or one in five) were referred from the level of the purok to the level of the barangay and the Lupon. At both the level of purok and that of the Lupon, most often conflicts are settled through a *kasunduan* (a pledge or an agreement).[4] How many cases are referred up in the system varies from purok to purok. In one of the packages that we will explore later in the chapter, not one case was referred in 2009 from the level of the purok to the Lupon. In another package, some cases were referred upward in the system. Clearly, this had to do with the nature of the conflicts, but also with the different purok. The one who did not refer any cases put much pride in that fact, whereas the purok working in the neighboring package emphasized the rules about when to refer, including cases of serious fighting and theft. This purok also put emphasis on respecting the wishes of those implicated and not forcing a local solution on them. Hence, if one party in the dispute wanted to refer the case to the Lupon, then the purok would follow this wish.

While there are differences between the different purok across Bagong Silang, it is also clear from our material that they share similar complex issues and dilemmas when carrying out their duties of order making. Prominent among those dilemmas and issues are the overlapping spheres of politics, family, and community. In the following two sections we first explore policing in the intimate worlds of family and community, and then examine the entangled nature of policing structures and electoral politics. We begin by following one specific purok leader, Mr. Garcia, to illustrate just how intimate a family affair policing on the ground can be.

## Policing and Community Intimacy before the Drug War

We met purok leader Garcia in 2009 on the first night of our fieldwork in Bagong Silang. It was Maricel who had taken us to Garcia. Maricel was the tanod responsible for the block where we stayed. There are five of these blocks in the package that Garcia is in charge of. We had been introduced to Maricel as someone who knows everybody in the block. Maricel took us on a tour, assuring us that everything would be ok: "Don't worry! Maricel will take care of you." The tour ended in the outpost where Garcia met us. At the time, Garcia was around sixty years old and a very friendly man, full of humor and capable of more than a few sexual innuendos. He showed us his books; in 2009 not a single case from his area had been referred further up the system; he had dealt with all the conflicts, he told us with pride. Garcia was, in principle, a volunteer, appointed by the head of the local government entity, the barangay captain, to perform an important community service. However, each tanod and each purok leader received an honorarium from the barangay captain (at the time a man named Padilla) and the then mayor of the larger city of Caloocan, Recom Echeverri. Although the amount was low, it came with recognition and access to resources as well as the possibility of patronage and ascending the political ladder. Both politicians were part of important political families on the levels of the barangay and the municipality.

Behind Garcia's chair, a placard indicated the names of Garcia and his ten tanods. Four of them were male relatives of Garcia, either his sons or sons-in-law; all of them were middle-aged. Garcia's situation was in no way unique in this regard. If we look at the overall profile of the slightly less than thirteen hundred purok leaders and tanods in Bagong Silang from the period between 2007 and 2010, more than 75 percent were male and 95 percent were above age thirty in a population with a majority of people below the age of twenty-five (Jensen, Hapal, and Modvig 2013). In this way, the purok leaders and their tanods constituted the kind of patriarchy that we discuss in chapter 4 in further detail. Although less conclusive, as a proxy for family relations, tanods and purok leaders often shared the same name or lived close to each other. When asked about this, Maricel and Garcia explained that a leader must be able to trust the people under him.

Unlike Garcia, Maricel was nominated because she allegedly knew her area extremely well. Hence, Garcia had sought her out to represent her area. This made policing highly intimate since it appeared to be frequently controlled by a small circle of individuals composed of middle-aged men related to each other by blood, kinship ties, or common history (*pinagsamahan*). However, intimacy worked in more complex ways than through kinship, as notions of neighborliness and common history often took precedence. Policing the ones you know requires a constant negotiation of such ties. In a package adjacent to Garcia's area, purok Ponte was in charge of local security. Ponte was appointed purok leader due to his close church relations to Barangay Captain Padilla. Ponte, in turn, appointed his daughter, a daughter in-law, and two of his five sons as tanods. The sons had a reputation for rowdiness when they drank—which they did quite often.

One afternoon, one son got into a fight and a neighbor stabbed him in the arm. The circumstances around the incident were uncertain, with Ponte's family insisting that it was a case of mistaken identity and others claiming that this was part of a conflict over debt. After the fight, the daughter of the house, also a tanod, went to the police to file a case, as it was outside the jurisdiction of the purok leader (her own father). In the days that followed the parents of the alleged stabber visited the Ponte family on several occasions, trying to make them drop the case. During these visits they invoked several concepts that all speak to issues of communal intimacy: the stabber was a *kababata*, that is, someone the brother who was stabbed grew up with; they had *pinagsamahan*, that is, a common history; and they invoked the notion of *pakikisama*, a kind of neighborliness. Of these concepts pakikisama especially is central.[5] To understand its centrality, we need to visit the path walk, a central part of communal life in Bagong Silang.

The path walk is the quintessential public space of Bagong Silang. There are thousands of path walks across the resettlement site, and life is lived more or less within the confines of these narrow streets. People's *kababata* will often come from the same path walk, and the history they have will emanate from what has happened here, good or bad. The path walk is densely populated, and little of what happens in anybody's house will go unnoticed by the neighbors. This is the space of *pakikisama*—or neighborliness, the ability to get along. As such, pakikisama is highly valued. As Maricel said: "It is deep, deep." It is what makes it possible for people able to survive; it is the ultimate support network, but it is also structured, not least by gender and generation.

However, there is a "darker" side to the concept. As one informant said, "I can't do anything about it. I need to get along with them. I live in this block; they also live in this block." Hence, pakikisama is ambiguous. On the one hand, it is ultimately virtuous—the ideological rendition of the good community; on the other hand, people are compelled to get along due to the claustrophobic proximity in which people live. To be outside these networks—to be seen as not knowing how to perform pakikisama—can be detrimental to one's survival, as we discuss in chapter 4. The Ponte family finally relented and dropped the case, specifically because of pakikisama, something a purok leader, in particular, cannot afford to ignore.

Pakikisama also has other direct effects on what is policed. In the block where Maricel worked as a tanod, the local drug dealer and the abortionist (and possibly others) were in blatant violation of the law. However, in both cases Maricel evoked pakikisama to talk about her relationship to them: they are supportive of people; they do people favors and in spite of Maricel's conservative morals, she thought that the abortionist provided a necessary service. In a replay of Herzfeld's notion of cultural intimacy (Herzfeld 2014), she explained: "I knew that Ken is a distributor of *shabu* [crystal meth] but it is not just for himself; he is able to help others. Ken helped many people here. People run to him whenever they need help. No difference with the abortionist: We were supposed to target her but then we had an opportunity to know each other. She helped a lot of people so then I stopped."

The drug dealer and the abortionist also knew that it was in their best interest to practice pakikisama because that—at least to some extent—protected them from being handed over to the police or the tanods. In this way communal intimacy structures policing. It animates who is a criminal, when an act is defined as illegal, and when and how action must be taken—even by those charged with upholding the law. Determining what crimes should be prevented is a moral issue rather than one of legality (Jensen 2015b). However, authorities like Maricel not only exonerated illegality for others. In her own life, she ventured into the realm of the illicit as part of very complex livelihood strategies. At the time, Maricel was a *kubrador*; that is, she took bets in the widespread but illegal game of Jueteng. Furthermore, her husband earned his income from organizing equally illegal cockfights. Maricel sometimes rationalized these activities as her keeping an eye on things, but most of the time she humorously and remorselessly admitted her moral shortcomings. Moreover, these activities brought her into the sphere of interest for the PNP as these acts contravened legal codes—but not, however, as a subject of the law but rather as a subject of extortionist police corruption, as we shall see in the next chapter.

Hence, policing is, and was, not just about law and order but also about morality. It seems clear that dichotomies of legality and illegality, state and civil society are constantly blurred in complex ways through processes that relate to family, community, and law enforcement. In the words of Judith Butler, they are interdependent and coproduced (Butler 2004, 130). At the same time as people seem to be well aware of the distinctions between the legal and the illegal, they simply ascribe different moral values to different practices, akin to Janet Roitman's (2006) notion of the ethics of illegality. Hence, abortion can be illegal, amoral, yet also the right thing to do. Second, the Barangay Justice System relied on politically elected families. To have a conflict with these families might not be very comfortable. However, people, including purok leaders and tanods, who are living in these areas have to negotiate local intimacies that are hard to ignore. One needs to think about common histories, a sense of neighborliness, and survival, as well as the law.

As we shall see in the next section, political fortunes change, leaving purok leaders and tanods out of a job, meaning that their position of power is temporary. In the packages in which we did fieldwork, the entanglements and the temporality of their positions seemed to make them accountable to the local population. Furthermore, as tanods and purok leaders came from the same deprived areas, their livelihood strategies may be in contravention of the very standards they were made to police. Morality was therefore constantly negotiated within the system of policing, allowing law enforcers and residents alike to go on with the business of survival. In this way, the Barangay Justice System is intimately entangled with family and communal relations, although not always in the ways that the policies intended. However, the war on drugs, to some extent, reconfigured these intimate relationships, adding a new layer of complexity, as the state demanded, even insisted, that loyalty to the war was paramount. It was this complexity that caught Kenny's father in the dilemma described in the opening paragraph of this chapter.

## The Politics of Policing

Besides the fact that policing is always a fundamentally political task, policing structures in Bagong Silang and elsewhere in the Philippines are also part of the political machines of strong families. This is not least because these political families and the state offices they control often hire them and pay their salaries (Sidel 1999, 26). This is particularly important in relation to the Barangay Justice System, where there are two political masters, the barangay captain and the municipal mayor, with the latter often being the patron of the former.[6] In this section, we first show how the Barangay Justice System and other policing structures were used for political purposes in the May 2010 election for the municipal mayoral position. In the second part of the chapter, we present cases relating to the political transition that took place after the barangay election in October 2010.

## A Political Machine

Purok leaders and tanods are supposedly officers of peace. However, they are also, and maybe even primarily, clients of their political patrons. To see how that plays out, let us return to Garcia's outpost. Apart from the placard with the names of the purok leader and his tanods, the walls were decorated with images of Garcia's political masters, barangay captain Cesar Padilla, who nominated Garcia as purok leader, and Mayor Echiverri. Garcia and his colleagues were called on and expected to take part in political rallies and functions, especially around election time. They were explicitly told that failure to support their patron would mean that the state apparatus would not pay their honorarium, which in this way resembled a private donation from the political master even if it was paid from the state coffers.

In all the rallies up to the May 2010 national elections, the purok leaders and the tanods constituted the bulk of supporters for incumbent Mayor Echiverri, as well as for the Liberal Party, on whose ticket the mayor had decided to run. Echiverri had recently jumped ship from the party of outgoing president Gloria Arroyo, Lakas ng Tao (Power of the People), as the times seemed to favor presidential candidate Benigno Aquino III, son of national icon Corazon Aquino, to become the next president. Echiverri's senatorial ambitions were known in many quarters. For that to come true, he needed to share a national platform with the stronger candidate when he reached his three-term limit as mayor in 2013. At the same time, he tried to pave the way for his son, RJ Echiverri, to take over as mayor in the 2013 national elections.[7] In this way, Echiverri incarnated the traditional politician, called *trapo*, which in Spanish and Tagalog means "dirty rag" and has been identified by a host of commentators as the one big problem in Philippine politics. What defines this politics is no loyalty to any party or agenda; it involves concern only for one's own fortunes and those of the family, and it is characterized by the mixing of private and public interests (Austin 1999; McCoy 1994; Hutchcroft and Rocamora 2003; Quimpo 2009; Sidel 1999).

In Bagong Silang, it was common knowledge that Padilla and Echiverri were political opponents. Still, because Padilla depended on Echiverri for his fortunes, he had to toe the Echiverri line and organize rally after rally for him. An insider in Padilla's office said that Echiverri had demanded absolute loyalty. If not, the consequences would be grave for future patronage. Subsequently, Padilla informed all purok leaders and tanods that he would not tolerate any absences from the rallies. Ponte's daughter explained, "If we don't come, we will not get our honorarium—not from Mayor Echiverri and not from Padilla."

The discussions about honorariums were frequently part of conversations with the purok leaders and tanods. Honorariums were often late and frequently smaller than expected. On one occasion, at the Christmas Party of all ten packages in Phase 5 in 2009, the mayor was supposed to come and show his appreciation of the service of the purok leaders. The excitement was tangible as Echiverri entered the covered court singing his signature song. All joined in. After ten minutes, he left again, leaving behind the money. The daughter of purok Ponte received the money on behalf of their package. With contempt, she looked at the 500 peso note (about 10 USD) that the ten tanods were to split and pretended to step on it. Furthermore, many of the purok leaders supported Padilla or other candidates rather than Echiverri. Maricel, for instance, was a staunch supporter of Echiverri's main rival, Oca Malapitan, who she hoped would win the 2013 election. This would allow her to cash in on all her hard work as an organizer for him. Garcia was originally a protégé of Echiverri. However, at a time of great distress and illness, he had turned to Oca Malapitan for support. Oca helped him, and thus he incurred what is called an *utang na loob*, a debt of gratitude, with Oca. Hence, Garcia was bound to support Oca, at least discreetly. Openly associating himself with Oca would have made him lose his position as purok leader. In the case of Ponte, there was little doubt. He had a long-standing relationship with Captain Padilla and his wife owed her job in the Barangay Hall to Padilla and to Echiverri. To go against this line would have been fatal for the financial stability of the family.

Despite the common knowledge that Padilla was not in favor with Echiverri, he supported the mayor as loyally as he could. Echiverri's election campaign was flawless; it didn't even cost him much money because of the poor opposition. Regardless of the weak opposition, however, he used all the state's resources for his own personal electoral gain. The policing structures were especially implicated. Purok leaders and tanods constituted the muscle of the campaign, and at every rally, station commanders of the Philippine National Police would speak about the heroic deeds of Mayor Echiverri. Like the purok leaders, they also owed their position and resources (allowances, vehicles, gas, phones, etc.) to the mayor. In the final election showdown, Echiverri used every police vehicle in Caloocan, probably to remind both the police and the general electorate who was in charge. Come election time, Echiverri won a landslide victory over a weak opposition. So did Oca in the congressional election. However, Padilla did not fare well, as Echiverri dumped him unceremoniously for his own candidate, Inar Trinidad, who went on to win the barangay elections some months later. This resulted in a sweeping transition, which also affected policing structures and their agents.

## Policing and Electoral Transition

When political patrons lose their office at any level in the Philippines, it usually results in a reshuffling of government offices from top to bottom. Posts are being refilled, offices are shut down, new offices are created, and budgets are revamped. All these shifts benefit new political patrons and allow them to repay the many debts incurred while attempting to be elected and also prepare them to win the next election. Hence, transitions are moments of great uncertainty for losers and those with weak political connections. In Bagong Silang, the Ponte family had much to lose when Captain Padilla lost the barangay elections to Inar Trinidad. Inar was seen by many as Echiverri's favorite candidate in Bagong Silang. Amid allegations of fraud, Padilla and his supporters were also embittered because of Echiverri's betrayal after Padilla's support during the 2010 national elections. Due to its size, Bagong Silang generates a lot of revenue through the Internal Revenue Allocation compared to other barangays, along with income from a variety of trading permits and issuing of IDs. There are also constant rumors of corruption by officials. In the Barangay Hall, there were, in Padilla's time, more than 250 employees. On top of this number, there were about 1,300 purok leaders and tanods. While some had to remain because of the jobs that they held or because they answered to different political patrons, a substantial number could not retain their positions. It was a matter of little surprise when purok leaders Ponte and Garcia were told to resign. In fact, all 115 purok leaders were told to vacate their office. The Ponte family awaited the fate of Mrs. Ponte, who worked in the Barangay Hall in the Barangay Council for the Protection of Children. It was to their great relief that Inar informed her that she could stay on. All throughout Bagong Silang, people were sacked from their position, especially if they had been close to Padilla. The official justification was that their loyalty was with the former barangay captain and not with the barangay. Keeping them in their post would threaten the current administration with too much politicking, which was detrimental to the "development" of the barangay. However, outgoing employees, like purok leaders and tanods, saw these actions as a purge to the benefit of the incoming barangay captain rather than an action in the best interest of the barangay.

It was not surprising that the puroks were replaced, as they almost always played a central role in the political machinery of the captain. They are often the only representative of the captain in each block of the huge relocation site. Besides the law enforcement, they perform important political tasks of presence and information to and from the Barangay Hall. In this way, replacing the supporters of the previous captain is an ideal opportunity to rid the council of dissent, to build relations, pay off political debts, and make one's mark. Inar came from the left side (*kaliwa*) of Bagong Silang and knew little of the right side (*kanan*), where Garcia and Ponte resided. As he knew little of the area, he nominated one of the erstwhile tanods in Garcia's area, who then replaced all of Garcia's kin with her own nominations. In Ponte's area, Inar nominated a political organizer of Echiverri.

After the election there was talk among some of the puroks of Padilla. They were certain that Echiverri had rigged the elections. They claimed to have done a good job in making Bagong Silang peaceful. In response, they formed a new organization, Samahang ng mga purok leaders at tanod ng Bagong Silang (the Organization of Purok Leaders and Tanods of Bagong Silang) prominently featuring several former purok leaders from the *kanan* of Bagong Silang. The organization tried to convince those who had been replaced to join to make Bagong Silang safe. However, not long after the organization was formed it became part of renewed political struggles between Mayor Echiverri and his vice mayor, Erice. Erice had mayoral ambitions and he needed a political machine to fight his battle in Bagong Silang, where he was weak. Immediately he seemed to have seized on the new organization as a potential cog in his electoral machine.

Shortly after Erice had begun to show an interest in the organization, unknown assailants killed one of its members. Whether his death was due to his membership in the organization is uncertain. As the word about the former purok leader had it, he was daring, talkative, sexually aggressive, and action-oriented. He frequently punished young people he thought were out of line. He might also have been involved in drugs. However, what spurred the rumor of his death being tied to politics was, first, that he died immediately after the formation of the organization and, second, because he was allegedly killed in a minivan with Echiverri's name on it. Regardless of whether his death was politically motivated, it had political consequences. For instance, Ponte's wife forbade him to join the new organization or even to get near any of the ringleaders out of fear for his life and her own livelihood. The death of the former purok leader also laid the organization to rest, along with Erice's hopes of mounting a challenge through it.[8]

While many of the purok leaders did not rely on the income generated from the honorarium, they still lost the source of recognition that followed with the post. Some of them had also invested personal resources in the position. Garcia, for instance, had decorated the room he used as an outpost, a building that one of the central Padilla supporters had loaned him. However, other, former purok leaders lost much more, as the case of a former purok leader, Ronel, illustrates. Ronel used to be a purok leader in the Phase 8 area (in *kanan*). During his tenure, he constructed a barangay outpost. When he lost his office, he wanted to retrieve his materials, including window frames and other building material. He went to the outpost but was met with resistance from the new purok leader. Ronel went on to beat him up so badly that he was arrested. However, due to his common history (*pinagsamahan*) with the officials at the barangay, Ronel was moved from the police cell and put in an office space at the Barangay Hall. Drawing on his connections again, Ronel managed to be set free the following day. Tragically, Ronel's father suffered a heart attack and died, presumably due to the shock of seeing Ronel taken into custody. However, the calamity did not end there. Angry with Ronel and seeking revenge, the new purok leader, along with his tanods, sought out Ronel and killed him. Subsequently, Ronel's pregnant wife lost their baby. The case illustrates the struggles over territory and resources locally and how they are tied up with state recognition. Ronel had constructed the barangay outpost out of his own pocket; that is, he came to represent, through his own resources, the state in his package. When he was no longer part of the state, he wanted it back with catastrophic consequences.

## Intimate Policing during the War on Drugs

So far, we have explored how and to what extent policing was caught up in family and community relations as well as local electoral politics before the onset of the war on drugs. While the Barangay Justice System is established with a statutory mandate, it is clearly animated by cultural intimacies comprising family relations, common histories, livelihood, and alternative ethics of legality (Roitman 2006). Furthermore, the Barangay Justice System is invariably implicated in electoral processes and political machines, to the extent that it often appears as though the political tasks take prominence over policing. As purok leaders and tanods are present everywhere in the massive barangay, they naturally attract the attention of political players. Hence, when the outgoing purok leaders wanted to establish an alternative justice structure, they were immediately implicated in the political schemes of would-be patrons. The moment this happened, the organization folded. At the same time, the purok leaders clearly had ambitions other than those of electoral politics. Some wished to secure themselves and their families and networks privileged access to resources and recognition from patrons and other community members that came with carrying out local policing. In this way, joining policing structures entailed both opportunities and dangers, all of which needed to be negotiated carefully by purok leaders and tanods. This intimate and effective relational economy is not inherently peaceful. On the contrary, violence is an integral part of the system at all levels, from the ways in which conflict is managed and how gender, age, and class articulate to conflicts over access to state resources and recognition. Nonetheless, despite the inherent violence and blatant injustice, the system of intimate and affective relationality was relatively predictable, following a certain schemata that we, along with Michael Herzfeld (2014), could talk about as based in cultural intimacy at the communal level. Purok leader Ponte and his family knew the rules of the game, understood how to play it, and were able to make decisions. Maricel also knew what her odds were. It was a question of employing the right combination of who you knew or with whom you could claim some kind of relationship; what kind of (monetary) resources you had at your disposal; and your capacity to navigate uncertain terrains (diskarte). In this way, the stability of the system reproduced existing power relations in terms of access to state power and in relation to social, gendered, and generational power structures.

The question is then how the onset of the war on drugs affected and reconfigured this complex intimate and affective relational economy. First, it is important to note that while the war on drugs constituted what we have called a critical event as well as a quantitative escalation in state violence (Kapferer 2010; Højer et al. 2018), the war was conducted through systems that were already in place, like the Philippine National Police and the Barangay Justice System. Many of the structures and institutional practices that we described earlier in the chapter were still in place and functioned as before the war. Police officers attend to complains, municipalities tar roads in which mayors and other figures in power engrave their names, tanods clean streets and path walks, purok leaders attend, even-handedly or not, to local conflicts, and residents go about their daily business of trying to survive and build a future for their children and families. Nonetheless, clearly significant changes have taken place, the most obvious of which is the rampant death in Bagong Silang. However, the death toll fails to capture important transformations in intimate communal relations that are at least as important. The transformations to which we have alluded throughout this book comprise, first, the destabilization of symbolic orders that render violence predictable (Jensen 1999; Feldman 1991). Second, the war functions through the reconfiguration or repurposing of the Barangay Justice System through what Palatino (2019) refers to as a "weaponization" of the system to play a significant part in the drug war (Lamchek 2017). The consequence, we argue, is that the drug war has led to a fundamental destabilization of both state-citizen relations and relations between neighbors in the path walks.

## The Unpredictability of Violence

Numbers in the drug war are very difficult to come by, and they are discussed intensely—not only how many have been killed but whom to count in which category (legitimate police operations, gang-on-gang violence, vigilante killings, killings by rogue cops, self-defense). According to official statistics from the Philippine National Police, a total of 27,928 killings were recorded between July 1, 2016, and July 31, 2018 (Philippine National Police 2018; Tina Santos 2018). Out of this number, 4,410 deaths occurred in "legitimate antidrug operations," while the remaining 23,518 deaths are listed as "homicide cases under investigation." In August 2018, an additional 444 deaths of drug suspects took place during antidrug operations (Philippine National Police 2018). Human rights organizations, members of the media, and academics protesting against the war have tried to assess objectively the number of deaths attributable to the war on drugs and extrajudicial killings, that is, deaths instituted by the state on behest of the president. In Bagong Silang, Balay Rehabilitation Center documented 106 deaths in a smaller section of Bagong Silang, mainly Phases 7 and 8 (Balay Rehabilitation Center and DIGNITY 2018). Other national documentation projects include, for instance, the Drug Archive run by Ateneo de Manila University, De La Salle Philippines, University of the Philippines-Diliman, and Columbia University.[9]

Documenting the death toll is clearly important for both political and legal reasons. As a repeat of his practices in the city of Davao (Altez and Caday 2017), Duterte claimed responsibility for cleaning up drugs but refused legal responsibility, suggesting that all police killings were part of legal drug operations in which the police kill suspects in self-defense. In this view, the state was not responsible for any other killings related to conflicts in the drug economy, intra-gang rivalry, or vigilante activities. Instead, the police investigated these deaths with vigor. Based on her interviews with police officers in Bagong Silang and in police headquarters in 2017 Warburg (2017) suggests that the legal defense and political pride both work through front-stage and back-stage performances, whereby the police can claim legality and justify extralegal violent policing at the same time.[10] Furthermore, those partaking in the war on drugs say they know that the police, despite their own (front-stage) discourses, do kill people. Warburg quotes one purok leader, Barretto in Bagong Silang, whom we shall see again in the discussion of the police's role in the killings of the people on his watch list: "I give the names to the police. They are included in the watch list, right? Then one of them is killed. Tokhang. . . . I give the area map, mapping of the house of the suspect. So, one day, [the police] kill them. *Patay!* [dead]" (Warburg 2017, 49).

While critiques of the war on drugs in academic circles, human rights organizations and the media have been largely unsuccessful in finding smoking guns concerning police involvement in the killings, there have been individual and spectacular cases where they have succeeded. One of those cases was the killing of Kian delos Santos, a minor, just across the bridge from Bagong Silang. Kian died in a violent attack on August 16, 2017. At first the police claimed that Kian had drawn a gun on the police, fired, and then was shot in self-defense. In his possession, they found a weapon, ammunition, and crystal meth. However, CCTV footage and witness statements soon established that Kian had been killed while he was defenseless and then framed by the police (Gavilan 2018). The killing of Kian led to huge protests from human rights organizations and politicians and finally to a conviction for murder of three lower-ranking police officers, who were sentenced to life in prison. While the sentences were severe, it led to no real accountability higher up in the system. Indeed, one of the commanding officers, after having been relieved of his duties, was later reinstated and even promoted within the police by President Duterte. This led to further suspicion that, in fact, the highest echelons of the police and the president approved Kian's killing (Roxas 2018).

All the conflicts and debates evolve around notions of knowledge. Who knows what? How can a death be counted and made to count? Moreover, conceptually, what constitutes real, true knowledge within different domains—the legal, the political, or the social domain (Choudhury, Jensen and Kelly 2018)? The documentation as well as the police reports and the official discourse all evolve around knowledge as objective and as an account of what really took place. Again, this is important for political and legal reasons. However, knowledge of or knowing about violence also has a subjective function in violent crises like the war on drugs. As we argued previously, while Bagong Silang was by no means peaceful or nonviolent before the advent of the war, there was a certain predictability to the violence. Most of the time, people could navigate social relations in ways that would protect them against violence. They knew more or less when to withdraw from conflict and when to push on. While this did not always work, most of the time it did. It was not a just social world. Women and younger men often suffered retributive, norm-maintaining violence (Benjamin 2018) from defenders, often older men, of a patriarchal order, as we explore in more detail in chapter 4. However, it was relatively predictable. This predictability seems to have been destabilized during the war. While the violence still reproduced patriarchal structures, it did so in much less predictable ways. Alan Feldman (1991, 79–80), in his analysis of violence in Northern Ireland, suggests that in situations of chronic violence, we need to understand how the symbolic order that explains violence breaks down and is, eventually, reconfigured anew. Let us try to provide some ethnographic detail to see how this worked in Bagong Silang in the midst of probably the most lethal phase in the drug war, late December 2016, in what locally was referred to as the "massacre in Phase 8" (Palatino 2019, 32).

On December 28, 2016, at the height of the drug war in Bagong Silang, two motorbikes, riding in tandem, blocked off the street of a house where a birthday party was taking place.[11] This was in one of the poorest sections of Bagong Silang, the part of Phase 8 called Bagsak.[12] Allegedly, the shooters barged in and started to shoot, leaving eight people killed, including a pregnant mother. Five of the victims were below the age of eighteen. Two of the victims were enrolled in Balay's educational programs. This much seems clear. However, intense discussions emerged around the identity of the perpetrators. The police, who came to the scene to investigate, asserted that according to their investigation, the shooting resulted from a drug-related conflict between two rival drug dealers in the area, each associated with different gangs or fraternities. Some residents, who were interviewed by Anna Warburg some weeks after the shooting, suggested that in fact the target had been a Muslim who had escaped a previous attempt on his life from a rival drug dealer and who had sought refuge in the house. He survived and those who were killed were, in fact, collateral damage. Other residents suggested that the killings resulted from strife between two rival fraternities.[13] Balay, which was well-connected in the area, suspected that the killers were in fact police. Reports did not even agree as to the gender of the assailants as some reports mentioned the presence of one woman and others reported only men. Finally, in May 2017 Steffen and Mariza, a friend from his fraternity days with whom he stayed during this round of fieldwork, went to interview people in Bagsak about the event, following his old fraternity networks. We got hold of the tricycle driver, a *brod*, who had taken one of the wounded to hospital. He had come to the house just after the shooting began and had found all the dead people in the house. He had then taken one of the wounded away to Tala hospital. According to him there had been two teams riding in tandem. So far this followed the narrative of the event. However, when asked about the perpetrators and the police narrative that it was drug-on-drug and not Tokhang and that people had identified a Muslim as the perpetrator and intended victim, one of the brods lowered his voice and said: "No, absolutely not, it was vigilantes but there were religious symbols there." When asked which one, he said, "You know that church, Iglesia ni Cristo. You know them? People said that they saw their colors, the green on white on their number plates so that's why we know it is them."

This deserves a few words. Some commentators call Iglesia ni Cristo (INC) a state within the state, given that reportedly it has as many as ten million members.

They have their own schools, universities, and housing areas. The church is known to command millions of votes. Hence, INC endorsement may constitute the difference between electoral victory and defeat (Serrano Cornelio 2017). Furthermore, they also have their own security organization, the Special Community Action Network (SCAN). In Bagong Silang, the SCAN has a reputation of violence beyond their mandate of maintaining order around INC functions. Allegedly, they can be called to intervene violently in INC members' conflict with neighbors. They are said to have hired out guns and goons to those willing to pay. According to several interlocutors in Bagong Silang, they were rumored to be involved in vigilante killings as part of the war on drugs. Consequently, their very name struck fear in people's hearts to an extent where conversations about the practices of the SCAN were conducted in a hushed voice, even when taking place inside a house. While these are rumors, they indicate the almost mythical place of the INC in local narratives. As one friend exclaimed after hearing such a rumor, "But you know it could be true."

Our task here is not to pronounce any of these narratives more or less credible. What they do suggest, however, is that the identities of the perpetrators and the victims have a shimmering and unstable nature (Jensen and Rønsbo 2014; Jensen 2015b). Depending on what narrative we choose, perpetrators and victims shift—vigilante, Muslims, gangs, collateral damage, gangsters, police, minors—even the unborn. This is not only of interest in terms of justice and accountability. It also affects how one stays safe. In order to stay safe, one needs to know from where the next assailants will come. It is about being able to predict violence. Each of these narratives come with a range of different protective measures. Do we stay inside? Lock all the doors? Prohibit our children from playing in the street? Or has the intended target been hit and we can rest again because the danger is past? In order to be able to make any decisions on one possibility or the other, people are constantly looking for signs of danger and certainty. In this way, the green on white colors of the motorbikes' license plates indicates—something. As our own work in South Africa (Jensen 1999) and, for instance, Helene Risør's work on security in El Alto Bolivia (Risør 2009) illustrate, people go to great and often creative lengths to "read" their environment.

In this way, the reading of signs and the telling of stories are ways of reconstituting the symbolic order that renders violence predictable. This also applies when the killings make sense within the logic of Operation Tokhang. Kuya Jerry had been killed in a drug bust. He was the cousin of an old informant whose death Kenny's father described in the beginning of the chapter. Ten police officers had chased him. In the end, he tried to escape by climbing a light pole to get across a wall. He had been shot in the leg in the process before being killed. The police claimed it was self-defense but a neighbor, also an old informant, had seen the incident. "In the leg . . . from below?" he asked rhetorically. However, everyone knew that Kuya Jerry was on drugs and sometimes sold small quantities to support his habit. When asked about the incident, his sister told us, "No, we know who it was and why. We are no longer afraid. We consider it a closed deal." In this way, the family told us that violence had been predictable. They obviously did not agree with the methods, however, "it was no surprise that Kuya Jerry died," as the mother continued, with grief in her voice.

This admission of guilt, while clearly not constituting any legal mandate for Kuya Jerry's murder, is, nonetheless, relatively rare. As we saw in the case of December 28, while police indicated that all had died, and not at the hands of the police, because they were involved in drugs, many residents insisted that it was collateral damage or a case of mistaken identity. They did not deserve to die. In this way, the notion of collateral damage in a strange way suggests that there are real drug personalities and that they, in some way, deserve the violence visited on them—but they are not us.[14] Of course, the notions of collateral damage and mistaken identities indicate that while the motives of the violence can be understood, people cannot either totally control or contain it. However, these notions also suggest that there is predictability to the violence. It can be explained, and it refers primarily to someone else. This same fundamental doubt also emerged in discussions of whether Bagong Silang was safer after the onset of the war. On the one hand, there were the pervasive narratives of mistaken identities, collateral damage, and the unpredictability of the violence. Anna Warburg (2017) also quotes one of her informants who noted the increased level of fear: "Before we used to go outside our house and talk, listen and tell stories even late at night, but we can't do that now, because we are afraid. We don't know who can be trusted anymore" (56). On the other hand, many people would insist that it was much safer now. Inday, one of our oldest informants assured us, 'Things are much changed now. Before there were too many drug *adiks* and we couldn't move at night. There was this fear. Now it is much better. We can walk up and down and feel safe."

Inday had been confined to her bed for a year because of a stroke and had only very slowly gotten back to some kind of normality. She was still very frail. We remembered that when we first met her, in 2009 and 2010, Inday did not appear scared to walk at night. Rather, she was always up and around and going out at all times. However, this is clearly beside the point. The insistence on it being safer, even in the midst of violence, is what allows people to go on living normal lives. Yes, it is violent. People die. But it is those people, the *adik* and the pusher, not me and my family. With Feldman's notion of the symbolic order of violence, we may say that people try constantly to reconstitute the symbolic order that allows them to feel safe and live normal lives. While this reconstituted symbolic order arguably breaks down ever so often in mistaken identities and collateral damage, it works on the premise that some people around here deserve to die (Kusaka 2017a).

## Reconfiguring Intimate Relations with the Local State

Tokhang relies fundamentally on the production of the so-called watch list or, put in context with the list, knowledge about real drug personalities. These lists were compiled by the police based on reports from the general population, from confessions signed by drug personalities, and from the purok leaders and tanods. As Anna Warburg asserts, these lists often became kill lists as the people on them tended to fall victim to mortal onslaughts, either in police operations or in assaults by unknown assailants and vigilantes "riding in tandem." The signing of confessions quickly stopped as people perceived it to be a "passport of death" (Warburg 2017, 50). This meant that the lists largely came from purok leaders and tanods. When we left them our informants on the eve of the drug war, we had established how implicated they were in intimate and affective relationality with their community and their political masters. This relationality did not grow less important during the war on drugs. On the contrary, they came to play a critical role in fighting the war package by package. As it was before the onset of the war, political projects worked their way down from the top. Mayor Oca Malapitan of Caloocan was a staunch supporter of the war and an ally of Duterte. He demanded that all his barangay captains play along. After the last barangay election in 2014, the political fortunes in Bagong Silang had shifted again. This time, they had favored Joel Bacolod, son of Councilman Bacolod and a member of one of the oldest political families in Bagong Silang.

The Bacolod family had lived in Bagong Silang since its inception, and it incarnated the traditional political family. Already when we did fieldwork in 2009–2010, Joel Bacolod was first *kagawad*. Kagawads are the councilors under the captain. They are elected independently of the captain, even if each candidate for the barangay captain fields a team of kagawads. Being first kagawad meant that Joel Bacolod had received the most votes of all candidates, even if he was not on the captain's list. True to form, not least as he conformed to trapo modes of politics focusing on building relationships and dispensing patronage to strengthen his and the family's political machine, he quickly got rid of most purok leaders to nominate his own team. Bacolod was also a strong supporter of Duterte, and especially of Oca Malapitan. Dutifully, he expedited the demand downward to assert that the barangay would participate fully in the war on drugs.

Informants told us that Bacolod had declared that he would consider those pu-rok leaders and tanods that did not perform well as assets to the drug dealers. This is a serious allegation that might lead anyone into trouble—with him and with the police. The gravity of the threat had been illustrated in the first months of the war on drugs when the barangay captain of adjacent Barangay 188, Edres Domato, had been killed along with his son, First Kagawad Edison Domato and every other kagawad in the barangay except for one. The Domato family was Muslim and widely believed to have links to the drug dealers in the area called Phase 12, which was infamous for its drug activities and its Muslim population. We shall return to Phase 12 in the next chapter. Suffice for now to say that the Domato family allegedly fell victim to assaults because they were assets of drug dealers. Hence, it was no small thing to decline to participate in drawing up the lists or to insist that there were no drug activities going on in their package. How-ever, it was also no small thing to inform on one's neighbors or to put them in harm's way by adding them to a list that was widely seen as a kill list. It is thus fair to say that purok leaders and tanods had to walk a tightrope between inti-mate and affective relationality with both their neighbors and their patrons.

When Anna Warburg arrived in Bagong Silang in January 2017, it struck her that many of the purok leaders she interviewed supported the war with a pas-sion.[15] This support was possibly less pronounced when Steffen arrived a few months later, in April 2017. While there are methodological reasons for what he found, empirically the field had also changed.[16] While a certain fatigue about the war may have set in (people indicated as much in informal conversations), more important for our purposes, in March 2017 unknown assailants killed one of the most vocal supporters of the war, purok leader Barretto, presumably because of his support for the drug war. If the killing of Domato illustrated how dangerous it could be to be an asset to the drug dealers, the death of Barretto proved that the opposite was no less risky. In the remainder of this section, we will explore how four purok leaders navigated these contradictory demands of deadly intimate and affective relationality. We begin with Barretto.

Barretto was an important man in his phase. Apart from being a purok leader, he was also chairperson of the local tricycle association[17] and had a past in the Philippine military. In his sixties, he personified the patriarchal values that we discuss in chapter 4. He was also a staunch supporter of the war on drugs. He exclaimed, "I accept peace and order, all the assholes, the . . . addicts. I have them arrested. There are many here. Those who are very addicted" (quoted in War-burg 2017, 64). He continued, "The really bad people here, the most bad ones [sic], they hurt people. I give the name to the police, then after a while, maybe two days . . . gone [moving two fingers across his throat]" (in Warburg and Jensen

2020a, 19). In this way, he invoked the standing language of the drug war that the adiks and the pushers hurt people and needed to be removed from society (Kusaka 2017a). Barretto knew that this might not be without risk to himself. He admitted, "Sometimes it is also frightening to report and report. I am being accused because I am the purok leader. Someone might go after me later on. . . . They might take revenge on me" (quoted in Warburg 2017, 59).

And they did go after him, presumably. In late March 2017 Barretto was killed in a drive-by shooting "riding in tandem." Immediately following his death, rumors as to why he was killed began to circulate. Some speculated that his death related to him being the chairperson of the local tricycle association (this was not unheard of). Others suggested in interviews that he was killed because he had failed to share the proceeds from the war on drugs, in which each useful piece of information was said to be remunerated by the state, something that Sheila Coronel (2017) also found. The majority of our interlocutors, however, suggested that his killing was related to his active involvement in the drug war and the number of people he had included on the watch lists.

While it is impossible to know the reasons for his death, it had effects on other purok leaders and on how they understood their own role. Ate Janet, for instance, an elderly purok leader in Phase 5, made the link explicitly. She had been elected purok leader because of her loyalty to barangay captain Bacolod. "It is always the same. The father and the son are so generous. They will always have time for you." Turning to Tokhang, we asked her if she had made a list of drug adiks. She looked at us suspiciously and said, "No, I don't think there is anything serious in my area." When asked to elaborate, she continued, "You know, I know their families. They are just simple people who are having a hard time. I know that they are only doing drugs for fun, sometimes. I don't think that is serious, so I reported that there was nothing to report from my area." We asked about Stella, a drug dealer from the package who had been killed. "She," Janet explained, "lived in the area but she was killed in Phase 8." Hence, Janet explained the presence of death by relocating it elsewhere. She said, "This area is peaceful, but drugs are coming in through here from Tala and Camarin, so that's how we sometimes have a little drugs." When asked what the police and the captain said to her about not reporting, she shook her head and said, "No, I just said that there was nothing to report. But if there was anything serious, I would report it. Both for drug dealing and drug use. I would have to." When asked how she distinguished between serious and not serious, she said, "Just like that, by looking if it is selling, or dealing and maybe if it is everyday." When asked if she felt pressured, she said, "Very much so. I am afraid. Just look at what happened to Barretto. You are in danger if you point to people. You have to think about your family first of all. So that is also why I did not make any list. I am very much afraid." The conversation with Ate Janet took place through an open window as she did not want to go out anymore and also didn't want us to enter the house. "I am sick all the time. All the stress. I tried to have the captain appoint a new purok leader, but he says I must stay on."

Ate Malou, a purok leader from Phase 1, experienced similar fears. We met her briefly with Karl, a friend of almost a decade and son of Emilio. We will meet Karl again in the next chapter where his family, some six years prior to the onset of the war, tried to get him out of a police cell unharmed. In 2017, he held a position as a nurse at the local hospital. Ate Malou adamantly denied that she was making lists. After leaving Ate Malou to her tasks, we asked Karl. "She is making lists," Karl said with confidence and in a hushed voice. "She just doesn't want to admit it." During one full day, we walked around with Karl in his area for him to tell us who was on the list. When we asked him to be discreet, Karl went, "Psst, house with red gate on the corner; on the list." When asked if he had seen the list, he said no. In this way, the list became the materialization of people's imagination of each other and the state: "If I were the state, Kuya Ambeth would be on the list!" Karl identified another twenty houses in the immediate vicinity of his home that he thought Ate Malou included on the list. Most of these were located in the excess lots near the creek, that is, the informal housing that had sprung up in addition to the planned houses in the rest of Bagong Silang. "There are so many drugs here," Karl said. While this may be true, it also confirmed Wataru Kusaka's analysis of how perceptions of drugs and crime animate and are animated by how local people distinguish between and recognize internal class division (Kusaka 2017a).

Juancho, also a purok leader from Phase 5, had refused to contribute to the lists. Juancho had become a purok leader because of his close school ties with the barangay captain. He was also very active in the Catholic Church and great friends with one of our friends, Mariza, who belonged to the same congregation. Similar to Ate Janet, he asserted that the people around him were good people. "I know some of them use drugs sometimes. For recreational purposes or because they are hungry and tired." This defense of drug use (and abuse) is frequently used. The job of staying alive in Bagong Silang is a tough one. Working days often last up to sixteen or seventeen hours for, say, jeepney or tricycle drivers. Drugs are often used to stay awake and to stave off hunger. Hence, what Juancho saw was not destructive consumption. Rather, he saw people trying to stay awake and alive. He pointed toward the creek and the excess lots. "It is often down there that you find the drug adik." He continued, "The people here—I know them. Some use drugs but not so much. I also think about their families. I am pro-life. Will I be responsible for killings?"

His explicit and open, religion-based stance had brought him into conflict with the local government leaders, including his patron, Joel Bacolod. They accused him of being an "asset" to the drug dealers. This accusation might well become dangerous as police targeted these alleged assets. Juancho was unfazed: "I told them to come and see for themselves. If they find anything I will redraw from my post." He had just arrived from a meeting at the Barangay Hall when we found him. The authorities had again demanded that they report and make lists but someone in the meeting had voiced protests. "Maybe it is changing," Juancho suggested. Furthermore, being a close associate of the barangay captain, Juancho may have felt slightly less exposed.

However, his deliberations as well as those expressed by the others enable us to see the real dilemmas of those charged with carrying out the drug war. Barretto, Janet, Malou, and Juancho's conundrums illustrate a larger issue as to how the drug war affects and reconfigures issues of communal trust in ways that might turn out to have lasting consequences. In other words, the war on drugs does not only concern state sovereignty and deaths. Rather, it affects and reconfigures intimate social relationships among residents and between residents and the state, not least through fear and, maybe increasingly, anger. As in the opening of this chapter, one informant next to Kuya Jerry's house reflected ominously about the purok leader who had entered Jerry's and many other names on the list, "Maybe Purok Tan does not survive for so long?"

These last cases illustrate the extent to which policing is caught up in intimate, communal relationality. In many ways, this did not change from before the war on drugs but the parameters of this relationality were reconfigured drastically. As we show, purok leaders and tanods had been central to political machineries before the war. They were being "asked" to perform loyally for their political masters as well as to navigate complicated communal relations. This was never easy or without risk, as the case of Ronel, who was killed by his predecessor in 2010, illustrates. However, the government primarily fought the war on drugs through the "weaponization" (Palatino 2019) of the local government. Along with the fundamental unpredictability of the violence and near-impossibility of assigning both victims and perpetrators to fixed categories, the demands to play along with their political patrons situated the barangay officials in dangerous and risky positions. Don't go along with the war and you end up like Domato; go along and you end up like Barretto! These conundrums and risks were not unique to barangay officials. Every resident in Bagong Silang faced similar dilemmas, although not in the same fashion and with the same acuteness. In this way, the barangay officials came to embody the fundamental dilemmas of the war. They reacted very differently to these dilemmas, whereby some bought into the war with fervor while others were much more cautious and worried. It was probably no coincidence that older and financially comfortable Barretto, who embodied what we could call the patriarchy on the street, was more vehemently active in the war, something which we will return to in chapter 4. In this way, the war played into and was fought along predictable lines of gendered violent politics at the same time as it inaugurated reconfigured forms of communal intimacy that may be the lasting effects of the war.

# POLICE VIOLENCE AND CORRUPTION IN THE WAR ON DRUGS AND BEFORE

Maricel, a political operator, tanod, and gambling and cock fight organizer, scurries off to pay yet another police officer demanding money to look away as the annual cock fights proceed at the back of the main road in Phase 5, Bagong Silang, in 2010. "Sometimes they come several times a day. I had officers coming in from Novaliches [some ten kilometers away] this morning," she humorously notes, shrugging her shoulders. Rafael confirmed this to Anna Warburg in early 2017 as she was conducting research in Bagong Silang on the war on drugs. "What do they claim their vision and mission to be? To protect and serve? Nah, that is not true. The only ones they protect are their families and themselves. Then all they really do is serve themselves. As for the community, nothing" (quoted in Warburg and Jensen 2020a, 11). The police had subjected Rafael to violent treatment in the past as well as recently, so he was in no way positively inclined toward the police. Rafael's comments and Maricel's experiences echoed persistent allegations against the police that they were corrupt and used their powers and the mandated violence to extort people. As the war on drugs picked up momentum and the bodies piled up, academic and political debates ensued about the shocking return to authoritarian rule and the production of a deadly sovereignty (Reyes 2016) whereby those deemed "disposable" (Tadiar 2013) could be killed without sanction (Agamben 1998). While we clearly agree with these criticisms, from our vantage point in Bagong Silang, two issues seem to warrant further consideration. First, while Duterte's war on drugs and the killing of Filipinos represent a radicalization and mark a new, deadly phase, the Filipino state is no stranger to killing its own people (McCoy 2009, 398). The second issue is that the focus on sovereignty and the production of authority through fear obscures the fact that police violence always was and continues to be animated as well by extortion rackets, which were radicalized in the war on drugs as Tokhang for Ransom (Coronel 2017, 176). However, rather than taking the practice of extortion as merely corruption, we propose to view these practices as part of intricate, often highly intimate exchange relations in which violence, or the threat of it, is key (Jensen et al. 2017). Drawing on anthropologist David Graeber's (2011) contribution, we suggest that violence is the means through which human relations are transformed into human economies of equivalence, that is, violence and the threat of violence produce relations and exchanges in which human life is priced in ways that the police and even residents (sometimes) believe are legitimate and useful.[1] In other words, violence, or the threat of violence, is what propels people to enter into exchange relations.

In this chapter, then, we ask how violence and exchange relations are connected in policing Bagong Silang and how these exchange relations have been transformed in relation to the war on drugs? In answering these questions, we propose two related arguments. First, exchange relations before and during the war constitute precarious encounters that need to be managed with the utmost care by both police and those they are extorting within a parallel, corrupt, and often violent system that mirrors the official criminal justice system. Second, the war on drugs, even if it was also couched in an anticorruption language, has transformed the parameters of exchange relations with the police in ways that made the system even more violent, expensive, expansive, and unstable. In order to conceptualize policing relations as exchange relations, as we suggested in chapter 1, we draw on Janet Roitman's important insights that we should not only focus on regulation or authority as such; rather we must focus on the relationships that are called forth and produced by regulation (Roitman 2004, 194). In her analysis of illegality and social relations in the Chad Bassin, she illustrates the prominence of social relations over institutional concerns of sovereignty and state power in the Agambean sense. Some caveats are necessary at this stage. First, when we employ Roitman's notion of regulation, we do not talk about regulation as expressed in normative frameworks of how regulation should be (what is in the laws and what institutions should do). Rather, we must understand regulation as actually existing policies and practices like, in our case, the drug war, the overburdened prison system or the fact that police extort money in exchange for release. These are not necessary indications of state failure; they are as much constitutive of state control. Second, when we evoke exchange relations from economic anthropology, we do not suggest that reciprocity involves equality or mutual consensus. Rather, as we also developed in chapter 1, following Anette Weiner (1992) and Marilyn Strathern (1988), exchange relations are always unequal and often coerced and violent. Finally, readers may wonder why we discuss the police practices before and during the war in terms of the relation between exchange relations and violence. Surely there must be other issues relevant to policing and the police. While that is true, policing in Bagong Silang did not often exist outside notions of exchange relations—whether good notions or bad. Hence, while we do discuss other issues of policing in this chapter, its emphasis resonates with how people in Bagong Silang saw the police and how the police, in turn, carried out their jobs.

We organize our argument chronologically and begin with briefly discussing historical policing in the Philippines with a specific focus on the Philippine National Police to complement the analysis of the Barangay Justice System in chapter 2. We then explore policing in Bagong Silang as caught between sovereignty and exchange before the war on drugs. This analysis will equip us to ask a different set of questions in the section about Tokhang as violent exchange and the art of making money during the drug war. We end by discussing reconfigurations of the relationship between exchange and violence to suggest that residents deal with a constant sense of unease and unpredictability while they draw on experiential strategies that seem overwhelmed by the transformation of their social world.

# History of Policing and Politics

Like other postcolonial societies, the Philippines provides an apt illustration of the deeply historically embedded connection between political power and policing (Albrecht and Kyed 2015). Police and order-making structures were aimed at maintaining the elite's position and, in the last century, winning elections (Sidel 1999). These structures, which had more to do with politics than with crime prevention, were propelled into independence and institutionalized in the role of the police in enforcing the law. The Philippines suffered three rounds of colonial experience—a Spanish period that lasted around three hundred years, a brief but painful Japanese occupation during World War II, and an American period lasting some fifty years. These rounds of colonialism left deep scars in Philippine society and were central in structuring the relations between policing and politics (McCoy 2009). During the colonial periods, policing vis-à-vis politics was mainly concerned with the pacification and criminalization of revolutionaries and other millenarian organizations (Illeto 1997 Bankoff 1996). In 1935, the United States gave the Philippines a measure of autonomy that lasted until the Japanese invasion in 1942. During the late American period (called the Commonwealth) and into independence in 1946 after World War II, the main aim of policing was the assertion and preservation of the power of the landed elite (Sidel 1999; McCoy 1994). When Marcos declared martial law in 1972, policing increasingly became about the suppression of political enemies inside the elite as well as the suppression of the increasingly discontent populace. In particular, the challenge by the Maoist New People's Army (NPA) caused a violent politicization and militarization of policing in the form of counterinsurgency that continued after the fall of Marcos. Although the NPA challenge had largely been subdued by the mid-1990s (Abinales 1996), it remained strong in parts of the country. In other parts of the country (Mindanao), different Islamic and Moro separatist groups ensured that politics and (counterinsurgency) policing remained thoroughly entangled.

During most of the twentieth century, the Philippine Constabulary was the central law enforcement agency. It was formed with the "special duty to suppress and prevent brigandage, insurrection, unlawful assembly and breaches of the peace" (de Campos 1983, 134). Until its integration in the Philippine National Police in 1991, its tasks remained unchanged. The post-Marcos reform of the police aimed first and foremost at decentralizing and demilitarizing the force; to put it under some level of civilian control, as well as to rid the police of the extreme forms of violence perpetrated during the Marcos regime (Quimpo 2008). In order to achieve this, the 1991 Act (Act 6975) created one national police force, the Philippine National Police (PNP). The PNP was put under a reconfigured Department of the Interior and Local Government (DILG). Furthermore, in order to make the police accountable, its command structures were decentralized so the police would answer to the authority of the municipal mayor (Gutang 1991). While the left-wing and human rights circles lamented the creation of yet another "militarized monster" through integrating the constabulary in the police, the constabulary saw the act as betrayal and a denigration of the service they had rendered to the nation. This sense of betrayal continued, and in 2010 a local inspector demanded to be called by his earlier military title and lamented the impotence of the police compared to the proud army institution and frequent savior of the nation. However, in line with John Sidel (1999), the law first and foremost returned political control of the police to local political families and strongmen.

Together with the continued politicization of law enforcement inherent, for instance, in counterinsurgency, the localized focus of policing had been a central and enduring trend in Philippine policing. Already the Spanish established municipal and provincial police forces (the Cuadrilleros and the Tercio de Policia) under the direction of local *principalia* (Philippine landed elite) and local, colonial authorities (Bankoff 1996). This was continued into independence. As John Sidel notes (1999), the entrenched interests of local *principalia* elites or families were given a national stage to exert their power through the electoral, representative system of the Americans, which was uncontrolled due to a weak state bureaucracy. This created a thoroughly localized political system based in power-ful families using the national state coffers to boost and perpetuate their own power and perpetuate their electoral success. This also involved the use of po-lice and private armies with which to quell resistance. Throughout the first half of the twentieth century this led to constant tensions between the interests of the landed elites and national interests, with the former as the perpetual win-ners (McCoy 1994), not least because the landed elites and the political families assumed control of the national government.

While the intention of the post-Marcos regime allegedly was to institute ci-vilian control over the police, in many municipalities and provinces the police came to serve a reconstituted cacique democracy (Anderson 1998; Sidel 1999), that is, a democracy in which (landed) elites managed to secure their hold on state power through electoral processes. Law enforcement agencies played a cen-tral role in this as the municipal mayor asserted authority over the PNP and, through the barangay chairperson, the lowest level of the state law enforcement system, the Barangay Justice System. At the same time that policing came under the political control of the local elites in the post-Marcos dispensation, in parts of the country, the police together with the Armed Forces of the Philippines en-gaged in a violent counterinsurgency against Moro nationalists, Maoists, and Islamic groups as well as defenders of human rights and land activists (Asian Human Rights Commission 2006; Hedman and Sidel 2000). This also touched Bagong Silang as the area constituted a frontline in the war with the NPA until the latter grew weaker through the "total war on communisms" declared by Pres-ident Aquino in 1987 and what has been perceived as a series of strategic blun-ders (Rutten 2008; Abinales 1996). However, at a minimum the war in Mindanao was important for developing counterinsurgency policing. The perpetual war in Mindanao against a string of nationalist and later Islamic and jihadist insurgen-cies militarized the army especially, but also the police (Santos 2010; Mercado 2010; Adam et al. 2014). In this way, policing in the Philippines was torn between local, politicized exigencies and a brutal counterinsurgency war. We can recog-nize exactly this tension in the war on drugs as well, not least when politics and policing increasingly were animated by logics and structures emanating out of Mindanao (Caday and Altez 2017; Warburg and Jensen 2020b). To illustrate this, let us return to Bagong Silang before the war on drugs commenced.

## Policing Bagong Silang

Since its inception as a relocation site in 1986, Bagong Silang has been perceived as a security threat—a hotbed of criminality and political mobilization. The relocation site was established to address the perceived overflow of people in the centers of Manila as well as a strategy to break up political organization elsewhere in the city. In time, Bagong Silang grew more peaceful, while not necessarily being perceived in less stigmatizing ways than as a violent and drug-infested place.[2] As we show later in the chapter, this created fertile grounds for Duterte's war on drugs. Policing was slightly demilitarized and much of the order making was delegated to the hands of the Barangay Justice System. The system was established within the jurisdiction of the barangay government (the lowest tier of governance in the Philippines). The chairperson nominates purok leaders, who then choose a number of tanods. The purok leaders and tanods are responsible for the local peace. Only when they cannot resolve conflicts locally through mediation or if the transgression carries fines above P5,000 or more than one year in prison will the case be referred to the Philippine National Police (PNP). In 2010, the PNP had only seventy officers in Bagong Silang—a number that increased to just about one hundred in response to the war on drugs, compared to about twelve hundred purok leaders and tanods.

In a survey carried out in 2010, 65 percent of the respondents referred to police performance as "normal" (Jensen, Hapal, and Modvig 2013). Given the rather notorious reputation of the police in Bagong Silang, this response appeared contradictory. In the vernacular of everyday life, the police are referred to as *buwaya* (crocodiles) or *linta* (leeches), both concepts that point to their extortionist inclinations. The capacity to extort money is based on their ability to threaten and ultimately use violence, including lawful or unlawful arrest. However, a more complex picture emerged once we began to explore the numbers in more detail. In follow-up interviews, we asked what respondents had meant with their answers. The majority replied that by "normal" they meant "*ok lang*," which in Tagalog translates into "just ok." This concept of "*ok lang*" is hugely complicated and endowed with important ambiguities. As such, it does not necessarily imply something positive, as is the implicit understanding in the survey question.[3] When queried further, people seemed to suggest that the police's performance was "as expected." Furthermore, through *diskarte* (the ability to survive through cunning and wits), connections, money, or a combination of the three, the police could be managed. Let us provide some more ethnographic flesh to this argument by looking at the example of Emilio's son Karl.

Karl had been arrested by the police one night in 2010, as he and friends of his had been drinking in the street. As the night progressed, fights broke out. A woman whose son was involved in the fighting had called the police to get them to stop the fighting. However, the police had come and arrested them all rather harshly, including her son, and brought them to the police station. Karl had asked the police, who were in civilian clothes, to show their police ID to identify themselves. The police took offense, thinking him *maangas* (arrogant), and grabbed him violently. Panic spread. At the beginning, Emilio did not know where Karl and his friend, along with two other friends, had been taken, so he had contacted the local purok leader, who was his relative, to ask if he could help find Karl. The purok leader and his tanods went first to a substation, but it was empty because all the police had gone to the hospital in response to a police shooting. They finally located Karl in the central police station. Emilio, who was quite worried, then sent one of his relatives to be around the police station in case something should happen to Karl.

Emilio called our friend and local operator Inday because he knew that she had relatives within the police station and would not be afraid to go because she was *matapang* (courageous). The police told Inday that one police officer had lost a phone and that they needed to pay P7,000. The phone was worth P14,000 but because it was used, the police only needed P7,000. Inday uttered the word, "Extortion!" The police then told her if they did not pay, they would inquest (charge) them. "What are the charges?" She asked. The police said it was a case of public scandal and assaulting a police officer. Inday said, "We are not paying. You just inquest them!" She called her relative in the police, a cousin. She told the cousin that a godchild of hers had been arrested and what the circumstances were. Her cousin promised that he would call the station and said she must just wait. In the meantime, Karl's brother and Inday went to the barangay to report the case. "This was to protect Karl," she said, indicating that the more reports were filed on Karl's whereabouts, the safer he would be.

When Inday was back at the station, her cousin called. Inday could hear her cousin (a superior) telling something to the officer. After the phone call, the officer told his colleague that they must release the boys, but the colleague contested this. He noticed that Karl had been *maangas* (arrogant) when he asked the police to identify themselves. "He should know that we are police when the van is outside, and we introduced ourselves as police." Inday quietly said, "But isn't it the right of people to ask for the ID, especially when the police are in civilian clothes?" The officer continued, "But there are also the costs. Who will pay for the bullets we used when firing warning shots [they had shot into the ground]? Who will pay for petrol?" Inday then asked, "So if we cannot pay, you will not release them?" "Not exactly," the police answered. Then Inday said, "Ok, thank you," and left. Outside the police station, she called the cousin again and explained the situation. He promised to take care of it.

Karl's brother had remained inside the police station. There were also the two mothers of the two other young men, including the one who had called the police in the first place. One of the mothers was already known by the police as the wife of an Overseas Filipino Worker (OFW) and therefore someone with money.

The police had had earlier encounters with her son, who was apparently a drug addict. Inside the cell, one of the police officers told Karl that the reason why it took such a long time for them to be released was because the police waited for the payment from this mother. Negotiations went ahead. In the end the mother paid P2,000 for the release, whereas the other mother paid P500. Afterward she told Inday, "I just wanted it to be over so [my son] would get out of the cells and be safe. That's why I paid." After this, the four were released.

The case illustrates that corruption is systemic and the extent to which some officers are complicit in the system. It is routinized to an extent that release almost has a price tag attached to it. The term for this kind of police behavior is *hulidap*, a term that combines the verbs *huli* (arrest) and *hold-up* (rob). It designates the practice of police holding up people through the threat of arrest. More importantly, however, it illustrates what people meant when they said *"ok lang"*; that is, people can manage the extortive tendencies of the police by employing intimate relationships; money and resources and a combination of cunning (diskarte) and luck. This is what allows some people to negotiate successfully with the police. Inday and Emilio may have been more worried during the course of the event, but Inday knew exactly what to do, what connections to employ, and how.[4] However, it is also these same relationships that the police prey on or colonize in their practices of extortion. While the police seclude people and threaten them with prison and violence, channels of communication must be open in order for those on the inside to activate their networks and relationships on the outside. This is what happened to the wife of the OFW. The task of the police is to manage these connections, of which some can be beneficial for the police and others can be problematic, like Inday's relation to her cousin.[5]

While hulidap is potentially viewed as *ok lang*, or, to some extent, manageable, this practice inherently relies on violence to extract money. However, the relative manageability of practices like hulidap are overwhelmed when the police use violence that is considered excessive. These excessive forms of violence relate to "salvaging" or extrajudicial police killings. In Bagong Silang, the image of extreme forms of police violence persists in the minds of people (Jensen, Hapal, and Modvig 2013). This perception has been enforced and reproduced by the violent policing and extrajudicial killings that occurred before the drug war. Hence, we might distinguish heuristically between two forms of state violence—the *"ok lang"* and the excessively violent. As an example of the excessive side of policing, take the following example, pieced together through interviews, police and media reports, and human rights documentation.

One night in 2011, around eight o'clock, José, Jay, and Renato went up to a man who owed José money. José brought a gun and asked Jay and Renato to be his "backup." While walking to the house of the man, the three young men encountered a police officer. The police searched them and discovered José's gun. Jay and Renato ran while José was detained by the police officer, who called him a *holdaper* (robber) out loud. Consequently, on the way to the police station, people on the street attacked José.[6] When he arrived at the police station, he was allegedly beaten up repeatedly. The police presented him with a paper with names on it and asked where these people were staying. The next morning, José, now weak from the beatings, was taken to the main police station, where a case was filed against him. While inside the jail, he considered filing a torture case against the police who maltreated him. However, as he feared reprisals against his family, he could not make up his mind. José's companions were later found dead. A news article that took notice of the incident dubbed the murder of the two as a drug deal gone wrong. However, suspicions lingered that they had died at the hands of the police.

The case of José is revealing in several ways. First, it seems clear that the fact that José was involved in criminal activity made him victimizable in the eyes of the police and the public. While this clearly did not exonerate the state officials or legitimize their actions, José's behavior made it easy to target him. Rendering this worse, in the eyes of the law enforcement agents, is the fact that they often cannot arrest young men but instead have to release them into the care of parents and social workers because they are younger than eighteen.[7] This sense of impotence arguably entices law enforcement officers to engage in extralegal activities that are legitimized in the name of protecting the normal law-abiding citizens from people like José.[8] José's case was hardly an isolated incident. One law enforcement officer confirmed the practice of violently and extrajudicially dealing with young people. In an interview in 2010 the officer said, "I won't lie about it. We do kill people. I myself have killed a lot of people in Bagong Silang." According to him, these practices are known and sanctioned by their superiors: "Let's just put it this way. Every action that we do, our superior knows about it."

While these statements are truly worrying, we need to be careful not to take them at face value. The officer seemed to be narrating the police and himself as powerful and vengeful agents, organized in strict hierarchies of death. In this way, the narrative resembled the image of a strong, effective, but gruesome military organization, much like the military in Mindanao. The statements were therefore arguably part of a narrative structure of strength and nocturnal secrets. While killings and torture also happened before the war on drugs, they might not always be carried out in the ordered, disciplined, and effective manner the law enforcement agent describes. But why does law enforcement need to carry out these acts of violence and render them intelligible through the narrative of the effective but gruesome policing structure? Another law enforcement officer explained this in 2010 by evoking a sacred and epic fight between good and evil that has been actualized during the war on drugs:

> The people we put down are not people anymore. They are demons that need to be removed from the face of the earth. We the police are like angels that battle those demons. We know what is right and we know that what those criminals do is not right. I am not afraid to die today. If I die today, I have the courage to justify to my God that I have done the right thing. I will even wish to be put in the front lines of his army to battle those demons. If He wishes that I be in hell, I have no problem with that. I have no regrets about the things that I did.

From this perspective, society is composed of "good" people and demons (*demonyo*). The role of the police is predictably, like avenging angels, to eliminate the demons to protect society—in other words, to keep the integrity of the "thin blue line." While some might be dismissive of the police's justification of the use of (excessive) violence and its accompanying assertion that it is meted out in a predictable, effective, and almost scientific way, we believe that it is reflective of a rather complicated and difficult policing situation. It is a narrative that stresses that justice will prevail, through the nocturnal death of the criminals, by the hands of secret and strong forces of order. Yet before the war it was not uncommon for law enforcement agents in Bagong Silang to despondently talk about their difficulties as "criminals" seem to disappear in the maze of houses and life. What accounts for this discrepancy? Given the police's institutional capacities and resources, law enforcement in Bagong Silang is at best challenging and at worst compromised. It is in this light that the rules for protecting order from chaos would seem stretched and porous.[9] The epic battle against evil therefore signifies a rationalization of violence in the light of a sense of impotence. Nonetheless, the image of the vengeful angel continues to animate policing. It is in this way we must understand the term "salvaging" or extrajudicial killing—the hard and dirty job of saving the nation one dead body at a time. This narrative, as we shall see later, provided a fertile ground for Duterte's war on drugs five years later.

## Violent Exchange

While some policing practices are "*ok lang*" and others are "excessive," this does not mean that the two are unrelated. On the contrary, they exist in and through each other. Through the epic narrative of vengeful angels, the practices of the crocodile are rendered at least partially invisible and its actions legitimized. In the case described earlier, Emilio was very aware of the connection between salvaging and the troubles in which Karl found himself because, as he said, he recalled his experiences with a week-long abduction and torture earlier in his life. In this way, violence—its history as salvaging and the concrete experiences of people— is central for the practices of the crocodile. The crocodile is only successful because of the fear of salvaging. Violence is the lubricant that allows the corrupt practices of the crocodile to continue.

While invoking the concept of corruption is surely one way of approaching the relations between police and policed, it is more complex. Let us revisit some of the central elements of Karl's ordeals. First, the identities of police and policed are inherently blurred and complex; and second, much more than money is being exchanged. The blurred and complex relationship is illustrated by the presence of Inday's cousin, who is a senior police officer (SPO) in Bagong Silang. Inday is indeed fortunate to have such relations, but such relations are not unique. Emilio also uses his connections to the local purok leader and his tanods; others would employ whatever relations they can muster. Hence, while Inday found it deplorable that the police acted as they did, she also cherished her relations with officialdom and wanted them to function when she needed them. Emilio is also fully aware of the value and even tried to enter into a debt relation with the police officer. Hence, the *buwaya* (crocodile) is the concept used to describe the negative side of a relational economy; as Olivier de Sardan (1999) notes in relation to the moral economy of corruption, this relational economy is also highly cherished and people will go far to protect their relations.

The case also hints at a more benevolent relationship between officers and residents. As we describe elsewhere (Hapal and Jensen 2017, 55), police officers understand their admittedly corrupt relationship with residents in terms of help—*tulong* in Tagalog. Take the case of police officer (PO) Carol. PO Carol was the officer in charge (OIC) of the Women and Children's Desk (WCD) in Bagong Silang. When asked about her duties and responsibilities, she pointed us to a flowchart that illustrated processes involved in reporting and filing cases. Explaining the functions of the WCD, PO Carol said: "Our work is clearly defined by the law; we just follow it." When asked about the difficulties they faced in policing Bagong Silang, PO Carol pointed to the sheer size of the barangay relative to their resources. According to her, as much as they wanted to prosecute all the cases, it was impossible due to lack of resources and time. Moreover, prosecution was not necessarily what a victim wanted. Most would not follow through and complainants only wanted the perpetrators arrested to teach them a lesson. To achieve some form of resolution in, say, cases of domestic abuse, PO Carol counsels couples to try to salvage their relationship and avoid a lengthy and costly judicial process. According to PO Carol, if they were to prosecute all of the cases in Bagong Silang, especially cases of domestic violence, the city jails and courts would overflow. PO Carol was proud of this form of *tulong* and claimed it as one of the achievements of their office. However, PO Carol also hinted that in some instances they ask for *piyansa* (unofficial bail) from the accused, especially if the case was problematic or if the accused was uncooperative. Nonetheless, she rationalized her effort as a legitimate form of assistance and said that the money was only an added incentive for going beyond the call of duty. PO Carol's experience resembles when one officer assures the brother of Karl that the boys will still be released. Nonetheless, it demonstrates how an overburdened justice system provides an important reason for people wanting to engage in the relational economy. Going to jail may simply have catastrophic consequences. In one case we experienced firsthand, Charlie was arrested and basically looked for someone to bribe for a full day in order to get out of the police station (Hapal and Jensen 2017). Drawing on Janet Roitman's (2004) insights, we might say that it is exactly the nonfunctioning justice system that sets in motion and structures the relational economy. In all these cases, the relational economy between police and policed is highly complex and defies neat binary distinctions. They suggest the simultaneity and coexistence of the angel and the crocodile in the minds of people, who want the police to apprehend criminals, protect the innocent and keep law and order (the angel) while at the same time being open to the relational economy of connections (the positive side of the crocodile). It was in the backdrop of this relational economy that Duterte's drug war hit Bagong Silang.

## Violent Exchange and the War on Drugs

In the previous sections, we showed that the Philippine police are no strangers to killing their own citizens as part of what is termed "salvaging"—a term that goes back to the Martial Law era and the counterinsurgency wars against Maoist, Moro, and Islamic insurgencies (McCoy 2009; Altez and Caday 2017). As part of an emic cosmology, police officers constructed a binary world of angels and demons as part of a moral legitimization of extreme forms of violence about which people were rather ambivalent, identifying salvaging as the worst danger and condoning and even participating in violence against for instance José. When the police officer, evoking the notions of demons and angles, insisted that he will want to be part of fighting crime regardless of the price he has to pay, he speaks of the danger of prosecution that he would face should he be caught in the act. This threat, however, was exactly what Duterte's war on drugs did away with, at least unofficially.

The war on drugs was organized as what is called the "Double Barrel" consisting of two different operations. "Oplan Tokhang," literally "Operation Knock and Plead," consists of police and local authorities going around to identify houses of what are referred to as known addicts and dealers, registering them, pleading for them to turn themselves in, and warning them of the dangers they are facing. The second element of the Double Barrel campaign is Project HVT (High-Value Targets), which targets drug lords, drug lord protectors, and drug financiers in order to reach the higher echelon of the drug syndicates (Lamchek 2017). Often it seems that it has been difficult to separate the two strategies. In discourse, however, the administration and the police have denied that they kill people extrajudicially and insisted that most of the killings have been drug-on-drug killings, unsolved murders, and police acting in self-defense. While this cannot be completely disregarded, in spite of mounting evidence to the contrary, the perception among our informants in Bagong Silang is that the killings are associated with Tokhang.[10] By being seen to have unleashed the police and promising to protect individual officers, Duterte seems to have legitimized, from the highest echelons of government, the extrajudicial killing of people like José. We might say that the angel was given license to be a real avenging angel.

However, just like before the war, the police oscillated between the angel and the crocodile, such that the former enabled and partly obscured the latter. While the crocodile thrived on the potentiality of angelic violence, the corrupt practices were never out of view for the people being policed. They knew and sometimes tapped into the relational economy of the violent exchange to an extent where it was "ok lang," or manageable. The question, then, is what happened to this relational economy of violence with the declaration of the war on drugs? A first answer is that it did not disappear—almost on the contrary, as Sheila Coronel (2017) illustrates in her insightful and well-documented account of "Murder as Enterprise." Only a few months into the war on drugs, South Korean businessman Jee Ick Joo was kidnapped by police officers, brought to the national police headquarters, and strangled, after which the police officers proceeded to extort money from his wife, who paid P5 million for his safe release. Only months later, after several payments, was it revealed that Jee had died and his remains had been flushed down the toilet, just doors down from the national police chief. This practice—the ultimate cashing in on the mandate to use violence—came to be known as "Tokhang for ransom." This, we may note, represents a turn to a much more sinister incarnation of the buwaya—one that steals and robs but with whom you cannot talk or negotiate.

The death of Jee forced the administration to suspend the war on drugs for about a month in January and February 2017 so the police could be "cleansed" of corrupt elements (Cone 2017; Valente 2017). The Jee fiasco led the president to accuse the police force of being "corrupt to the core" and even claimed that at least 40 percent of the force was engaged in illegal activities (Malakunas 2017). Despite governmental attempts to root out corruption, there have been persistent reports of continued corrupt practices. One rather blatant example was the discovery of secret detention centers where suspects would be held until their families paid up (Cayabyab 2017). What this suggests is that while there have been attempts at rooting out corruption, it has not worked. In fact, it seems that the more the angel is allowed to be an angel, the better are the conditions for the crocodile. In the remainder of this chapter, we will present empirical material from Bagong Silang that allow for tentative conclusions to be drawn on the relationship between violence and money in the war on drugs. We begin by exploring how one makes money on the war on drugs. A good place to start is the notorious area known as Phase 12.

Drug trade and the production of *shabu* (methamphetamine) in Bagong Silang have always been closely connected to Phase 12, which is about 1 kilometer from the eastern border of Bagong Silang and part of adjacent Barangay 188. During fieldwork between 2009 and before the onset of the war on drugs, we never succeeded in going there. People would flatly refuse to accompany us or connect us with anyone in the area, as it was deemed to be very dangerous. Apart from the relations to the drug trade, it was also feared for the majority population of Muslims from Mindanao, which, for most people in the Christian Philippines, and not least in Manila, were seen as incarnating danger and violence. However, after the war on drugs had commenced, people said that it was no longer so dangerous and we could go. This was despite the spate of killings in the barangay, including that of Domato, then local chief of Barangay 188. In 2016, Domato was gunned down and killed by unknown assailants (Ramirez 2016). Later reports indicated, however, that the police could be behind the killing of the Domato. The volume of deaths in the barangay led the police to describe the barangay as a killing field (Galupo 2016). However, some residents of Phase 12 said that "those big timers" had left their houses and gone back to Mindanao. When we finally went, the adventure—none of us in the company had been before—was facilitated by Bondo. A few months into the war, he had been asked by one resident in Phase 12, a Muslim drug dealer, to take care of his house while he and his family went to Mindanao, probably in fear for their lives. When asked when they would return, Bondo laughed and said "after six years," indicating the end of Duterte's term. However, he was not sure they would ever return.

Bondo knew the drug dealer because he had been coming regularly to Phase 12 to collect garbage for reselling. Bondo and his family were dirt-poor, staying in what are known as excess lots near the creek. As it is a particularly unhealthy environment, they had jumped at the chance of actually inhabiting a house with a television and sanitation. Bondo explained that this was far from the only house where this had happened: there were "many houses," he said. His benefactor had approached him one day as he was coming through with his cart, saying that he would like Bondo to stay in his house while he was gone, just out of pakikisama, which is characteristic of reciprocity or mutual obligations between people of relatively equal status (Jensen and Hapal 2015). However, it is something of a rarity between rich and poor, where utang na loob (literally, inner debt), constituting vertical, debt relations, is much more common. Arguably, the war on drugs potentially equals out some hierarchical relationships.

Bondo indicated other houses abandoned by the owners. He said that the police went to these houses and emptied out all the stuff inside. Allegedly, they brought it to the police station. Bondo pointed to a big house and said: "They come at night. You could see the lights there and cars outside and then they would be gone along with all the things in the house." When asked if anybody said anything about it, Bondo shrugged, "What can you say? It's the police."

We asked if there had been any killings in Phase 12. Bondo said, "No. But, there have been arrests (huli)." Bondo explained, "Some of them pay piyansa [unofficial bail] and they come back. Others have not paid so they are there now in the jail. . . . The [value of the] piyansa differs. It is higher for Muslims, maybe P50,000. For Christians it is lower." Piyansa, or bail is, of course, a formal practice within the justice system. However, it is not uncommon for it to be circumvented by corrupt practices at the precinct level. We tried to assess whether the arrests were part of the formal system. Bondo and the other people present laughed, saying, "No, there are no judges there. The people stay in prison for three weeks and if they can pay, they pay the police officers there. Nobody knows about it. After three weeks they must go to the real prison." Going to the real prison and being booked in the formal system is no laughing matter, as one might never get out, both because of the threats of the war on drugs and because the criminal justice system is overburdened and for all purposes has collapsed.

In Bondo's narrative, there are several issues at stake that are important to our understanding of how to capitalize on the war on drugs. First, the war on drugs not only impacts the relationship between the police and people in poor neighborhoods. It potentially transforms other social relations as well. Bondo was extremely lucky, and the life of his family might have been transformed for good. He had something to exchange—his ability to stay put—which he translated into a livelihood. Bondo is far from the only one. Jay, a tricycle driver from Bagong Silang, had seen better days before the drug war. He had been the personal bodyguard of the former, now killed, barangay chairman, Padilla. He had also been a security guard at a local hospital, a job he lost in 2012, and he had been a member of Special Community Action Network (SCAN), the Iglesia ni Cristo (Church of Christ) private guard that we discussed in the previous chapter. The four-year lull ended with the initiation of the war on drugs. Through connections he had with local political networks, Jay was nominated as a local tanod and then became part of what is called the Community Investigative Services (CIS). CIS was established as a national program of surveillance in relation to the war on drugs, under the command of a retired army general. Jay showed us with pride his batch and his ID with his own photo and that of the general. In Jay's account, this was all very secret, a system outside the other surveillance system organized around the barangay, purok leaders, and tanods. He was also to be remunerated relatively handsomely for his efforts. When asked why he joined, he answered, "For the connections, of course!" and further explained, "It's a good connection to have." Jay's case illustrates that resources cannot be reduced to a question of money only. Like Bondo's case, social relations—both vertical and hierarchical—are absolutely central in terms of survival or improving one's life. The war on drugs radically reconfigured the possibilities of relationality. While much focus has been on the negative relations to the state and the toll on human life, it is necessary to recognize that people like Bondo and Jay have benefited quite literally from the war.

Furthermore, Jay talked at length about more direct benefits, saying that members of the CIS were paid for all good information about drug addicts and pushers. All over Bagong Silang, stories of payments to the police for killings abounded. Amounts as high (or as low, depending on one's point of view) as P10,000 were frequent—Jay said they were promised P7,000—and fed into the narratives of the police killings. In her essay "Murder as Enterprise," Sheila Coronel (2017) explores these rumors and finds them credible. Needless to say, if true, this provides a very strong motive for engaging in the killings, and equally as important, it provides residents in Bagong Silang for an explanatory model for understanding the killings—although not one that is likely to improve the relationship between the residents and the police. In this way, Phase 12 and the other cases presented here illustrate that the war on drugs is not only about killing but also about profiteering. While the case of Phase 12 can be attributed to the location, both Bondo and Jay's cases suggest that monetary exchange constitutes social relations that people manage or move into—or out of.

# Relationships and Violence in the War on Drugs

It is clear from the preceding analysis that money can be made from the war on drugs in direct ways as well as in terms of reconfigured relationships. In this final section, we will explore in more detailed ways the quality and significance of these reconfigured relationships. As the story of the *piyansa* (unofficial bail) suggests, we can identify something akin to a parallel system mirroring the formal criminal justice system, in which you can be released if you pay bail. If we think along with this heuristic idea of a parallel system, we might say that the emptying of houses represents civil forfeiture. As we show in this chapter and elsewhere (Hapal and Jensen 2017, 61), in the parallel system one can also pay fees for licenses and fines for smaller transgressions, have one's children disciplined by the police for a price, and, finally, even be subject to the death penalty. Except for the latter, these practices are couched in an ambivalent language of assistance (*tulong*) and violence. Money, violence, and exchange are central to this system. Police practices constantly oscillate between those of the avenging angels of Duterte's war on drugs and those of the crocodile with whom one can negotiate.

How do we think more theoretically about this? The war on drugs lends itself to analyses of the state of exception and the production of bare life as suggested by Giorgio Agamben (1998). However, such analyses fail to account for the negotiations and exchange relations that go on. Hence, we find it useful to think through our material in more economic, relational terms. Janet Roitman (2004, 194) suggests that we must understand the relationships that are produced by state regulation—of, in our case, criminal justice, prisons, anticorruption efforts, and the war on drugs—rather than state regulation as such. This might seem like a small detail. However, it moves our focus away from the policies—whether informal or formal—to focusing on what happens when they hit the ground and become part of residents' and police's attempts to survive or thrive through relationships. It is these relationships that are central for how people engage with the system. If that is the case, it is important to understand what relationships are produced by, say, prison conditions—for instance, the need to get out or, more importantly, to stay out of prison. These relationships and the negotiations they lead to were incredibly complex even before the war. However, as captured in the ambiguous notion of *ok lang*, there was a certain predictability to them—not always leading to good results but at least with a promise of resolution. The war on drugs has, we argue, radically reconfigured the parameters of these relationships and how residents may negotiate them through money, relationships, and diskarte.

The first element in these reconfigured relationships is that the price of survival seems to have gone up significantly. If we compare the amounts that we registered before the beginning of the war on drugs, they were significantly lower than the amounts we and others (Coronel 2017; Lamchek 2017) registered after the onset of the war. It is, of course, very difficult to establish the amount with any certainty, not least because narratives, rumors, and forms of gossip per definition are unreliable sources. With this caveat in mind, the data from Bagong

Silang and Phase 12 indicates that those related to the drug economy had to pay substantial amounts. It is also clear that many people decided to run rather than pay the price of survival. This was especially true for Muslim residents in Phase 12. This suggests that the war on drugs was not only about drugs but also part of larger political struggles.[11] It suggests that while money is important, we cannot reduce the war on drugs and policing practices to money alone. Rather, the relationships and exchange relations are animated by political categories as well.

While we cannot be sure whether Muslims fled because they were certain to be killed or had to pay exorbitant amounts, it is fair to assume that this was a question they themselves posed, at least if we compare with other contexts of violence in for instance South Africa and Bolivia where wars on crime and drugs have been fought.[12] Studies here suggest that the unpredictability of violence is in fact equally important and constitutive for social relations. The studies illustrate how violence constitutes a problem, especially if we are not certain from where and by whom it will come. In exploring civil war in Northern Ireland and Guinea Bissau, Henrik Vigh (2009) usefully suggests that in conflicts the social terrain is fundamentally shifting, unstable and illegible. Hence, people invest great efforts into rendering violence predictable and knowable. While some human rights organizations exert much care in bringing all deaths back to the police via a chain of command (Human Rights Watch 2017), the realities are often much more complicated. In one case that we described in the previous chapter, in which seven people were killed in one shootout, we were told of three different potential perpetrators—the police, competing Muslim drug dealers, and the Iglesia ni Cristo acting as a vigilante group. With each of these perpetrators or violent social networks, to paraphrase Arias (2006), different chains of events emerge and with them different dangers. Hence, as the event had not been stabilized, violence remained unpredictable (Jensen 1999). The lack of certainty and the plurality of perpetrators remain some of the important sources of the unstable terrain. This is compounded by the presence of competing police units and the constant shuffling of police officers.

Duterte has made it policy to rotate police officers to root out corruption. Hence, most police officers in Bagong Silang have been shifted around to and from other places. In the time between the onset of the war in June 2016 and May 2017, four different station commanders had been assigned to Bagong Silang. Mindanao seems to play a particular role in this (Warburg and Jensen 2020b) as corrupt police officers are sent to Mindanao for "re-education" and punishment. Obviously and logically, there is a reverse movement from Mindanao to Bagong Silang. This has two possible implications for the war on drugs—one in terms of policing strategy and one in relation to relationships between police and residents.

In relation to policing strategy, the station commander in April 2017, according to a barangay employee and long-term friend, made a speech at the State of the Barangay Address (SOBA), where he complained about the lack of collaboration from the barangay. According to the informant, he said, "If you do not want to collaborate with me, I am more than willing to bring the hell from Mindanao to Bagong Silang." This opens up the possibility of counterinsurgency tactics being employed rather than local policing as usual. While this uncertainty is palpable, perhaps what matters for our present analysis is that residents will be pressed to know what kind of policing they will encounter in the next encounter with the police. Will it be the avenging angels, saving the nation, or will it be someone they can talk to?

The sheer number of replacements and the circulation of officers compound this question. Dealing with the police in the past in a manner that was "ok lang" had been premised on money, connections, and diskarte, as the case of Karl suggested. This also entails knowing someone in the police force that might know the police officers in question. However, the circulation of officers renders these relations potentially more difficult and less simple to access. In this way, unpredictability increases because relations are more tenuous and need to be stabilized repeatedly. This does not mean that establishing a relationship cannot happen. Mariza, a key interlocutor, when asked about this, suggested, "You know, they maybe be strangers one day, but it will not take them long to establish contacts again—maybe only two days [laughing]!" The humor aside, Mariza's comment indicates that while the circulation does create the intended alienation of police officers from their communities (producing de facto barracks-style policing), there is a willingness on the side of both police officers and residents to establish these contacts. They are imperative for the survival of the residents as well as the thriving of the officers. We can also speak of this as intimate and affective forms of relationality that need to be reestablished after having been severed—again and again. While this willingness to (re-)create intimate and affective relations arguably seems to exist on both sides, the sheer number of circulated officers and the different potential perpetrators, as well as the different strategies and objectives of police officers all contribute to increase the unpredictability and illegibility of the encounters. Stella, the drug dealer from Ate Janet and Mariza's area, provides an illustration of tenuous relationality and the increasing expenses associated with survival. Stella had been accosted by police officers from the local police station and "asked" to pay P180,000 so as not to be arrested. Hours later, the same officers had returned and warned Stella that another unit from outside Bagong Silang had her on their list. For another P100,000 they helped her escape—but to no avail, as she was executed on her way out of Bagong Silang. Together with the increasing amounts of money necessary for survival, residents are right to ask with trepidation "Who and what will I meet next time? What will it cost, and will I be allowed to pay?" The point is not that the war on drugs has introduced new tactics necessary for surviving a violent and corrupt turn in policing. The point is that the strategies residents in Bagong Silang employed to cope with violent and corrupt policing—money, relations, and diskarte—have been undermined to the extent that people are right to doubt their effectiveness.

# THE VIOLENT PRODUCTION OF URBAN DIVIDES

Juancho, a purok leader whom we met in chapter 2, indicated toward the section at the end of the paved road toward the creek that was engulfed in darkness. He said, "Most of the *adik* live down there in the excess lots."[1] We were sitting in his house after sunset in May 2017. During the day, one could see the steep fall into the creek below. The banks of the creek were full of makeshift houses on stilts to compensate for the steep incline as well as tackle the water when the creek flooded. It is, and was, a precarious and dangerous place to stay. Juancho was adamant that most of those living in the excess lots were good people who used drugs to cope with a tough everyday life.[2] Despite his kindness, which we witnessed on several occasions with the poor people of the excess lots, he arguably also spatialized the drug scene, differentiating between areas where drugs were found—like there—and others where there were no drugs—like here. Many of our interlocutors would agree with Juancho that most drug abuse could be found in the excess lots. While this is a truth that can certainly be challenged, the perception points to the extent to which the spatial layout of Bagong Silang is crucial in understanding the violent politics that enabled the war on drugs. The notion of excess lots only makes sense in relation to the planned lots of the resettlement site that is Bagong Silang, and the resettlement site is only intelligible in relation to displacement processes that have dominated and structured urban politics in Manila (and elsewhere around the world) starting in the 1960s (Garrido 2019; Ortega 2016). Hence, in order to appreciate in a deeper way the processes around policing, we need to situate them in the often violent production of what we can call urban divides—between the center of urban politics and development and Bagong Silang, and internally in Bagong Silang. In other words, we need to understand how Bagong Silang came into existence as an effect of both displacement and resettlement, how the emergence of the place framed particular forms of sociality, and what kind of violent politics the divides produced and enabled, including the war on drugs.

While the human toll and the anxieties we discussed in the previous two chapters are both tragic and worrisome, they do resonate with historical structures. Since its inception as a resettlement site for thousands of squatters in the early 1980s, life in Bagong Silang has been violent and deadly to varying degrees. In the 1980s and until the early 1990s, it served as a buffer zone for the state's counterinsurgency operations against communist rebel forces situated north of Metro Manila. Later, but prior to the drug war, it had been subjected to violent policing to bring order and curb criminality. In parallel, and related to this, Bagong Silang had also been an exclusion zone, a surplus people zone, and a relocation zone which testifies to the bifurcation of Philippine society, where some people are worth less than others (Kusaka 2017b). The violence and exclusion illustrate its marginality and, more importantly, the disposability of its people (Pratt, Johnson, and Banta 2017; Tadiar 2013). While we do not suggest that displacement and resettlement caused the war on drugs, we do suggest that the production of marginalized places and disposable people has informed and animated how the war on drugs was undertaken in Bagong Silang and places similar to it.

Despite its dire impact, the war on drugs has enjoyed almost unwavering public support (Social Weather Stations 2019). This sentiment is somehow reflected in Bagong Silang as many would insist that their community had become safer as a result of the war on drugs and the targeting of amoral and dangerous drug personalities. Prior to the war, it was the promise to eradicate amoral and dangerous characters in the community that convinced some of our informants to vote for and support Duterte's crusade. It was a promise that appealed to the perception that the main problem in Bagong Silang, apart from poverty, was that it had long been *magulo* (disorderly). *Magulo* is a catch-all policing term, which resembles Wacquant's 2008a description of the "advanced marginality" of urban spaces, which are perceived as places where "violence, vice, and dereliction are the order of things" (44).

Following on from these introductory remarks, we raise two arguments to explore why the war on drugs has assumed a deadly character in places like Bagong Silang and what has allowed it to garner popular support despite the palpable violence it has brought. First, we argue that the war on drugs must be understood as the continuation of structural forms of violence against the urban poor (Arcilla 2018; Garrido 2019). We focus on the violence embedded in the practices of displacement and resettlement that produced Bagong Silang. Arguably, displacement invokes some of the same discourses of disposability (Tadiar 2013) that animate the war on drugs. The war on drugs has created zones of exclusion and death in which life can be taken with no repercussions as, for instance, Reyes (2016) suggests. In the analysis of Loïc Wacquant (2008b), displacement and resettlement produced territorial stigmatization that enabled, even legitimized, the drug war. Second, as a complication of the first argument, we cannot simply reduce displacement to disposability. We need to pay attention to what happens within the resettlement site, and not least how some residents have become ardent supporters of the drug war. We do not suggest that the people of Bagong Silang brought the war on themselves. We simply note that the war was waged on fertile ground and that internal divisions provided the backdrop that justified its necessity. To unpack this structural backdrop, we investigate how Bagong Silang's communal relations and moral frameworks are embedded within intersecting structures of class, gender, and generation (Crenshaw 1990). We suggest that these structures may explain why state violence and death, in the past and in the war on drugs, seem to have been administered in a predictable manner, targeting young (or younger), poor, unemployed, or undereducated men.[3]

This chapter consists of two main sections that elaborate each of the two arguments. The first section historicizes the processes of displacement and resettlement that produced Bagong Silang and relates it to the wider discourse of displacement and disposability that informed the war on drugs. We may say that this section explores the production of class divides at the metropolitan and local levels. The second section moves the analysis into Bagong Silang to explore how internal class, gender, and generational structures animated notions of morality, violence, and community in Bagong Silang as we found it before the war on drugs. Exploring how these were entangled is imperative for understanding what the war did to the sense of community as well as understanding how the war mapped onto and was articulated within notions of moral community and in relation to conflict and violence. We argue that even before the war on drugs, violence was not the opposite—the radical other—of communal forms of intimacy; rather, it was constitutively linked with them. Furthermore, people's sense of community was deeply ambiguous. On the one hand, community and neighborliness were praised and lauded as almost objective characteristics of the equality of people in Bagong Silang. On the other hand, social life was characterized by deep sentiments of mistrust and violent practices. In fact, notions of community often hid and even legitimized older men's violence against women and the young.

# Displacement and Resettlement

From its creation in 1982, Bagong Silang was born in promises of new beginnings for the informal settlers in Metro Manila as well as of a cleaner and modern Manila. Yet Bagong Silang was also called La Kubeta—or "The Toilet." As we described in chapter 1, rumor has it that the name was coined by a British journalist who was taken on an aerial tour of Bagong Silang in the mid-1980s as the regime attempted to promote its commitment to eradicating poverty and cleaning up Manila. Bagong Silang was one of the projects of former first lady Imelda Marcos, who was charged with transforming Manila. What the journalist saw were endless rows of toilet bowls. Stretching across the hills, marking off thousands of meticulously bordered ninety-square-meter plots with path walks in between, the bowls became the materialization of the regime's fantasies of modernity, a planned city (Tadiar 2004). The name of La Kubeta can, however, also be easily associated with its position within the urban economy of Manila. This was, after all, where thousands of squatters from the city were flushed out, so to speak, some twenty-five kilometers away from the city center, in what was referred to as *bukid*, or countryside. Between 1982 and 1990, the government resettled thousands of families in Bagong Silang from among the poorest, densest, and most politically turbulent areas of the city. Some came voluntarily, but most of our informants were forcibly displaced to Bagong Silang. For them, the new birth meant starting over again from scratch and often without the crucial social ties that see people through days and nights of poverty. The case of Emilio illustrates this.

In 1982, Emilio and thousands of other squatters were dropped off three kilometers away from Bagong Silang.[4] The thick mud made it impossible for trucks to go all the way to the site. The squatters had to walk to the resettlement site and struggled to carry whatever they managed to salvage from their houses, which the government had forced them to demolish. Whatever they left behind was fair game for thieves and opportunists. As they made their way inside Bagong Silang, Emilio and his companions met resistance from the original inhabitants. Prior to being a relocation site, the land belonged to the Tala Estate, a leper colony established during the Commonwealth Era. Located in the Tala Estate was Dr. Jose N. Rodriguez Memorial Hospital, formerly known as the Central Luzon Sanitarium, which cared for lepers. Through Presidential Proclamation 843 of 1971 the land allotted for the leper colony was reduced from 808 hectares to 130 hectares. Emilio recalled that the lepers were not happy with this development and saw the new settlers as stealing the land that had been granted to them: "We were obstructed. They asked us, 'Why do you come here? The lots here belong to the lepers.' The lepers threw rocks and shit at us." After walking for three kilometers, the bitter and unpleasant sight of stretches of land dotted with toilets greeted them.

**FIGURE 8.**  A toilet given to the first wave of relocatees of Bagong Silang. From *Bagong Silang*, directed by Jayneca Reyes, 2016. Courtesy of Jayneca Reyes.

"There was nothing! We were thrown here like animals," said Emilio. The houses promised to them were nowhere to be found. He continued, "There was nothing for us. It took us years to recover. There were no jobs; others died . . . no roads, no electricity, no water." Others arrived in Bagong Silang in even less well-planned ways. During this period, other informal settlers all over the city were evicted. Some managed to secure a space in Bagong Silang through land invasions. Such is the case of an area in Phase 8, Bagong Silang, called the *bagsak* (dump). According to Arnel, a community organizer we will meet again in the next chapter, "The reason why that place is called *bagsak* is because it is the area where we dumped [our] *yero* [galvanized steel], nails and materials to build walls . . . it is where the houses were [eventually] built." In this way, class differentiations between residents began to emerge from the very inception of the resettlement site.

The successive demolitions carried out by the government was part of its "last campaign" to rid Metro Manila of squatters (Van Naerssen 1993; Karaos 1993; Honculada 1985).[5] Evictions had begun in earnest in the early 1960s, as a result of a huge rural crisis (Kerkvliet 2002a) and picked up speed through the 1960s and 1970s. The first wave of demolitions to putatively end squatting in Manila also became the beginning of Bagong Silang.[6] The evictions began with the informal settlements along Commonwealth Avenue and the Batasan Pambansa Complex. Informal settlements in Tatalon, Pook Ricarte, Tondo, and other places soon followed. These demolitions cannot be divorced from larger attempts of the Marcos regime to curb rebellion and establish an orderly society, a vision articulated in Marcos's New Society or (*Bagong Lipunan*). Central to this vision was the transformation of Manila into the "City of Man"—a shiny and new version of Manila that was to be a showcase to the world and prove that the Philippines was a modern and legitimate player in the global economy (Tadiar 2004). Perceived as "economic saboteurs," "mendicant," "land grabbers," or "eyesores" (Doherty 1985), the squatters were seen as obstacles to this vision; they needed to disappear in order to pave the way for grand monuments and infrastructure.

Meanwhile, the relocatees were barely surviving in Bagong Silang. Many returned to the city center to squat. Apart from securing food and water, their priority was to construct some form of shelter or house.[7] According to Emilio, the materials provided by the government was only enough to put up a frail structure, which he calls a "skeleton." Apart from providing some building materials, the local National Housing Authority provided little assistance. By 1985, there were few improvements in Bagong Silang. According to Precious, whose family was among the first to be relocated in Bagong Silang, "It was very difficult. Most of the families sold their rights for P500 or P200. That is with a house already!" She recalled:

> It was as if we won't last here. We wanted to go back to Manila. There were no jobs. There was nothing . . . it was just bushes, you will only see toilets . . . half of the houses were made of galvanized iron sheets, half were hollow blocks. There were no roofs. We went to NHA . . . they gave us a toilet bowl, the type which you need to squat, you cannot sit on it. When you get your toilet, [the NHA] will give you the dimensions of your lot. That was it. It was two years of suffering. If you want to get some drinking water, the nearest source was three to four kilometers away. If you want to go to Manila, the cost of transportation is too expensive. You need to walk [for about two kilometers] until you get to the terminal. There was no electricity. My father bought electrical wire and illegally connected it to the nearest source. By 6 p.m. [the voltage was] only 110V (from 220V) and you cannot watch TV.

The situation of the relocatees was extremely difficult. As Lita, a community leader, recalled, "It was as if you cannot speak to the people here." As people became desperate and hungry, incidents of theft and violence became frequent. According to Emilio, a family could not leave their food unattended since it would likely be stolen. Hanged clothes became likely prey. Fighting erupted between groups of informal settlers from different areas of the city and different regional groups erupted. Lita and her family fared slightly better due to the cohesion of their group, along with support given by their organization and then-mayor Boy Asistio. For Lita, patronage networks were indispensable for survival.

The ending of Marcos's dictatorship in 1986 after countrywide insurrection co-incided with the beginning of Bagong Silang. Yet, despite Marcos's ouster and the restoration of democracy, the struggle for land tenure, decent housing, and humane relocation for the urban poor continued to pervade Metro Manila politics. The continuing struggle of the urban poor, notwithstanding various political victories including the ouster of Marcos, reflects their enduring marginalization, both a precursor to and product of their displacement and resettlement. While the practice of displacement and resettlement (from a longitudinal perspective) have been informed by different and changing rationalities, including counterinsurgency, environmental concerns, infrastructural development, neoliberal gentrification, and aspirations of modernity and a world-class city, all were underpinned by the state's attempt to produce and maintain urban divides. These divides ostensibly sought to establish and maintain discrete boundaries informed by binary notions of order/disorder, purity/danger, and wealth/poverty (Jensen, Hapal, and Quijano 2020). Urban studies in the Philippines, especially focusing on Manila, have explored the logic of the divides in detail and have illustrated the extent to which class structures urban development in ways that further enrich the wealthy and put the poor at a further disadvantage (Garrido 2019; Arcilla 2018; Ortega 2016).

At the margins of these divides, in places like Bagong Silang, where we see manifestations of advanced marginality, "isolated and bounded territories increasingly perceived by both outsiders and insiders as social purgatories . . . where only the refuse would accept to dwell" (Wacquant 2008b, 67). It is no wonder that despite the many years since Bagong Silang was established, the title of La Kubeta has remained an enduring and visceral description, resonating with many residents' feelings about the place they inhabit. While this is clearly an apt description of the forms of marginalization and violent politics that later would enable the war on drugs, we need to look into the social structure that developed on the back of displacement and resettlement to explain how that war came to be fought as it was. Hence, the remainder of this chapter will explore internal class differentiations and how they articulated with gendered and generational forms of domination to produce particular forms of moral community that treasured equality while also allowing for systemic forms of violence, culminating in the war on drugs.

## Internal Class Divides

At the time of this writing (2019), Emilio was sixty-one years old. He and his family no longer lived in what he called a "skeleton house." In fact, despite his deteriorating health and recurring episodes of depression, Emilio lived a quiet and comfortable life inside his walled and concrete home, thanks to his wife and sons, who managed to "escape" Bagong Silang and work overseas. The same is true for many of the residents of Bagong Silang. Hardly any spot in Bagong Silang has not been developed, improved upon, or built on. The local government has eagerly told and retold this narrative of Bagong Silang's transformation. For instance, in the State of Barangay Address (SOBA) in 2010, Lito Depanes the barangay secretary (the highest ranking nonelected official in the barangay) had prepared an evocative slideshow illustrating how far Bagong Silang had come. Old, grainy photos of Payatas, Tondo, and other urban slums were followed by colorful pictures of present-day Bagong Silang, thus signaling the road traveled and the progress made. Since Lito's address, Bagong Silang further developed and now boasts fast-food outlets like Jollibee and Mang Inasal, both materializations of Philippine progress, as well as a Puregold supermarket, 7-Eleven, and Ministop. Roads are being built and paved, streetlights are being installed, and metal gates guard the entrance to path walks—each clearly marked with the tag of the politician that saw it come into existence. With an estimated population of 250,000, Bagong Silang constitutes a significant part of the electorate. Winning Bagong Silang is central to any electoral success in the city and for the congressional seat of North Caloocan. This has created a new, local elite to run the resettlement site as public servants as well as politicians. This elite and the vertical political networks of course reach into every area of Bagong Silang and can only be understood in relation to the resettlement practices and the patron-client networks that resettlement enabled.

However, despite these material improvements and the emergence of an elite tied to political structures, the majority of the population struggles to get by. In 2010 more than half the households of Bagong Silang lived below the poverty line and a similar number of people had no or inadequate employment (Jensen, Hapal, and Modvig 2013). These indicators of marginalization intimately relate to the urban divide created by the resettlement that left Bagong Silang far away from much of the formal, urban economy. Furthermore, Bagong Silang's past will always be embodied in enduring, spatial structures.[8] The plots are still the same. The path walks are the same. Even the toilets are often the same. For example, Bagong Silang continues to be organized and uses names and codes of resettlement. Areas within Bagong Silang are still called "phases," and each phase corresponds to the chronological expansion of the resettlement site. Each phase is then subdivided into packages. Across Bagong Silang there are 115 packages (in Tagalog, purok). In each package, a purok leader is chosen by the local chief executive, commonly known as a barangay captain. As we described in chapter 2, the purok leaders play a crucial role in the barangay as representatives of the barangay captain and as cogs in the wheels of political machineries that extend to the city and even the national level. Each package would be made up of three to five blocks with approximately one hundred households in each. This entity, the block, would be the one that most people identified as their community. A block is composed of two to three path walks, or narrow alleyways. Along the path walks, rows of conjoined bungalow houses are built on ninety-square-meter plots. These plots have remained relatively the same, except for households who have managed to build vertically.

Perhaps the most important legacy of resettlement is that it continues to shape and structure the lives of the residents of Bagong Silang. The enduring legacy of resettlement has led to a profound sense of "stuckness" in what Wacquant (2008a) in other contexts has described as "social purgatories," referring to places of advanced marginality like Bagong Silang.[9] This stuckness becomes palpable if one considers that apart from working overseas or trying their luck (*sapalaran*) in the metropolitan center, there is no other real option apart from living their lives in Bagong Silang, often at the economic mercy of those who managed to migrate abroad or find jobs in the formal economy, often at incredible costs to themselves (Jensen 2014; Barber 2000). This is partly a consequence of Bagong Silang's marginal position in the urban landscape, but also a result of how resettlement programs are designed. Relocatees are prohibited from selling the houses or lands granted to them by the government, or else they forfeit their "rights" to them and will likely be forced to squat in precarious places within the metropolitan center. Without the necessary resources, Bagong Silang is a place from which it is very difficult to escape (Jensen, Hapal, and Quijano 2020). Furthermore, for each successive generation with no or limited social mobility, the only real option is to further cram bodies into an already densely packed space. This explains why the practice of encroaching in "excess lots" or subletting houses designed for a single household is a pervasive practice in Bagong Silang. The combination of lack of space, density, and immobility has led to the production of communities whose relations are both intimate and tenuous.

However, the precarity of life in Bagong Silang is not experienced uniformly, certain areas are visibly poorer than others and are consequently perceived as *magulo*. Take, for example, Phases 7 and 8, where the area known as *bagsak* (the dump) and many of the excess lots are found. Phases 7 and 8 are located on the northern side of Bagong Silang. Bordered by the Marilao River, these phases are literally at the edge of Metro Manila, beyond which is the province of Bulacan. Phases 7 and 8 have had the reputation of a crime-ridden and drug infested area. During our different stints of fieldwork there were several instances where dead bodies of suspected criminals were found at the borders of Phases 7 and 8 along the banks of the Marilao River. Along the borders, we saw shacks and makeshift

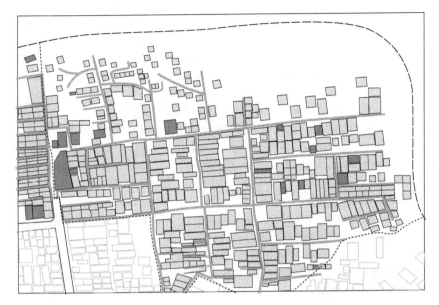

**FIGURE 9.** All household structures located in an area in Phase 8, Bagong Silang called the *bagsak* (dump). Those colored in gray are excess lots.

**FIGURE 10.** The Marilao River, the natural border between North Caloocan and the province of Bulacan. Courtesy of Jayneca Reyes.

houses or "excess lots." In fact, during a mapping exercise in relation to a survey, we had to add hundreds of structures around creeks and rivulets and even in the graveyard, where people had constructed shacks around and in between graves. These structures were not accounted for by the official maps that we acquired from the National Mapping and Resource Information Authority (NAMRIA). These excess lots illustrate how Bagong Silang has grown and became denser to the point that people have encroached on the limits of its borders or in informal areas. What this points to is the production of a class society in Bagong Silang, many of whose members were victims of a second, internal displacement within and out of family homes—what we could call backyarders.[10] They cannot claim a space of their own and must move out of the family home, into excess lots, or out of Bagong Silang, with its promise of social relations, as humiliating as they can be.

In this way, displacement and resettlement processes are not one-off events but rather a continuous struggle. This is true for more than the backyarders. Bagong Silang might soon be experiencing a new round of displacement. In the past five years, malls, shopping centers, and condominiums—all considered edifices of growth and development—have sprouted up in North Fairview, an area just five kilometers away from Bagong Silang. A train line passing through its margins is currently under construction. The city is moving closer and it just may potentially facilitate people's inclusion in the formal economy or, at the very least, provide palpable opportunities. However, the old relocatees in Camarin, an adjacent barangay to Bagong Silang, claim that the NHA has informed them that it will suspend the collection of mortgage fees indefinitely. A huge infrastructure project sponsored by the government is under development, and they are directly in its path (Reyes 2016). The boundaries of the urban economy appear to be changing, its margins looming ever closer to places like Bagong Silang and Camarin. Perhaps this may lead to greater inclusion and further personal development, which many in Bagong Silang desire. Yet given the history of the urban economy so far, it may very well be that the looming expansion of the city will lead to another round of displacement and suffering, as people in Bagong Silang and the rest of the urban periphery are, yet again, in the way.[11] Rumor has it that this time around, people will be resettled in Cavite, far to the south of the ever-expanding metropolis, and very far away from important social relations.

As a way of concluding this section, we may say that displacement and resettlement have enabled, animated, and reproduced the formation of class differentiations. First, the displacement out of Manila drew lines of class, rendering Bagong Silang into what Neferti Tadiar (2007), in talking about urban development in Manila, has called a "monument of reified class antagonisms" (317). In this way, Bagong Silang came to embody that far-away, disorderly place in which the debris of metropolitan dreams was flushed out of sight, and in dire need of *disiplina* (discipline), that is, in need of the capacity to act correctly according to normative social orders (Kusaka 2017a). Again, displacement did not produce the war on drugs, but it enabled it, creating a fertile ground for its operations, out of sight, *magulo*, and perceived as irrelevant for the urban elites, a model of what Loïc Wacquant calls "territorial stigmatization" (Wacquant 2008a). Moreover, however, displacement and resettlement also animated internal class divides. As the political bailiwick of strong political masters, an elite developed to run and structure the huge resettlement site. The sheer number of people, no matter how poor they were, created markets that in time included residents as consumers. Furthermore, housing regulations and the density of people stuck in place meant that new rounds of internal displacement out of families and out of other areas of the city ensued with squatting in the excess lots. For a few, like Kuya Bondo, whom we met in the last chapter, the war on drugs created new opportunities as he was able to move from the excess lot into the big house. However, for the majority of the people inhabiting the excess lots, the drug war created new risks, as they were the most likely victims of the suspicions and violence, not least from those members of the new elite in the resettlement site, who came to operate the watch lists and implement the drug war locally. As we shall see in the next section, these class differentiations more often than not were articulated, together with structures of gender and generation. To see this, we need to begin in the path walk.

## Communal Relations, Intimacy, and Conflict

The path walk is the smallest, but arguably the most important, spatial unit in Bagong Silang in terms of people's ability to survive and the ways in which affective relationality and communal intimacy are played out. Each block, the smallest administrative unit, consists of three to four path walks. As shown in the following photo, the path walk is about three to four meters wide and lined with houses on both sides facing the path walk. Bagong Silang is made up of hundreds of these path walks, and most social life is carried out within their perimeters. In 2010, the average time of residence in Bagong Silang was a little more than fourteen years. As few residents have stayed more than twenty-five years (since the time of its construction as a resettlement site), Bagong Silang is a relatively stable area in terms of residency. Many people have lived within the confines of the path walk for years and therefore have intimate knowledge of the other people around them. Intimate knowledge of their neighbors, as seen in our

**FIGURE 11.** Path walk with a steel gate. From *Bagong Silang*, directed by Jayneca Reyes, 2016. Courtesy of Jayneca Reyes.

2013 survey (Jensen, Hapal, and Modvig), is associated with "trust." However, as we indicated in chapter 1, "trust" in the context of Bagong Silang is a contentious term and is subject to communal relations influenced by how the resettlement site, materialized in the path walks, was designed. In the survey, 95 percent expressed that, in general, they trust people living in their path walk and that they get along with each other too. This suggests that there was a high level of solidarity or, at the very least, cordiality. However, this is never unqualified. When we asked what people meant by trust, they indicated that they trust their neighbors because they afford neighbors no opportunity to cheat them. Furthermore, the high level of trust was not extended to outsiders (residents of adjacent blocks and beyond), who were generally mistrusted. In fact, when asked about people outside their respective blocks, the respondents indicated that they did not trust them and cited them as a source of violent and criminal activity. In this way, it is fair to suggest that trust never exists outside notions of mistrust. In his evocative study concerning what he calls an ethnographic theory of mistrust, Matthew Carey (2017) suggests that rather than being the opposite to or antidote of trust, mistrust indicates a wariness toward people and a "sense of the unreliability of a person or thing" (10).[12] It is this wariness that we note clearly in how residents in the path walk conduct their lives.

As houses are small and densely populated, life is often lived in the path walk, and people have intimate knowledge of the practices and activities of everyone else, including the informal practices of survival. These practices are, at best, dealt with in a civil manner; they are tolerated, if not ignored, as a means of *pakikisama* (discussed in the next section). In many ways, the sheer density and intense proximity of houses and lives in Bagong Silang compels one to "deal with it," often in cordial ways but not entirely without conflict. As an illustration of the complexity and density of life, we mapped one path walk in Phase 9 where we did fieldwork with one chapter of a fraternity in 2010. While it is not representative, the map is typical of life in many path walks throughout Bagong Silang. The path walk comprised thirty-five plots, of which three were double-story houses with a total of 183 residents. Five lots had been subdivided as families grew, resulting in complicated, often conflictual, forms of cohabitation. On eight plots there were more than eight people, with one plot holding twenty people. In terms of livelihoods, seven households were supported in part by remittances from migrants working abroad, mostly in the Gulf. Others gained their livelihoods through working as tricycle drivers, construction work, or other forms of informal economic activities, including owning smaller shops, renting out property, or operating smaller shops at the local market. Several of the households were related by family and intricate hierarchical relations existed around survival whereby some residents would employ less fortunate family members. One man, Kenny's father, worked as a tanod for the local purok leader. Two households were involved in illegal activities like drug peddling and fifteen households had jumpers, that is, illegal electricity connections, while others had no electricity at all. Finally, several different fraternities had representation in the path walk, sometimes leading to violent clashes. While this description by no means is exhaustive, it illustrates some of the complexities.

Maricel, whom we introduced in chapter 1, provides further testimony to this complexity, and it might be useful to revisit her story again. As we recall, Maricel used to be a barangay tanod, a guard associated with barangay policing structures, and an assistant to purok leaders. Several young men also belonged to rivalrous youth groups, the fraternities. However, despite these contradictions, people have a real need to get along. We related how Maricel, at that time a tanod, talked about a local drug dealer and an abortionist in her path walk. While she acknowledged that they were engaging in illegal activities that she was to police, she decided to refrain because of their services to the community and the history they had together. Furthermore, Maricel was herself involved as a kubrador (collector) in jueteng, an illegal numbers game played all over the Philippines, and her husband organized illegal cock fights in the court next to our house. Both activities landed her in constant situations in which police would extort money from her. She is an example of how people inhabit a world where life often contrasts with dominant notions of morality.[13] Despite the obvious illegal nature of these activities, the localized forces of order, the local tanod, declined to act, not least out of pakikisama. Maricel's case illustrates an important point. While pakikisama is associated with hospitality and cordiality, it is also fundamentally conflictual. Communal relations, as we shall see in the cases in the following sections, are not only (if at all) conforming to ideological renditions of Filipino virtue. Rather, they are also performances of navigating, getting along and surviving in the community. In this way, communal relations are not solely characterized by solidarity and trust; instead, it also coexists with contentious relations laden with mistrust.

## Communal Conflicts

One way to explore communal conflicts is to look at the figures from the Barangay Justice System (in Tagalog Katarungang Pambarangay). We explored the Barangay Justice System as part of the general policing structure of Bagong Silang in chapter 2. The Barangay Justice System is part of the conflict resolution or mediation structure at local level instituted through the local government act that is unique to the Philippines. Each purok leader in the 115 packages that make up Bagong Silang is mandated to mediate in interpersonal and communal conflicts where the offenses are punishable by not more than one year of imprisonment or a fine not exceeding P5,000[14] or offenses concerning children.[15] During the years 2008 to 2010, approximately 6,500 cases were annually reported to the purok leaders across Bagong Silang. When the purok leader is not able to mediate, the cases are referred to the Barangay Justice System and the Lupon ng Barangay (the Barangay mediation council, called Lupon hereafter). In 2008 and 2009 approximately 1,500 cases were dealt with annually by the Lupon. This means that less than one in four cases were referred further up the system. Some purok leaders never referred cases further up. This was the case with the purok leader who presided over the area in which we and Maricel stayed. He showed us his books (blotter reports) and proudly announced that he had dealt with all of the seventy-seven cases that had been reported to him in 2009.

Despite the fact that they do not represent the majority, the cases referred to the Lupon provide a privileged entry point to understand communal conflicts, not least because they often comprise conflicts between residents who know each other intimately. The Lupon accounts are also better than the reports from the purok leaders because motives and cause of conflicts will have been established by the Lupon chairperson. About 64 percent of all cases between 2008 and 2010 were nonviolent, whereas 36 percent had resulted in some kind of violence. As the Lupon only hears cases that carry a penalty below a one-year sentence, serious forms of violence tend to fall outside these figures. In the Lupon records, violence includes, for example, slight physical injury, grave threats, assault of public authority, and public disturbance. This violence often has very intimate roots, as indicated in the following cases.[16] For example, a thirty-five-year-old man went to the office of the purok leader because he was allegedly beaten up and attacked with an ice pick by three neighbors after a drinking session. Finally, he was able to escape from the three men. The next day one of the three men and his wife went to the purok to lay a charge against the thirty-five-year-old for public disorder, assault, and harassment going back some time, as there was already a bad relationship between the two families.

This incident correlates to our survey findings, and it might be useful to briefly revisit its conclusions (Jensen, Hapal and Modvig 2013). Violent episodes in Bagong Silang were interpersonal and intimate in nature. The victims were primarily male, young, out-of-school (usually referring to school drop-outs) or unemployed, and poor. Two out of three victims knew at least one of their victimizers. Indeed, almost half the perpetrators of violence were neighbors of the victims. Furthermore, most of the victims mentioned that they still see their perpetrators in places where they often go. Importantly, most of the violent incidents were perpetrated by adult males whereas youth and children constituted less than a third of the perpetrators of violence. This data runs against the popular perception, which was also registered in the survey, that perpetrators of violence come from the "outside" and that most of the "trouble" in their vicinity is caused by young people. In fact, adults were more likely to perpetrate violence than young people, and youth and children were more likely to suffer from violence than adults. While there are contradictions between the perceptions and experiences of violence as captured in the survey, they in fact explain one another, as older men, arguably, feel legitimized to discipline younger, troublesome youth.

Fast forwarding to the war on drugs, we might say that these numbers echo what happened in 2016, when older men in some level of authority—either public or locally—were central in targeting younger men through the Barangay Justice System. While not all purok leaders were male and old, in 2010, more than 75 percent of the purok leaders and tanods in Bagong Silang were male and 95 percent were above age thirty in a population with a majority of people below the age of twenty-five. Hence, barangay leaders were overwhelmingly older men like purok leaders Garcia, Ponte, Baretto, and Tan. At least we might suggest that it was not a huge surprise that they involved themselves in the violence, given their prewar practices. Furthermore, the difference between the levels of trust and perceptions of violence as emerging from outside the intimate sphere on the one hand and the wariness that people exhibit toward their neighbors on the other hand might seem paradoxical at first. However, again this helps us understand some of the logic of the drug war, as it was fought locally between embedded forms of morality. These violent cases that we identified in the research project on violence in 2010 illustrate the extent to which conflicts are local and intimate and how they develop over time, as one complaint is often followed by a countercomplaint.

Not all conflicts related to disciplining youth. In fact, many conflicts revolved around resources. According to the Lupon figures for 2008–2010, a third of conflicts related to resources. Resource conflicts include unpaid debts and loaning practices, theft, destruction of property, territorial disputes, and fraud. The following excerpt from one of the blotter reports describes such a conflict, involving a family inside the survey area: "One female member, Violette, goes to the office of the purok leader to file a complaint about the theft of a cellular phone allegedly stolen by her drinking companions. The event was resolved with the promise that the phone would be replaced with a new phone. However, the next day the brother of Violette files a complaint against her for destruction of property. The event is not resolved. Harsh words are exchanged, and the brother leaves with the hope that Violette will stop taking his possessions."

The general level of poverty in Bagong Silang, where survival is an ever-present concern for people animate these conflicts. They often emerge as people try to get by and deal with very real "here-and-now" issues, often through seizing the chance of immediate gains through cunning or luck. This is what is referred to as *diskarte*, a concept we will return to later in the chapter. Normally diskarte denotes a positive ability to survive, but often it takes the form of hustling (Wacquant 1998), at the expense of the immediate surroundings. Arguably, this is what happened between Violette and her brother.

While resource-based complaints are material in nature and relate to survival, another set of conflicts relates to problematic relations. The data from the Lupon ng Barangay suggests that many conflicts concern slander and gossip. In the Lupon reports, these forms of complaints are registered under, for example, "slander," "oral defamation," or "unjust humiliation of honor." According to the reports to the Lupon, about one third of cases that are not related to resource conflicts fall within this category. These figures are conservative because complaints about what is referred to as alarm and scandal. This is often associated with drinking sessions, but might also result from different forms of personal humiliation. Furthermore, they are likely to not all be reported, except if there are particularly compelling reasons to report it to the purok leader. One reason could be as a counterclaim. This kind of complaints relate to one final set of Tagalog concepts, *tsismis* (gossip) or *sabi-sabi* (hearsay).

In summary, localized conflicts are common in Bagong Silang and their presence question normative notions of trust and togetherness in everyday, localized life. About one third of the conflicts turns violent, and, correlating to quantitative findings, they are often intimate. Many of the conflicts relate to resource issues, which confirms that matters of survival—inherent in notions of diskarte, for example, which is often at the boundary of legality as well as abuse and hustling—animate the kind of sociality that may emerge in these densely populated areas. Other conflicts relate to issues involving gossip, rumor, or other forms of verbal affront. This suggests that in communal life in Bagong Silang, conflicts and mistrust, sometimes turning violent, coexist with strong notions of trust and neighborliness. To explore this in more detail, it is useful to revisit the central concept of neighborliness and communal intimacy, pakikisama.

## Pakikisama as Communal Intimacy

We need to discuss pakikisama in relation to other concepts like abuse of intimacy (abuso) and survival (diskarte), as they emerged in our discussions with people in Bagong Silang. Pakikisama is a central concept in the understanding of culture and identity in Bagong Silang as well as the rest of the Philippines. It is also inherently ambiguous, and, we would argue, sometimes slightly misunderstood in accounts of Philippine social life. Before we get to this and how it matters for understanding conflicts and violence, let us introduce the concept.

Marunong siya makisama! In other words, this person knows how to get along with others. This is about as positive a compliment anyone can get, outsiders as well as insiders. It signifies the person's ability to engage positively with his or her neighbors, help them without expecting anything in return. be cordial, and not act or feel superior. This is how Maricel described pakikisama as opposed to diskarte, which is the ability to survive in situations of adversity: "Diskarte is about how you would be able to live and earn a living every day. Pakikisama is a different thing. In pakikisama it is when you are going to help. That is our way of helping, without wanting anything in return."

In relation to Inday, a neighbor just down the road from Maricel (and our closest informant), who was said not to know pakikisama, Maricel noted, "It's like whenever we're together I want that we will be equal. Yes, I agree that she knew many things but if we're together she should know her place. She needs to learn to level with me." Maricel was recognized as legendary in the difficult art of pakikisama. She continued: "Pakikisama has a variety of meanings. We can say that it's pakikisama when we are here [talking as friends]. We drank together wherever. We're good with that, in sharing stories. But once someone asks help from you, and you'll use your diskarte so that you'll be able to help the people, by hook or by crook, it is real pakikisama. Also, if you desire to help a person out of pakikisama, you must do it. It is not enough to talk about it. I must be judged by my actions, not by my words."

Hence, pakikisama, among other things, is intimately linked to practices of helping rather than simply being cordial to those around you. However, there is more to pakikisama than just altruist wishes to help; rather acts of pakikisama enter into an exchange economy. First, it is clear that Maricel helps because she also wants to be treated in the same way should she ever get into trouble. Furthermore, Maricel invokes the "need" to help. In this lies a contradiction. Whereas help ideally might be said to denote benevolence and the intention to give without expecting anything in return, "need" evokes the opposite. This is a crucial element in how people in Bagong Silang talk about pakikisama. Rather than talk about the knowledge of pakikisama or the ability to be neighborly, it might be more correct to talk about the need and obligation to do pakikisama. Pakikisama as an obligation emerges out of a necessity to get along in order to survive and get along with people one knows from having a long history of suffering, friendship, and conflicts (captured in the concept of *pinagsamahan*). In this way, pakikisama is an investment in communal, social relations.

Intimacy is central in notions of pakikisama; it is about intimacy of space—the need to get along with people in a close and dense space, and it is about temporal intimacy—getting along with people that one has shared a long history with and will have to share most of the future with as well. In this way, community as pakikisama—as a central feature of communal life—denotes benevolence, necessity, and obligation at the same time. It relates to the communal conflicts that we described previously, not least as it is seen as a guard against conflicts. This corresponds to much of the literature on pakikisama. Frank Lynch (1962) defined it as the need for smooth interpersonal relations. In his account, pakikisama is about avoiding conflicts and maintaining face. The father of Philippine psychology, Virgilio Enriquez, focused more on the obligation and the potentially hierarchical connotations and defined pakikisama, inter alia, as the yielding to the leader or the majority, companionship, esteem, and "alter-fellow" (Enriquez 1993). Despite the obvious merits of these discussions and definitions, they tend to focus on pakikisama as an almost objective fact of social life in Bagong Silang and beyond that is evoked to explain why people in the Philippines do as they do. Vergilio Enriquez (1993, 56) criticizes this but ends up suggesting another term that better captures the Philippine psychology, *pakikipagkapwa*.[17] Whichever concept one chooses, both arguably tend to essentialize Philippine culture. One way of avoiding essentialism is to look at how the concept is put to use in everyday life. Seeing the concept in a constructivist light suggests that it functions as the ideological marker of insider and outsider.[18] Those who are said to know how to do pakikisama become insiders whereas those who are known to be incapable of pakikisama face the real risk of exclusion from the intimate space of community. The extent to which people are ascribed the ability to do pakikisama marks the boundaries of inclusion or exclusion of the community. These identities are often negotiated through rumor and gossip in the path walk. As with local politics conducted through rumor and gossip, it is not always what one does that counts but how one is perceived by others. This dynamic may be seen in the conflict Maricel had with Inday, the woman Maricel mentioned as unable to do pakikisama. Inday defended herself and explained her alleged lack of pakikisama in the following way:

> When I did pakikisama with them it was being abused [abuso], or actually it was my husband who did all the pakikisama yet it was being abused. My husband was permitting those things done to him but for me it was an abuse of his pakikisama. It was an abuse because it was done many times. I think there are many other ways to show pakikisama like showing your respect to the person. Actually, my husband was not really known here at first because he rarely stayed here. Now, he was very famous to them because of that. But he was known in pakikisama due to his gambling activity. I told him that he was famous because he has money and when he has no money they will no longer call him. My husband is actually very good at pakikisama yet he was being abused because of it. He is known to be good in pakikisama.

In the excerpt, Inday goes back and forth between her pakikisama and that of her husband. This relates to the domestic sphere or conflicts. Her husband's pakikisama resulted from his gambling and drinking, and how he shared with those around him. He worked outside the area and only came home once in a while, when he would spend his money on himself and his neighbors. Inday, on the other hand, confronted him to stop what she considered his wasting of scarce resources that could go toward sustaining the household, including paying for expensive school tuition. This made her appear to the neighbors as someone without pakikisama while she stressed the abusive relationship and argued that pakikisama was also about respect for the other people. This was not a perception of pakikisama that was widely accepted at that time, and Inday's relationship with the path walk was strained. However, as an illustration of the negotiated and unstable character of pakikisama, it seemed that fortunes shifted one year later, as Maricel had lost her privileged position in the path walk while Inday had improved her status. This was to a large extent due to changes in the political life of Bagong Silang. In the barangay elections in 2010, Captain Padilla lost the election to Kuya Inar (Brother Inar). As we describe in chapter 2, this meant that purok leaders were replaced and Maricel lost her position. Parallel to this, the new captain initiated a consultative forum where Inday managed to involve herself. These changes disadvantaged Maricel and gave Inday new political options that she pursued with vigor. This case illustrates several features about pakikisama that are useful to our understanding of communal life. Although pakikisama is seen as a fundamental (essential) characteristic of communal life or personal quality in Bagong Silang by scholars as well as people living there, it is also a highly unstable signifier, subjected to local political struggles, in which it is employed as one of the central elements in determining insiders from outsiders.[19]

Inday's explanation of her husband's ability to do pakikisama also illustrates the extent to which the concept is gendered and, as Felipe Jocano (1976) suggests in his seminal study, *Slum as a Way of Life*, generational. Jocano notes that the concept is used to calm down young people when humiliated by older ones ("Get along with him/her, s/he is old" [199]). In Inday's comment we also note that in many instances pakikisama is tied to practices outside the household in relation to neighbors, be that consumption of alcohol, gambling, or political ties, which are often male activities. She, on the other hand, emphasizes respect and proper comportment. This means that although pakikisama is employed by both men and women, there is a specific gender dimension to it, as there is a potential tension between the prerogative of pakikisama and household survival. At the same time, pakikisama is viewed as essential also to household survival. It is these contradictions that emerged in the conflict between Maricel, Inday, and Inday's husband.

Finally, there seems to be a hidden or obscured relationship between violence and pakikisama. Pakikisama clearly represents a positive and benevolent core of communal life, as people take seriously the imperative to help others. It forms part of people's ability to survive and their resilience in times of adversity. However, parallel to the benevolent side, pakikisama also may lead to violence. In the case of Inday, she was disciplined by her husband for not knowing the rules of (masculine) pakikisama. In her own explanation, she stated that she did not accept notions of pakikisama that were linked to the consumption of alcohol. The presence of alcohol as constitutive for pakikisama was one of Virgilio Enriquez's chief concerns (Enriquez 1977). This suggests that the gendered tension between household and communal life is real and potentially violent. Pakikisama is also related to violence and conflict in a more complex way. As we saw in the survey and from interviews with policing structures, most violence takes place between people who know each other, with the old victimizing the young at times when many people are present in the path walk (weekends in the middle of the day). These periods are privileged moments for the exercise of pakikisama. In this way violence is de facto obscured, as it is perpetrated by adult men who, like Inday's husband, are the prime performers of pakikisama against outsiders, youngsters, and women. In this way, sometimes communal intimacy and notions of pakikisama become battle zones in which gerontocratic patriarchy still holds sway.[20]

# Communal Intimacy and Violence in the War on Drugs

In this chapter, we have explored how Bagong Silang came into existence through processes of displacement and resettlement that fundamentally animated the ways in which life could be lived far away from centers of economic power and in an area that has been territorially stigmatized (Wacquant 2008a). In this way, Bagong Silang and other resettlement sites came to incarnate "reified class antagonisms" (Tadiar 2007) between the urban poor and the elite where the latter seldom had any respect or regard for the former (Kusaka 2017b). Unsurprisingly, this urban divide has always been characterized by forms of violence—either physical abuse or in the form of violent displacement and marginalization, of which the war on drugs was but the latest instantiation.[21] However, while the forms of metropolitan exclusion help us understand the violent onslaught on places like Bagong Silang, they do not explain the extent of the support inside the resettlement site nor what form it took. To understand this, we need to pay attention to how internal class differentiations also developed on the back of resettlement and how these class divides are often articulated along with gender and generation. While residents of Bagong Silang think of their community life as characterized by equality, trust, and solidarity, people coexist and cohabitate in ways that are as often conflictual and tenuous as they are trusting and mutually benign. In this way, the forms of intimacy resemble the agonistic forms of intimacy that Singh (2011) describes in his study of India. We can see this in the characteristics of violent episodes recorded in the survey data and the records of the Lupon. More often than not, reported incidents involving violence are perpetuated by insiders against insiders and animated by conflicts over scarce resources and affronts to one's dignity.

The tenuous and conflictual communal life in Bagong Silang in many ways emerges from the planned, spatial design of Bagong Silang and the dense and intimate path walks that make up communal life. The sheer density and proximity compel and alter communal relations. We demonstrated how community life was ideologically constructed around the notion of pakikisama. This emic concept invoked notions of neighborliness, friendliness, equality, and the ability, but also a real need, to get along with those around you. As one respondent exclaimed, "We have no choice. We live here and they [our neighbors] live here as well. We just need to get along with them." However, pakikisama also denoted a terrain in which insiders and outsiders were produced. To be acknowledged as one who knows how to do pakikisama equaled being an insider, whereas someone constructed as not able to do pakikisama faced the risk of exclusion from the local polity. This suggests the extent to which pakikisama is negotiated and contested. As Singh (2011, 446) argues in relation to his analysis of agonistic intimacy, whether it turns violent or not, benevolent or malign, depends also on politics. If we relate this to the war on drugs, we may say that communal forms of intimacy in the form of pakikisama potentially are unstable. Maricel provides a good illustration. At the point where we left her, she was influential in the path walk, being known for her ability to engage with her neighbors. However, when the war on drugs was introduced, her year-long struggles with drugs came back to haunt her. She was among the first to sign up on the list, but as the watch list turned into kill lists (Warburg and Jensen 2020a), she escaped the area for another part of Manila. What this illustrates in relation to pakikisama is that while her abilities were well established, they did not protect her against the violent politics of the drug war. Suddenly, overnight almost, she went from being a sanctified member of the community to being its enemy. Furthermore, the public nature of her affective relationality, which had protected and elevated her, became a liability as she could not guarantee that somebody would not turn her in or betray her otherwise. In this way, pakikisama is not stable and will be reconfigured as state violence folds itself into communal forms of intimacy.

Furthermore, the concept of pakikisama emerged as a classed, gendered, and generational term whereby some men were in a better position to assert authority in the path walks.[22] This gendered and generational aspect of pakikisama not only created insiders or outsiders, it also created categories of people whose practicing of pakikisama (and forms of activities associated with it) are deemed legitimate. Hence, for Inday, without access to local participatory processes, the realm of pakikisama where her husband engages is anything but accessible. She relied on him. Neighbors recognized his skills in doing pakikisama really well—to the extreme frustration of Inday, as he spent vast sums of (household) resources on maintaining his standing in the block. On more than a few occasions, especially in the earlier years of their marriage, her protests led to him physically abusing her. The gendered and generational aspects also apply to youths and children who, by virtue of age, are excluded from (masculine) pakikisama. In chapter 6, we describe how these children and youths attempt to address their exclusion by tapping into what we call "a world of significance" and creating effective peer relations that resemble pakikisama. As we shall see, these relations were equally enforcing of gender and generational notions of morality. In relation to communal intimate life, the gendered and generational character of pakikisama suggests that it is difficult to talk about Bagong Silang as a homogenous social space. Rather, it is hugely conflictual, not least around issues of what is moral and proper. What is moral and proper however, as our discussion of the gendered dimension of pakikisama suggests, was shaped by older men of authority, disciplining those who have gone astray, often through violence.

The gendered and generational character of pakikisama explains how the relationship between community and violence was rendered invisible, as the violence is perpetrated by those (mainly men) who were "good at doing pakikisama." Violence is rendered invisible by pitting poor, young men and their families against a patriarchal, moral community and is therefore framed and justified as acts of disciplining (Kusaka 2017a). The intersecting identities of class, gender and generation arguably structure also how different putatively "guilty" people are judged. Elsewhere, we have examined the reactions of social media users to the deaths of a minor, Kian delos Santos, the archetypical victim in the war on drugs whom we also encounter in chapter 2, who was killed just across the bridge from Bagong Silang, and self-confessed drug lord Rolando Espinosa (Hapal 2019). On social media, Kian's death was met with sarcastic remarks or regarded as another nameless casualty in the war on drugs. For instance, many Facebook users were quick to accuse Kian of being a drug pusher whose death was justified. Others blamed Kian's parents, whom many saw as also involved in the illegal drug trade. All these accusations were made despite evidence that Kian was in fact executed by police officers who were later (for once) convicted of the crime. In sharp contrast, many Facebook comments expressed sympathy for the "repentant" drug lord Rolando Espinosa. Some expressed forgiveness for or valorized Espinosa. This was quite surprising given reports that Espinosa was a "big fish" in the illegal drug trade in the Philippines. The sympathy or scorn for both Kian and Espinosa may be due to their respective class positions, but the treatment of the former, at least based on our analysis, reflects a discourse where the young are treated as objects of (violent) disciplining. The forgiving treatment for Espinosa on the other hand suggests that, despite his illicit activities, he continues to enjoy a degree of recognition that he can rejoin the "good" society if he repents, rendering his crimes and violent potentials invisible. In this way, the intersections of class, gender, and generation as embedded in structures of authority and violent institutions both transcend and animate how the war on drugs was carried out in Bagong Silang.

# COMMUNITY ACTIVISM
## From New Birth to the War on Drugs

"He really conned us," Emilio said jokingly, as he talked about how Duterte had "tricked" Emilio into voting for him. "No end to contractualization. No peace talks. No land reform. Just dead bodies," he added. We were sitting in Emilio's comfortable house in Bagong Silang while sharing a meal. Emilio had supported Duterte because he thought Duterte would govern with an activist and almost revolutionary agenda. Emilio had cause to think so as Duterte labeled himself a president of the left with the support, even, of the exiled head of the Communist Party of the Philippines (CPP), José Maria Sison. While Emilio supported the drug war, it was Duterte's progressive agenda that really caught his imagination, as did Duterte's promise to clean up the government. Emilio's sentiments echoed the views of other community activists who have been our interlocutors for the past decade.

Most of our activist interlocutors and friends participated in militant action against demolitions and in the larger antidictatorship movement during the 1980s. In their prime, many of them had occupied leadership positions in various community organizations in and outside Bagong Silang and were at the frontlines of demonstrations and rallies. Through the years, their roles have changed with the transformations of Bagong Silang. Ronald occupies the dual role of an activist and a political strategist for a politician. Junior, Lita, Vicky, Lando, and Arnel have had to find ways to straddle between the *masa* (masses) and the politicians, partly to get the best deal for the poor and partly as a means to secure their own well-being by staying relevant to both parties. Others like Emilio have since retired due to illness but continue to remain active in community discussions.

These activists are, in many ways, our most important interlocutors. We interviewed several of them for the first time in 2009. Both of us have boarded with some of them in their houses and we know their families. Karl conducted interviews with them and followed them in their work in relation to the research on which much of this chapter builds. Steffen reinterviewed them in relation to the war on drugs in May 2017. They are the main protagonists of the story. They are gatekeepers of our various fieldwork periods and engagements in Bagong Silang, and they embody difficult communal contradictions from displacement and resettlement to the war on drugs. These contradictions are inescapably intimate, as they have long histories with those whom they represent and those in power with whom they have to engage.

Since its establishment in 1982, Bagong Silang has been an arena of intense political contestations between and among various political actors. Relocatees waged massive demonstrations against government agencies responsible for the living conditions in Bagong Silang. Popular struggles in Bagong Silang transcended its borders; many organized groups found themselves participating in movements that were national and multisectoral in scope. After democracy was restored in 1986, some community organizations shifted their focus. They began to perform the functions of local development agents by facilitating people's access to basic necessities, credit, and services, without abandoning their militant stance. Since then, community organizations and their militant repertoires have become increasingly marginalized, partly due to various sociopolitical developments that have shifted the development discourse toward maximizing formal government processes. This does not suggest that the political landscape has become less contentious. The charged political world has been the landscape that community activists have navigated to stay relevant, for themselves and for those whom they represent.

Ronald is one of the activists who had to navigate through the intensely contested political landscape in Bagong Silang. During the 1980s, Ronald was at the forefront of youth organizing in Bagong Silang. Soon after, he fully committed to the goal of achieving political change by taking up arms against the regime. By the mid-1990s, Ronald returned to Bagong Silang to support his struggling family, as he was unable to provide schooling for his children while fighting in the countryside. When we met him in 2017, Ronald was working for a barangay official as a political strategist. While his position entailed the performance of administrative work and service delivery, his main skillset was his ability to connect with groups and organizations in Bagong Silang, some members with whom he had worked directly when he was a youth organizer decades before. These connections were useful not only in delivering much needed services, they were also crucial in soliciting support come election time. Being a political strategist, Ronald was part of an electoral machine vying for political dominance in Bagong Silang and in the city of Caloocan. Ronald and his wife, who was also an activist and currently an employee of the Caloocan city government, shared how they distributed money for an aspiring politician during the 2013 elections. According to Ronald, "We had sacks full of money. . . . People lined up in front of our house and we gave it all to them." Ronald maintains that he is still an activist but justifies his involvement with politicians with the need to survive. Beyond survival, Ronald believes that his employment with the barangay official is a valuable platform where he can act on his progressive ideas. He believed in changing the system from within.

Junior, a fellow community organizer in Bagong Silang working for a local nongovernment organization (NGO) did not take kindly to Ronald's activities. Commenting on these activities Junior said, "The politics in Bagong Silang is different. Money talks . . . if the price is right." Junior questioned Ronald's principles and insinuated that he was a hack and a sell-out. Like Ronald, Junior was an activist in the 1980s. After being tortured and imprisoned, Junior left his militant past and instead worked with various human rights organizations in Bagong Silang. This made Junior well acquainted with local political networks in Bagong Silang. Junior's connections proved useful when, in 2013, together with Balay, we were conducting human rights seminars for purok leaders. Junior led the negotiations with then incumbent chairman Padilla to grant us access to the purok leaders and provide a venue and food for the seminar. Padilla obliged. After all, he was in the middle of an intense reelection bid at the time. Junior knew that Padilla would support our seminar so that he could reinforce his good standing with his purok leaders, who were crucial cogs in his electoral campaign. Our series of seminars went smoothly. Occasionally, Padilla and his slate would come by and check on us by the end of the seminar. We felt obliged to be courteous, give them refreshments, and have them greet the participants. Padilla's short greeting, however, became a ten-minute speech about his accomplishments and plans, one of which was raising the salaries of his purok leaders. Aspiring council members soon followed with a five-minute speech of their own. Often, we found ourselves tempted to interrupt Padilla's speeches. However, Junior told us to let them be and explained, "This is how the game is played here in Bagong Silang . . . this is how you build partnerships." Secretly, however, Junior was campaigning for Padilla's opponent, Inar, who promised to provide space and support for Junior's organization.

While Junior was quick to judge Ronald's involvement with politicians, he was no less compromised, tapping into patronage politics to advance his (and his organization's) developmental agenda. Their actions however were not surprising. Patronage politics is central in how policing and politics are organized in Bagong Silang. Community activism is not immune to this either. However, we cannot reduce local politics to simple instantiations of large political narratives but rather must pay attention to politics from below. This view allows us to see Ronald and Junior's actions as more than hegemonic versus counterhegemonic struggles (Kusaka 2017b) and instead points to how political languages, in this case patronage and revolutionary politics, are entangled. In the case of Ronald and Junior, we see that patronage and revolutionary politics are not necessarily invoked and acted on in an antithetical manner. Instead, Ronald and Junior navigated the political field using both languages. The entanglement of political languages, we argue, is central to understanding the history of community activism in Bagong Silang. Activists like Junior, Lita, Vicky, Lando, and Arnel, all of whom have sought to struggle for inclusion and equality, found themselves in rather complicated and often changing relationships with other actors espousing political agendas of their own. More importantly, the entanglement of political languages provides important insights into how community activists such as Emilio, who, despite having strong convictions on revolutionary and emancipatory politics, have come to support Duterte's war on drugs. Duterte's war on drugs and its underlying discourse were able to tap into aspirations for sweeping and genuine change that activists like Emilio have sought throughout their lifetime. It is this promise that led them to turn a blind eye to the carnage that was to come, hoping that Duterte would be the one to deliver on the progressive agendas. Emilio's support for the war on drugs is no different than the way he has tapped into and acted on other political languages that he deemed congruent with revolutionary politics. However, as we discuss throughout this chapter, while these attempts embody their desire for inclusion and equality, Emilio and activists like him often find themselves in compromised positions. As Emilio indicated, Duterte's promise of change bore no fruit, only dead bodies.

We explore the practices and discourses of community activists in two sections. The first section adds to the histories of displacement and resettlement discussed in chapter 4 by focusing on organized community action in the face of demolitions and resettlement. We discuss the militant and combative political language in Bagong Silang that emerged in the 1980s and retrace its gradual transition from militant to transformative languages—making governments work without being less critical. The transformation from militant to transformative languages coincided with the transition from dictatorship to democratization in the 1980s. We also touch on other transformations in the postdemocratization context, which featured an explicit attempt to engage in politicking that anti-Marcos icon Popoy Lagman referred to as "jump[ing] into the pigsty (Teehankee 2001, 75)." Here, we describe how some community organizations began to deal with politicians to access resources or obtain concessions. This form of *trapo* politics culminated in their participation in electoral processes either directly or by supporting a political champion. This shift toward politicking and politicians is reflective of their adoption of some form of patron-client language framed as a means of making demands. It also meant a decline of strong egalitarian politics at the expense of hierarchical forms of politics.

The second section on entanglements discusses how various political languages, at different times and to different degrees, are invoked by various community activists. Community activists have used the languages of militant, transformative, and patronage engagement as means of navigating an otherwise unforgiving situation. This does not suggest that community activists are less principled or opportunists. Instead, it reflects the process of appraisal, opportunity seeking (*diskarte*), and the allocation of efforts or energies (*pagtaya*)—processes that are compelled by both local and intimate relationships and wider sociopolitical developments. We conclude by relating this examination of entangled political languages to the rise of Duterte and the seemingly widespread support for the war on drugs, especially at the local level. We suggest that the populist rhetoric of Duterte appealed to both militant and patronage-based political languages adopted by community activists in Bagong Silang. Duterte's disdain for the *dilawan* (a derogatory term for the opposition to his rule) also reflected the community activists' implicit frustration over formal, bureaucratic, and professionalized processes that have, in many ways, marginalized them from political processes. Ironically, however, the congruence of Duterte's rhetoric—a reflection of their need for inclusion—has led to a bloody war on drugs that has impacted their communities profoundly. While some of them have regretted their support, their support of Duterte's populist rhetoric played a part in legitimating the war on drugs.

# Transformed Community Activism in Bagong Silang

Whole populations of informal settlers were displaced just before the end of the Marcos regime as part of its effort to beautify Metro Manila. The first wave of demolitions began with the informal settlements along Commonwealth Avenue and the Batasan Pambansa Complex. Informal settlements in Tatalon, Pook Ricarte, Tondo and others soon followed. Informal settlements all over Metro Manila became fertile grounds for antidemolition mobilizations. Some community organizations of informal residents like those in Commonwealth and Tatalon took a hardline position—resist demolitions! For others, the goal of the protests was to gain concessions, guarantees or even delay demolitions as they attempted to further reinforce their ranks. As the resistance against demolition intensified, the government responded with brute force in a replay of violent suppression of activism for the urban poor during the 1970s (Karaos 1993).

Take the case of Arnel. Arnel was a community organizer in Tatalon, Quezon City before we met years later in Phase 8, the area called *bagsak*. For weeks, Arnel and his comrades resisted government efforts to demolish their houses. One day, marines stormed into their community. The aggressive response by the government was nothing new, Arnel explained. As he saw it, the intensity of government action was due to the renewed confidence of the landowner, Greggy Araneta, who married presidential daughter Irene Marcos back in 1981. In response, Arnel, together with his comrades, poured gasoline in the creek and prepared Molotov cocktails. They were prepared to burn the creek running through Tatalon and throw bombs at the marines as soon as they breached the inner areas of the community. The marines, however, opened fire and killed several people instantly. Outgunned by their adversaries, Arnel and his comrades surrendered. Together with civilian operatives, the marines tore most of the houses down. Emilio, whom we met earlier, recalled a similar experience: "We were surprised by the army to the point that we can't fight. We were told that we must demolish our own house. By 'hook or crook,' if you do not demolish your own house the soldiers will be the one to take it down. They do not care; they will just tear your house down. That was how demolitions were done."

Outright resistance was not the only strategy deployed by the informal settlers. Take the case of Lita, a resident of Tondo near the Manila Port, whose organization's mobilizations aimed at getting the best deal possible out of displacement. Their position was not necessarily reflective of their capitulation. Rather, it was an implicit recognition of the inevitability of their eviction and the relative impossibility of acquiring land tenure within the metropolis. For informal settlers like Lita, agreeing to the government's relocation program was a calculated move to cut their losses or dampen the adverse effects of relocation. This was not without any form of agonizing; nor was it without violence or harassment from the government. Nonetheless, informal settlers like Lita who "volunteered" to be relocated were then given the chance to tear down their houses themselves and salvage some construction materials. Some were given subsistence allowances, construction materials, and means of transportation to Bagong Silang.

Beginning in 1982, thousands of informal settlers were resettled in Bagong Silang. After their relocation to Bagong Silang, Arnel recalls that many informal settlers maintained their community organizations and resumed their militant activities. Others were able to reconnect with their progressive allies from within and outside their areas. As Arnel put it, "We [community leaders and organizers] were like snails picked from the field [*mga pinulot na suso*]. . . . We had heard about each other's organization before being resettled in Bagong Silang but it was here where we were able to connect and work with each other." By referring to these leaders and organizers as snails, Arnel alluded to their displacement. However, their resettlement also led to the formation of a strong urban poor bloc in Bagong Silang. According to Emilio, Bagong Silang became the base of operations for many organizations tasked with "politicizing the masses." The government, particularly the NHA, was aware of the politically charged and militant character of some relocatees. The NHA attempted to break the ranks of these organizations by scattering the lot assignments of the members of militant organizations, but without much success.

According to Emilio, the government's inability to provide the necessary services and basic needs to the relocatees together with feelings of discontentment and anger fueled community activism in Bagong Silang. In the case of Emilio and his comrades, they began to undermine the NHA's capacity to collect payments for the houses. They argued to the relocatees that the houses must be given for free. Apart from undermining the NHA, they also demanded better services. The relationship between community organizations and the local NHA soon became outright hostile. After several years of struggle the NHA yielded by agreeing to grant a moratorium on mortgage payments. This gave the relocatees of Bagong Silang some time to recuperate and focus on more pressing needs. According to Emilio, the NHA only began to collect payments during President Joseph Estrada's term (1998–2001), almost sixteen years after Bagong Silang was established.

While the NHA was a detested entity, this feeling did not extend to government in its entirety. For instance, the late mayor Boy Asistio of Caloocan was an "endeared" figure in Bagong Silang and a political patron for some of the relocatees and activists. Emilio and Lita credited Mayor Asistio for distributing rice, grocery items, and nonfood items during the height of the relocation in Bagong Silang. Lita claims that it was through Mayor Asistio's assistance that her relocation (and the relocation of the members of her organization) was not as painful as that of other relocatees. According to Emilio and Lita, Mayor Asistio was also a key figure in preventing the demolition of houses built in Bagong Silang on invaded land. Indeed, our interlocutors referred to Mayor Asistio as a *kaibigan* (friend). In this way, patronage politics was always present in Bagong Silang as entangled with revolutionary languages.

According to Emilio, while community organizations focused on local issues, they also became part of a larger politicized, multisectoral network around the urban poor sector. Emilio recalled that they, together with other community organizations, formed the first branch of the Pagkakaisa ng Maralitang Lung-sod (PAMALU, or Unity of the Urban Poor) in 1983. Being part of a wider net-work partly explained their ability to access development aid and socioeconomic support during and immediately after resettlement. On the other hand, the ur-ban poor movement capitalized on the situation in Bagong Silang, using it to promote a progressive political agenda and expose government shortcomings. The mutually reinforcing relationship between local organizations and the wider political movement resulted in the mitigation of some of the grievances and suf-ferings. Furthermore, it elevated the plight of relocatees into the public sphere and by implication led to the strengthening of the urban poor movement. As Emilio recalled, "It was Bagong Silang that was the first to be exposed at the in-ternational level through the BBC . . . they named it the *kubeta* [toilet] village. Through this, they learned . . . national groups learned and [then] the Kongreso ng Pagkakaisa ng Maralita ng Lungsod [KPML, or Congress of the Solidarity of the Urban Poor] was formed." KPML served as the umbrella organization for most of the urban poor organizations in city centers across the Philippines.

Increasingly, engagements with the larger urban poor movement also entailed participation in the antidictatorship movement during the 1980s. Relentless waves of demolitions in Metro Manila likewise heightened the politicization of the urban poor sector. Lita, a veteran of antidemolition rallies when she was still in Tondo, remembers rather fondly her participation in these mobilizations. Ac-cording to her, "We were the first to rally on *kalderong walang laman* [literally empty cauldrons, signifying demonstrations over lack of food]. We were blasted with tear gas. We rallied every day. We had several buses. Our president asked: 'Lita, how many buses?' I say, 'Six or four.' All the buses were filled. You need not convince them. If you say that there is a rally the people will support. When we got here, we continued."

According to Emilio, urban poor organizations in Bagong Silang and else-where continued to participate in mobilizations after the fall of Marcos. The mili-tant stance was largely due to the slow and poor delivery of services by the Aquino government. According to Lando, the new sociopolitical context pro-voked cautious optimism among community activists in Bagong Silang despite slow implementation. However, this cautious optimism immediately turned to distrust as demolitions continued and perceived political opponents, especially left-leaning organizations, were repressed.[1] According to our interlocutors, the government crackdown led to the incarceration, torture, or death of several com-munity leaders. This left many community organizations reeling from the sheer brutality of the state.

According to Arnel, apart from state repression, strife within the movement also disrupted organized community action in Bagong Silang. By the 1990s, the so-called split divided the Philippine left into competing factions and led to the fragmentation of its support (Fuller 2007).[2] Many party members, organizers, and supporters were demoralized, frustrated, and bewildered because of the split. Its impact was quite evident in Bagong Silang as it led to the division of community organizations. Lando, who was at that time already a veteran community activist and Arnel's close friend, recalled, "Before we could fill-up twenty mini-buses. Then it became problematic when . . . the *pwersa* [movement] got divided." While organized community action in Bagong Silang persisted, the postdemocratization context saw the rise of different repertoires and its expansion into less militant and combative forms. For example, some organizations focused their efforts on site development and welfare, building people's capacities and engagements with governance structures and formal political processes, such as elections. In this way, the struggles in Bagong Silang began to move away from the wider revolutionary agenda.

In the absence or lack of government services, some community organizations like those headed by Lita and Emilio facilitated site improvements while others implemented various socioeconomic and welfare-oriented projects such as housing support, health services, and access to credit. Through these activities, community organizations assumed quasi-state functions. For instance, Emilio claimed that community organizations occupied a central role in the development of the waterworks project in Bagong Silang. Despite facing serious challenges, the waterworks projects were managed by community organizations. The water services continued to operate until the 1990s. Additional water tanks were built, and services began to expand to other areas in Bagong Silang. However, in the late 1990s, "when Malonzo [the former Caloocan City mayor] saw that it was earning 1.8 million Pesos a month he kicked us out. It is where Malonzo got rich," said Emilio.

Support from external donors was key to the establishment of these socioeconomic and welfare-oriented projects. Since the 1986 transition, the amount of development aid provided to the Philippines steadily increased as an expression of support to the newly instituted democratic regime. A significant proportion of the aid was channeled through NGOs and community organizations due to their supposed flexibility, innovativeness, and efficiency. Contrary to this view, donors perceived the performance of the government in implementing aid-funded socioeconomic projects to be "sadly lacking" (Lopa 2003, 3).

Foreign funding had far-reaching consequences for development programs and projects run by community organizations in Bagong Silang and elsewhere in the Philippines. NGOs and community organizations attempted to align objectives and strategies with the demands of external donors. It also entailed learning the technical skills and language required to access these resources. Complementing the projects, capacity-building activities sought to promote people-centered development, participation, and the deepening of democracy. This entailed a formative process of *pagmumulat* (conscientization) and skills developments, eventually leading to action or mobilization. Unlike their militant counterparts however, these activities, while no less critical, aimed at activating residents to contribute to their community's development through participation in democratic (albeit state-dominated) processes. The cautiously optimistic view about the newly instituted democratic regime also led to the growing realization that community organizations should not ignore the government and its processes. This was in no small measure due to foreign donors who were occupied with state capacity and the demand that the state assume responsibility (Mosse 2004). Hence, instead of simply fighting the government, the new political climate required a reconfiguration of strategies toward a more constructive and transformative relationship with government. The rise of transformative engagements was also due to feelings of frustration and fatigue concerning militant forms of action. Arnel, who lost all his front teeth from the beatings he endured while participating in demonstrations, echoed this frustration:

> For the longest time we have been fighting. They sometimes think, "Here we go again, but it is as if nothing has changed." The issue we are facing, it keeps on recurring. It does not go away . . . so we concluded that we would have no gain if we just attacked. With other organizers we conducted case studies . . . to explore why it was very difficult to address the issue of housing. We concluded that we must be open to dialogue and not only limit ourselves to the barricades. We do not always have to fight. We needed to talk to them since we might end up agreeing. There is a process and our claims have basis. That is why, by the 1990s to 2000s, there were a lot of dialogues.

Transformative engagements between government and civil society organizations also flourished with constitutional and legislative reforms that widened the democratic space in the Philippines. The 1987 Constitution (Article XIII, Section 16) guaranteed the "effective and reasonable participation at all levels of social, political and economic decision-making [processes]." Subsequently, this space was institutionalized through the establishment of the party-list system within the House of Representatives; the creation of basic sector-oriented agencies or offices within national bureaucracy; and the passage of the Republic Act 7160 or the Local Government Code of 1991. The passage of the Local Government Code was an important milestone for community activists in Bagong Silang and the urban poor movement in general. The law delegated greater powers and autonomy to local governments in an attempt to promote effective, efficient, accountable, and responsive governance structures in terms of delivering services. Among other things, the Local Government Code mandated the creation of local development councils where sectoral representation (for instance, that of the urban poor) was required. The law likewise devolved vital functions such as urban planning, housing, welfare, health, and poverty eradication to local governments.

While the law was lauded in terms of instituting democratic and development-oriented reforms, its application in real life was not without its problems. According to Porio (2016, 31), "Some have argued that decentralization has also led to the further entrenchment of traditional elites and their local allies."[3] Despite the Local Government Code's problematic implementation, it still provided an avenue or an arena for community organizations and activists alike for meaningful engagements with the government. Vicky, a veteran of militant action, opined that it might be more productive if community organizations work with government through its programs and participatory mechanisms instead of waging a struggle against government. Vicky's remarks stem from her frustrations with combative strategies against the state, which she now saw as frequently counterproductive. Presently the community leader for a chapter of a political party, Vicky emphasized the need to get inside the system (*kailangang pumasok*) in order to be in a better position to influence and affect change. According to her, "The question is where is our [the people's] destination? How do we get there? Before, we were trying to make people angry so you could mobilize them. Now, it is different. For me, instead of keeping on hitting, it is better to participate. That is my brand of organizing. That is how I raise their awareness. I do not organize people so I could use them because I have a particular agenda. To understand the full extent of the problem you need to understand its inner workings."

According to Emilio, many organizations relied on dialogues and transformative forms of engagement in the arena of governance and politics by the 1990s. Many of the organizations saw participation in programs and making the government accountable as a viable option to provide services and address socio-economic issues. They reserved protests and other forms of militant action for tactical purposes, mainly to draw government agencies to the negotiating table. The increased engagement with government agencies and foreign donors did not come cheaply for community activists. They often found it difficult to perform according to the new professionalized environment of community development, participation, and empowerment—words that sounded much like their own repertoire but with significant differences in what they meant in practice. With Wataru Kusaka (2017b), we may say that the civic sphere invaded the space of the mass sphere with all the consequences in terms of changing languages and culture. In many ways, working with politicians was sometimes easier but that also elicited a high degree of ambivalence. Sometimes they were referred to as *kaaway* (enemy), and engagements with government agencies and their political masters drew hostile responses.

Amid the rise of transformative engagements, community activists increasingly perceived electoral and parliamentary processes as legitimate arenas for struggle. This began when certain blocs within the left began to believe that advancing democracy, promoting reforms, and combating elite domination might be achieved through participating in the electoral struggle and parliamentary processes (Quimpo 2008). The justification to participate in these processes is best exemplified by Popoy Lagman's comments. According to Lagman, "*Kung kailangan na lumusong sa babuyan upang ipamuka sa mga baboy ang kababuyan nila ay gagawin natin* [If we have to jump into the pigsty to expose them, we will]" (in Teehankee 2001, 75). Lagman was the former head of the Manila-Rizal Regional Party Committee of the CPP-NPA. Due to ideological differences, he split from the party during the early 1990s. With his departure, Lagman took with him the support of many community organizations in the Manila-Rizal area. Most of the activists claimed to be affiliated with the Manila-Rizal Regional Party Committee. Eventually, the Manila-Rizal area became the base for the formation in 1993 of Sanlakas, an alliance of multisectoral organizations.

Many left-leaning organizations, activists, and NGOs did jump into the pigsty. In 1995, political organizations expressed their support for or endorsed some candidates running for national and local office (Quimpo 2008). By 1998, leftist organizations such as ABA, Akbayan, and Sanlakas were able to win seats in the House of Representatives through the party-list system. Their respective bases of support were key to these victories. Equally important were community organizations whose members served as *kampanyador* (campaigners) and mobilizers at the local level. Similar to their experience in 1995, some left-leaning groups continued to field or endorse candidates at the local level. However, Quimpo (2008) observed something apparently contradictory regarding the manner of endorsing or fielding candidates. According to him:

> Some leftist parties and groups . . . have put candidates in the local elections, but they have done so in a most curious fashion. Often a candidate who was a bona fide member of a leftist party ran under a traditional party in the local polls, while at the same time campaigning for the leftist party in the party-list vote. In effect, he or she was affiliated with two parties—trapo and leftist! Where the candidate's main allegiance lay was open to question. The leftist parties tolerated this dual-party affiliation since they believed they did not yet have the wherewithal to field successful leftist or progressive candidates without some backing from a trapo party. (150)

Quimpo's observation of left-leaning organizations and their community organizations invoking both trapo and leftist politics illustrates our point that political languages—that of patronage and revolution—are entangled. However, this was a precarious proposition, especially for progressives. By jumping into the pigsty, one is susceptible to be swallowed by the corrupt political system (*malamon ng sistema*). Despite its "dangers," especially at the local level, the left-leaning groups decided to participate in the electoral and parliamentary process. By getting inside the political system, political organizations thought that they would be in a better position to contribute to the advancement of both utilitarian and politico-ideological objectives.

Similarly, community organizations in Bagong Silang began to endorse aspiring barangay chairpersons and council members. However, community organizations proceeded with caution. As Elmer, the president of a prominent urban poor organization in Bagong Silang, insisted, "Getting our support is not automatic. It depends on his or her programs and whether these are consistent with our principles or beliefs." Arnel, on the other hand, adopted a rather pragmatic perspective. According to him: "that's how they [politicians] are. If they can, they will give it to the people; they [politicians] are dole-outs . . . especially when they have ambitions to ascend to a higher position."

In this context, activists like Vicky attempted to capitalize on the handout tendencies of politicians, especially during elections. The idea was to use their organization's support base as leverage to achieve concessions and open the arena for *paniningil* (demanding). As Vicky said, "They need us. That is why they come to us. But what is in it for us? Yes, it must be 'give and take,' but we should have the advantage." Activists tacitly know that local politicians are, at the very least, ambivalent about dealing with the urban poor sector. An unpopular program or policy might cost them their electoral fortunes. Some community leaders like Arnel and Vicky were keen to exploit this. Arnel reenacted a conversation with a politician: "I said, 'Sir why don't we establish an in-city [housing program for informal settlers in Bagong Silang]? Let us look, there are a lot of vacant lands then let us establish an in-city [housing] for the informal settlers along Bagong Silang's waterways. Let us put them there. . . . I am sure you will get their votes."

Dealing with politicians entailed engaging in a reciprocal relationship—a "partnership" with politicians so to speak. In this partnership, politicians provided access to various resources. As politicians open these opportunities, community organizations and activists have to reciprocate and grant politicians access to their members. It reflects a type of relationship constituted by two agendas that do not necessarily complement each other. It has also paved the way to rather blunt practices talked about as *walang delicadeza* (literally, callous) since both parties are just *nagagamitan* (using each other). As Emilio commented about some community organizations in Bagong Silang, "they were able to milk the politicians . . . around half a million in exchange for votes. It was *matindi* [intense]! The politicians will believe these organizations because they are representing many people. That is why some organizations are *mabaho* [literally, stinking] here."

Despite this, some activists like Arnel insist that engaging with politicians provides access, leverage, and the opportunities to organizations and its members. Community activists like Arnel and Ronald attempted to capitalize by becoming political strategists of politicians. Arnel justified his involvement with a city council member as his attempt to influence the policy and program making process to better suit the urban poor of Caloocan City. This, however, led them to assume dual roles; that of a political operator and that of a community activist, roles that frequently entail conflicting agendas.

Lando on the other hand simply engaged politicians through the electoral process where organizations endorsed candidates believed to be pro–urban poor. Come election time, organizations campaigned for candidates who would champion and advance their cause. However, these attempts, at most, yielded mixed outcomes. For instance, Lando recalled: "We have a lot of experience with politicians. For example, look at Abaca. He said that he was a member of KPML. After we helped him win, he just left us. He said that he was a member of KPML; that he knew our organization very well. We helped him in his campaign. Yes, he did get some of our leaders as his staff. They were not able to stand Abaca because he was such an asshole. They left eventually. Now, he is reconnecting with us again. After the way he fooled us before, why would we talk to him again!"

It is illustrative of the lack of choice that despite Lando's frustration with cunning politicians, activists continue to deal with politicians especially when an opportunity presents itself to forward a particular developmental or political agenda, as well as personal opportunities. In some cases, supporting politicians proved to be a major problem for community organizations. To mitigate this, Lando's organization attempted to field candidates within their own ranks. These candidates soon realized the immense challenges involved in entering politics. According to Lando, "Back in the 1990s we had Norman, a KPML member, who ran as a barangay councilor. He won the elections. However, in the end, he flipped; he was swallowed by the system. He sold his victory." In the 2013 midterm elections, Lando's organization attempted to have one of their leaders run for public office. However, without any form of political machinery, community organizations often find the process to be too costly, exhausting, and full of vitriol. During the campaign period, it is not uncommon for stories of corruption, ties to dubious characters, infidelity, homosexuality, and even sterility to circulate within the community. These stories are spread in an attempt to undermine specific candidacies. Despite their supposed wide mass base, Lando and his organization lost in the 2013 midterm elections. According to Lando, the reason why they lost is that elections in Bagong Silang are, in many ways, a battle of resources. Hence, despite their development work for decades, some leaders and members gravitate toward politicians because of their promises and the immediate benefits involved. He explains:

> Sometimes, our community leaders go where the resources are. In some cases, the politicians give two kilos of rice just to support community leaders while campaigning. That is already huge for them. So even if the leaders and members say that their campaigns are also for the organization, it is secondary. The primary thing is what they can get. It then becomes very difficult. After the elections, you scold them for not prioritizing the organization. But they might leave you. So you need to patch things up, another round of explanation. They still have not understood or cared about the concept of what a community organization is.

While community action continued to be one of the main activities to affect socioeconomic programs, build constituencies, and forward politico-ideological agendas, gone are the days of grand and massive rallies in Bagong Silang. Militant action, in some cases, is frowned upon especially by local officials in Bagong Silang as they often associate it with trouble (*gulo*) and opportunism. As militant action declined, the implementation of various "niche" development projects aimed at addressing a specific issue proliferated. These projects often directly engage local government through partnerships. Unlike their militant counterparts, these projects are positively received, especially by the barangay—treating them as vital *tulong* (help). However, some have criticized these projects as apolitical, isolated from each other, and inept in addressing corruption and the root causes of poverty.

# Entanglements

At this point, we have presented a mosaic of the history of organized community action in Bagong Silang, exploring nearly four decades of struggle. We began with the militant roots of organizing prior to, during, and after relocation and then turned to its evolution into transformative actions and electoral engagements. In recounting its history, we illustrated how community organizations in Bagong Silang employed various strategies and navigated through the sociopolitical landscape, which has led to the use of political languages that are both conflicting and entangled with various political agendas. We see this in the case of Ronald, who rationalized his involvement with a politician as an act of survival while maintaining his activism. We also see this when activists jumped "into the pigsty"—navigating through the world of politics while at the same time attempting to maintain their legitimacy and integrity through principled and ideology-guided actions. Yet, to assume that this entanglement of political languages was a byproduct of the postdemocratization climate is, in our opinion, a mistake. As seen in the case of Lita, the invocation of patron-client networks alongside militant action was present even at the height of the Marcos regime. In many ways, what we see in Bagong Silang's history of organized community action is that various political languages—languages that have revolutionary, transformative, and patrimonial appeal—have been invoked, circulated, and entangled in people's discourses and actions.

While various political languages may have been simultaneously at play in Bagong Silang, some languages have dominated at certain points. This may be largely due to the prevailing political climate at any given point in time. This is evident in the transition from militant action to transformative engagements. While both repertoires are underscored by critical and progressive perspectives, they are differentiated by their vision of development and their attitudes toward the state. For instance, militant repertoires were a direct response and critical reaction to the excesses of the Marcos regime. The growing influence of Marxist-Leninist-Maoist thought (Guerrero 1972) and the entry of the ideas of Alinsky (1971) and Freire (1984) concerning critical pedagogy militant repertoires fueled organized community action. This, in turn, prompted a critical reexamination of Philippine society, the formulation of alternative visions, and accompanying strategies to achieve it. This facilitated the politicization of various societal actors, which eventually coalesced into a movement of multisectoral networks. These networks adopted a conflict-based analysis and repertoires of action, not least due to the ineptitude of the state, its excesses, and the repressive nature of the Marcos regime. On the other hand, transformative repertoires were shaped in response to the sociopolitical developments immediately after the EDSA revolution in 1986. These developments included the widening of the democratic space, the institution of politico-legislative reforms such as the Local Government Code, and the perceived "burgeoning" of civil society dominated by professional NGOs rather than community activists and leftwing cadres. Open democratic struggle rather than directly opposing the government characterized transformative repertoires. This is rendered more complicated because there was a palpable swelling of competing and complementary visions and trajectories of development.

Demarcating repertoires of action alongside changes in the sociopolitical landscape reveal the backdrop that allowed its evolution. Indeed, the democratization process and its political consequences constitute one of the widely used explanatory models to account for the evolution of development discourse and action in the Philippines (Silliman and Noble 1998). However, the swelling of visions and the expansion of repertoires of engagements were not merely a result of the newly widened democratic space. They were also partly influenced by the fragmentation of the leftist monolith, which arguably had dominated the counterhegemonic perspective and ideology (Abinales 1996). Likewise, one cannot discount the flooding of development institutions and aid which, on its own, carried its rather persuasive brand of developmental agenda, strategies, tools, and vocabulary. Frustration and fatigue over militant action, while contestable, cannot be readily dismissed. Finally, the resurgence of traditional politicians (trapos) postdemocratization provided yet another political language that people and even activists gravitated toward.

Notwithstanding changes in the sociopolitical structure and the positions actors occupied, this transformation is informed by the liberalization of development discourse and practice—a flea market of political languages for counterhegemonic strategies and pathways toward emancipation and development. Hence, while class-based struggle continues to be a robust language in interpreting the maladies of Philippine society and pathways to address them for many, the liberalization of development discourse has brought along other languages. These strategies, which may be transformative, reformist, rational, or identity-based, have all gained some currency. For better or for worse, this has opened opportunities for alternatives beyond ideological and conflict-based repertoires to flourish. Indeed, the explosion of developmental vigor was often lauded as a positive consequence of democratization—the plurality of repertoires as an indicator of a vibrant and burgeoning democracy.

The coexistence or contemporaneity of different political languages may be seen in the process leading to the passage of the Urban Development and Housing Act of 1992 (UDHA), a struggle in which some community organizations in Bagong Silang participated. UDHA was an important struggle for the urban poor since it addressed two pressing issues: demolitions and habitable relocation sites. The process of passing of the UDHA entailed a two-pronged approach: legislative advocacy and lobbying at the top and mass mobilizations at the bottom. At the top, the strategy aimed to convince legislators and provide important legal inputs to ensure the swift passage of the law. At the bottom, the strategy aimed to widen the base of support for the legislation through mass mobilizations. Taken together, the top and the bottom—which Jun Borras (1998) calls the "bibingka approach"—created the necessary pressure to pass the law.[4] The "bibingka approach" involved mass mobilizations from below and programmatic, policy-level and legislative initiatives from above, creating simultaneous pressure (Borras 1998). The approach presented a promising strategy, which "involves the symbiotic interaction between autonomous societal groups from below and state reformists from above despite potential or actual differences in immediate motivations and long-term goals between them" (66). According to Borras, the formulation of the approached was a result of the lessons from the "post-1992 change in the balance of power . . . the emergence of enclaves of state reformists within various departments of the government branch . . . [and] the collapse of the hegemonic and sectarian communist-led national democratic movement" (66).

While the experience of passing the UDHA demonstrated what Kusaka (2017b, 42) calls a contact zone between the two, the experience of activists in Bagong Silang regarding socioeconomic and welfare-oriented projects paints a different picture. While opportunities were plenty in terms of accessing resources to pursue these projects, activists had to reconfigure their ways of working and learn the technical language of planning, log frames, indicator setting, and evaluation. Failing to do so risked alienation from external grants. Others relied on technical expertise of NGOs for support and resources. Furthermore, organizations had to reconfigure their thrusts beyond militant action to include advocacies and direct engagements with participatory governance mechanisms. In this sense, community organizations had to conform to the language of transformative engagements or lose their relevance in a changing landscape of development work.

This environment led to the growing influence and the moral and technical ascendance of NGOS, a central part of which belonged to what Kusaka (2017b) calls the civic sphere. NGOs, primarily composed of a professional staff, served as intermediaries or development brokers between the masses, governance structures, or the elite (Caroll 1998; de Sardan 2005). The increasing focus on strengthening civil society and democratic institutions, some of which asserted a nonpolitical and nonpartisan position, have rendered militant forms of action more accommodating. Consequently, terms such as *mass movement* and *mass mobilizations* were replaced with new and, arguably, sanitized or politically neutral terms like *participation*. The discursive shift promoted the transition from militant action to open democratic struggles where governance structures and participatory mechanisms served as its arena. Program development, legislative advocacy and transformative engagements were in vogue while mass work on the other hand took a back seat and were largely reduced to representation of the community. This has led sociologist Randy David (1988) to lament the depoliticization of development work post-EDSA. Porio (2016) furthermore suggests that inasmuch as transformative engagements aim to develop institutions and promote development, it may also result in "helping local elites to strengthen their dominance" (31) and legitimacy. In this way, activists become partly and unwittingly complicit in the perpetuation of traditional politics.

Meanwhile, as the postdemocratization setting led to the plurality of coun-terhegemonic political languages, it also resulted in the further entrenchment of traditional forms of political languages that relied on patrimonial networks. This is clearly evident in the cases of Ronald and Arnel. Both Ronald and Arnel work for politicians as local operators. As operators, they are the bridge between the *masa* and the politician. This function is especially important during elec-tions as political fortunes may rely on the skill and reputation of a local opera-tor. As gatekeepers, local operators become conduits of resources as in the case of Ronald as he handed out money to people during the 2013 elections. How-ever, Ronald and Arnel are not only local operators for politicians; they also claim to represent community organizations in Bagong Silang. They justify their em-ployment with politicians as an opportunity to advocate for sectoral issues and shape policies. In critical moments, Ronald and Arnel continue to participate in mass mobilizations to fight for their rights. They claim that principles of equal-ity, democracy, and empowerment inform their decade-long experience of mil-itant action. Ronald and Arnel's actions reflect the entanglement between patronage and revolutionary politics; between hierarchy and equality. It has long been an entanglement, even at points in history where relations with the state were hostile. Take the case of Lita. Inasmuch as Lita was at the forefront of the militant mobilizations during the 1980s, she assumed the role of a political op-erator for then Mayor Asistio and relatives in the barangay government. Lita's husband likewise occupied the position of a *siga* (local strongman)—a status fur-ther strengthened by their political connections. Using her connections with the government, Lita was able to provide the members of her organization with access to important state services. Likewise, Lita was able to access resources from the networks supporting the urban poor sector. This allowed her to become the first president of their organization once they were relocated in Bagong Silang.

Seeing the case of Ronald, Arnel, and Lita as either reflections of co-optation or an aberration of the overall democratizing agenda is not helpful. For one, while their engagements with politicians seem to resemble patron-client ties, these relationships are not absolute but rather temporary, fleeting, and tenuous. Furthermore, dealings with politicians were undertaken with great caution— engagements or lack thereof seem contingent on personal histories and the be-lief that it will be beneficial for them and the people they claimed to represent. Residents and their activist peers recognize Ronald, Arnel, and Lita as legitimate members of community organizations and the larger urban poor network even if people know of the complicity with trapo politicians. Most people understand that the harsh living conditions in Bagong Silang in the past and the present com-pel these putatively amoral practices. Adding complexity to this compelled process are the variegated histories, relationships, and overall appraisal of people's situation in Bagong Silang not only by activists, but the relocatees themselves and outsiders. In many ways, we cannot reduce their practices to for instance the urban poor as a monolithic bloc. Rather, it echoes Mbembe's (1992) claim that the postcolony consists of a "plurality of 'spheres' and arenas, each having its own separate logic, yet nonetheless liable to be entangled with other logics" (5).

# Political Languages and the War on Drugs

What does our analysis of political languages in Bagong Silang mean for Duterte's war on drugs and the popular support it enjoys in Bagong Silang despite its horrific consequences? Let us bring back Junior, our critical interlocutor at the beginning of this chapter. Junior had worked for various NGOs when we met him in 2013. Among these were organizations promoting the rights of children, especially those in conflict with the law. While Junior maintains that he is a staunch human rights advocate, he has approached his advocacy in a peculiar way. On one occasion, we discussed whether rapists, thieves, and murderers who have been tortured or ill-treated must receive services and support from human rights organizations. This was a controversial topic as human rights work in the Philippines has largely focused on activists and human rights defenders. Extending services to so-called common criminals was, at the very least, a contentious proposition. In our conversation, he joked, "It is better to kill them [criminals]." Another activist chimed in and said, "I am fine with children in conflict with the law. They can still change. But as for drug addicts and rapists . . . I refuse to work with them." By 2016, Junior was working for a human rights organization. However, he welcomed the candidacy of Duterte. He had hoped that Duterte's iron fist would teach the criminals a lesson, especially the rapists and drug pushers. He also believed that if anyone were to bring about a sweeping and revolutionary change to the Philippines, it was Duterte.

Duterte was speaking Emilio's language—that of a progressive social transformation through revolutionary means. In conversations in 2017, Emilio insisted that he had voted for Duterte because the latter promised labor market reform, land reform, and serious peace talks with the New People's Army (NPA) on top of the war on drugs, which he also supported. Lita echoed Emilio. Now in her seventies, she was employed as a tanod when we met up with her again in 2017, that is, as a guard appointed by the barangay captain. This means that she had been enrolled in the war on drugs as one of those making lists of suspected drug personalities. In conversations with Anna Warburg during fieldwork in

Bagong Silang in January and February 2017 (Warburg 2017; Warburg and Jensen 2020a, 2020b), she confirmed her support for the war on drugs. However, at the same time, she was deeply ambivalent about the war. Like many others, she would lower her voice whenever expressing anything resembling a possible critique of the war. She arguably did this because her neighbor was a police officer and because her political patrons—from purok leader to barangay chairperson to mayor—were all staunch supporters of the war.

How come people such as Junior, Emilio, and Lita, whose personal histories have shown commitment to revolutionary change for people's empowerment and development ended up supporting Duterte and his war on drugs? This is a question that many human rights activists have posed, and it was also the question we posed to Emilio as we were sitting around the dinner table enjoying his lovely cooking. Emilio no longer supported Duterte or the war on drugs, as seen in the vignette that opened this chapter. However, the question clearly betrayed our own particular preconceptions about politics, which were more often in line with human rights activists and critical media in Quezon City than the understanding of the people in Bagong Silang. Our activist friends, including Emilio, enjoyed Duterte's brazen and ruthless rhetoric. On many occasions we had discussed the peace and order situation in Bagong Silang with Emilio. Many of his stories depicted Bagong Silang as a place that is *magulo* (without order). His view echoed Duterte's language and his analysis of the ills of the Philippines. It was a view that Bagong Silang is rife with criminality and illegal drugs. If Bagong Silang were to develop, it needed *salvaging* from the lurking threats of drug addicts, pushers, and criminals, not least through tougher policing. In our work with Balay, we had documented cases of torture and extrajudicial killings beginning in 2010, often with the help and support of Emilio and Junior. While Emilio expressed hesitation and disgust at the brutality of the killings, he still accepted the deaths of so-called criminals. It was an implicit acceptance of the idea that it was morally legitimate to get rid of the bad elements of society.

Furthermore, Duterte spoke of revolution or radical change that he, as the ultimate patron or a patriarch, was able to deliver. Given the histories of both complicit and contentious politics that we describe in this chapter, the propensity to subscribe to populist rhetoric has always been present in community activist circles in Bagong Silang. Lita demonstrated this right from the beginning when she celebrated the benevolence of Mayor Asistio. In many ways, Duterte came to echo people like Lita, the "action-oriented" local executive, now just amplified and propelled to the presidency. Apart from addressing the impending crisis, Duterte's paternal language demanded keeping the "house clean." This urgency and an endearing yet strict figure, requiring order, no matter the cost, was arguably largely absent in the past administrations, which were often seen as professional and capable yet impersonal and distant. Duterte's use of both revolutionary and patron-based language, relates to what Curato (2016) refers to as the politics of anxiety and hope. Unlike Duterte, the past administration spoke the language of democracy which for many of the poor, is anything but a charade, especially given how Estrada was deposed and Arroyo's subsequent perversion of the government (Kusaka 2017b). Given the erosion of democracy's appeal, it is not difficult to understand why Emilio, Lita, and Junior, along with millions of other disillusioned people, gravitated toward Duterte.

Emilio changed his mind as he saw the devastation of the war on drugs on his neighbors. Furthermore, he noted that Duterte had managed to follow through on none of the other progressive agendas. He did so with a laugh indicating surprise at his own naïveté. Lita, on the other hand, was also becoming extremely worried that her neighbors saw her as informing on them. For Junior, the deaths he calls "positive"—meaning people who were known to be drug pushers—were justified, but he regretted the "collateral damage" that the violence inflicted on innocent people. In Lita, Emilio, and Junior's cases, we see how different political languages are present and conflictual. These languages are partly born out of affective relationality and at times are bold political claims and visions. In the case of Lita, she was negotiating between the different political languages, which in her case could not be separated from her meager income as a tanod, depending on her relations to politicians, her neighbors—police officers and drug personalities, and her comrades in the leftist movement. Furthermore, despite her support she did not feel strongly about the war to the same extent as she did for left-wing, progressive activism. In many ways, Lita was treading lightly—a misstep might cost her not only her job as a tanod but also the important social ties she had carefully and laboriously built throughout the years, social ties that are intimate but use different vocabularies, so to speak. For Junior, Emilio, and Lita equally, however, the paramount issue continues to be social justice. In 2017, they had become increasingly unsure whether Duterte was the answer to this question of social justice.

# FRATERNITY DENIED

It was Sunday afternoon in early May 2017 and Al was explaining why we had not been able to find him. At that stage, we had left countless messages with people. We had known Al from 2009 and he had been a crucial gatekeeper into the fraternity. One day, in late 2009, he had shown up with around twenty *brods* (members) from several fraternity chapters around Bagong Silang. Al had indicated with a gesture, "Now, you can start interviewing." Al was slightly older than most other members of the fraternity—an *elder* in the fraternity lingo. Al was and is full of stories of daring escapes and exploits, revolution and gang fighting, not all of which was credible. He also embodied the typical victims of the drug war almost a decade later. "In the end I had to run away," he said and explained that some of his friends had warned him that he was on the local list of drug personalities. He looked tired, slightly intoxicated, and worn out, possibly because of the strain of having to hide and being away from his family, but also because of a hard life, revolving around long hours in traffic and very long working days as a painter. Remembering some of those extraordinary fieldwork days that could not have happened without Al, it was hard not to feel sad on his behalf.

One of these days was a hot afternoon in 2010, in Phase 10B in Bagong Silang. Bobs lets out a muffled cry as his body takes yet another lash from the initiation whip, in this case a large wooden cricket bat used in the initiation rituals of the Tau Gamma Phi fraternity. Tau Gamma Phi, or the Triskelion Grand Fraternity, is a university-based sodality group in the tradition of Greek-letter fraternities in the Philippines and the United States. The room is full of young men, sitting, smoking, joking, and talking while the more experienced of them take the bat to Bobs's upper thighs. Bobs is standing like a crucifix, arms stretched out, facing the wall. A dramatic banner on the wall in front of him portrays a lion holding a bloody sword with the words, "Kaunlaran Community Chapter, Triskelion Grand Fraternity, 2009." The banner is the only colorful artifact in the drab and dilapidated house.

A reader would be justified to ask why it is relevant to explore Bobs's ordeal of getting into the fraternity in a book about the war on drugs in Bagong Silang. However, his ordeal allows us to understand important questions about masculine identity, coping with precarity, inequality, and injustice in what we, in this book, call the politics of violence. First, the fraternity allowed the young men access to what could be called a world of significance in a situation where hopes for social mobility were, and still are, slim and the future seemed to hold little beside an eternally perpetuated present of nonachievement (Jensen 2014; Jefferson, Turner, and Jensen 2019). While this eternal present has been perpetuated, it has of course also been fundamentally disrupted in deadly ways by the war on drugs. Of the young men in the drab room a decade ago when Bobs was initiated, at least two have been killed and several others, like Al, have had to flee the neighborhood and the watch lists. This means that we, by visiting the fraternities, get a privileged point of entry into the lives of those who, six years later, would become the most likely victims of the war on drugs: lumpen, unemployed young men, marginalized and forever on the border of the illicit economy. Second, the fraternity incarnated a fundamental dilemma of poor urban settlements—namely, that while they are the most likely victims of the war on drugs, they preempted the war by disciplining members caught smoking marijuana, for instance. This of course echoes Kusaka's (2017a) analysis. Kusaka suggests that many residents of the poor urban areas that became the main battleground of the war endorsed it as a way to care for them through discipline. Indeed, many of them, even drug addicts, saw the war as an offer to redeem themselves, to get out of drugs. In many ways, the fraternities incarnate just that analysis. Through disciplining the bodies and the minds of groups of chaotic and unregulated, violent youth, the fraternities allowed their members to grow up, to become adult and mature members of the community. As we show later in the chapter, the fraternity constituted an apprenticeship of patriarchy of the street akin to what we explored in chapter 4. In this way, the fraternities brought into a view the distinction between those who were good people and those who constituted trouble. This was, as Kusaka (2017a) shows, exactly the same distinction that animated the war on drugs. A final reason why we should care about the fraternities is that they expressed in very direct and explicit ways the call and demand for equality and dignity. As we saw in the previous chapters, on communal relations and community activism, relentless unequal social structures of patron-client relations most often compromised and defeated these calls for equality. Hence, studying the fraternity helps us understand those who became the most likely victims of the war. Furthermore, the fraternities embodied subaltern forms of politics that we found in Bagong Silang. In this way, the fraternity offers a view into a particular political culture, caught in tensions between equality and hierarchy before and during the war on drugs. In this way, the story of the fraternity is also a story of fraternity denied.

We organize our discussion in three parts, which we introduce briefly next; they comprise the problem of equality, the persistent presence of revolutionary discourses, and the relationship between violence, secrets, and rituals. These three analyses allow us to gauge the contours of a political culture that not only dominates the fraternities but arguably also forms the backbone of a subaltern politics, organized around equality, calls for dignity, and the constant and ambiguous presence of violence. In the final section, we return to how this (historic) account of ritualized violence helps us understand violence and politics in the war on drugs. We begin with the issue of equality. The Philippines is a society of structural and cultural extremes, in which there is a constant tension between the significance of equality and notions that relate to social hierarchies. However, in much of the literature, social hierarchies take precedence. One example of social hierarchies is the analysis of *utang na loob*, which translates directly as "inner debt," or "debt of gratitude." One incurs a debt of gratitude the moment a person higher up in the social hierarchies helps out in a moment of crisis—often in relation to disease, death, or financial trouble (Kerkvliet 2002a). Although it is incurred in a moment of crisis, people often try to indebt themselves because the debt creates social ties that a patron is hard-pressed to ignore (Mauss 1966; Graeber 2011). These hierarchical social forms seem more pronounced in earlier periods, but they have reemerged in relation to electoral politics as a reconfigured patronage and a kind of political semantics with which many people think about and analyze events and processes. Benedict Anderson explored Philippine politics through the prism of cacique democracy (Anderson 1998), arguing that while the electoral system seems highly competitive, it is always the same people—from the political families in the specific national, provincial, or local polity engaged in political patronage—who win. Anderson's work was preceded and followed by other works focused on social hierarchies, not least in relation to family structures (cf. McCoy 1994; Sidel 1999). While social hierarchies are important and often seen as a kind of life condition, we think that elite democracy scholars like Anderson, at least in the work related to cacique democracy (1998), underestimate the power of equality. As we show later in the chapter, discourses of equality as social justice have also made themselves felt. Over the last century or more, these have taken the form of civil society protests, peasant movements, squatter federations, and revolutionary and anticolonial struggles, to mention a few. Rather than being mutually exclusive, it is more correct to see the opposing political strands of thought related to social hierarchies and equality as intertwined and contemporaneous. As we saw in the two previous chapters, they are dimensions of a complex political language in which equality and social hierarchies coexist in a complicated and conflictual manner.

Second, in relation to the persistence of revolutionary discourses and calls for equality, there is what can be termed revolutionary passion. Successive struggles have stressed the injustice of economic systems, violent dispossession, and unequal access to resources of different kinds, along with the de facto disenfranchisement of large segments of the population. These rather rational forms of resistance politics are clearly present. However, at least in some instances the political language of equality is infused with or animated by what might be termed passionate dimensions or impulses with strong religious connotations. For the literary critic Neferti Tadiar (2009, 9), such impulses are historical and social experiences. We return to Tadiar's argument later in the chapter as we explore three examples of the relationship between equality and passion: the relationship between the central religious text of the Passion of Christ (*Pasyon* in Filipino) and the revolutionary movements in the late nineteenth century; the peasant movements of the 1930s; and some of the revolutionary practices of the late twentieth century. This analysis of equality and religious passion allows us to see historical trends that link the Manila fraternity and the ordeal of Bobs with a longer political history of struggle in the Philippines. The land struggles of the 1930s and the fraternities of Manila's underbelly are not necessarily intuitively comparable. However, we suggest that they draw on similar logics that have characterized political struggle in the Philippines for more than a century. Fighting for justice has not simply been a question of righting wrongs but rather has been infused with calls for equality and particular forms of religious passion and conviction. Tragically, these calls have seldom translated into justice. Rather, and most recently and lethally, in the war on drugs, they have translated into new forms of suffering, not least for Bobs and his fellow brods. In the first two sections of the main text of this chapter, we explore the historical relationship between equality, social hierarchies, and (religious) passion in the twentieth century Philippines. While this analysis does not provide a fully fledged historical account, it allows us to gauge the connections between the struggle for equality and religious or millenarian convictions. In the second section, we explore how Bobs, Al, and the other the young men in the fraternity make a case for equality.

Third, Bobs's trials suggest an intimate connection between ritual, violence, and politics that, again, mirrors in strange ways the emphasis on bodily *disiplina* during the war on drugs. The rituals function as the threshold of the fraternities.

Beyond them lie secrets and inclusion as part of a world of significance that belies the present misery. Drawing on Maurice Bloch's 1991 seminal analysis of rituals, the initiation is necessarily violent and painful. On the one hand, rituals become privileged points of entry for exploring how violence is harnessed and directed in particular directions by an organization—that is, they reveal how organizations attract young men. On the other hand, in their everyday practice they also reveal the inherently temporary nature of the ritual and the fraternity as the world of significance appears to be dwarfed, again, by the realities of everyday life in the resettlement site. In this light, the rituals are best understood through Judith Butler's (1993, 15) notion of reiterative performativity, through which we can examine the ongoing negotiations between the young men, the fraternity, and the surrounding society. If indeed the ritual is less an entrance into a secret society and more akin to a performance, then it makes sense, as a privileged point of departure for understanding the importance of the fraternity and the young men's choices, to ask who the audience is. Such questions are the subject of the third section in the main text, where we revisit Bobs and the ritual in order to explore what kinds of meaning are performed and how relevant audiences received the performance.

In summary, studying the contemporary fraternities in Bagong Silang provides insights into the political processes and political culture in the Philippines beyond the fraternities themselves. Echoing scholars like Nicole Curato (2016) and Wataru Kusaka (2017a, 2017b), we are able to see historical visions that transcend the idea of Philippine politics as mere functions of patrimonial relations at the same time as it is clear that these patrimonial structures are ever present. We are also able to see just how embedded violence is in politics—the violence of politics—at many levels, not least in the kind of sacrifices it takes for the poor to earn their place at the table. We can also see just how desperately violent that denial seems to be in the war on drugs. This is similar to previous chapters on resettlement and community activism. Like other residents, the brods desire to be included and have what they consider their fair share, as well as to occupy a world of significance. While they work hard to earn the respect and to be able to shape their world in ways that make sense to them, it never seemed to be enough, with dominant structures weighing in to determine their world, even determine who gets to live and how.

# Equality and Passion in the Philippines

In her succinct analysis of subaltern voices in the Philippines read from a critical engagement with literary texts, Neferti Tadiar (2009) evokes the concept of historical experience to capture the often complex assemblage of elements from the past that enable legibility of the present and some sort of template for the future. She notes, "By 'historical experience' I do not mean only people's collective responses to objective social and economic conditions in which they find themselves: I also mean the collective subjective practices they engage in that help to produce and remake these objective conditions" (19). Hence, for Tadiar, historical experiences are dynamic, ever-changing, and productive. Experiences are not only inscribed on subjectivities; they produce new political realities. Tadiar explores how messianic experiences and enactments are central elements in the revolutionary struggle. This messianic—or passionate—quality to the struggle derives part of its strength from historical messianic experiences of the revolutionaries, not least those drawing on religious discourses of justice. The historical experiences of passion were clearly not only relevant in the revolutionary struggles of the second half of the twentieth century; they were also central to earlier revolutionary struggles for justice and equality. While they draw on comparable religious practices and discourses, they must be analyzed against the historical background in which they are put to use. Three brief illustrations will demonstrate how passion and equality have played themselves out in the Philippines in a continuous struggle for justice over more than one hundred years. The first is the war of independence; the second is the struggle for just land tenure in the land reform movement of the 1930s over the Maoist revolution of the late twentieth century; and third, the relationship between passion and equality and it they plays out in the fraternities in contemporary Manila.

In his seminal study on *Pasyon and Revolution*, Reynaldo Ileto (1997 explores popular movements between 1840 and 1910 to conclude that religious conversion played a central role in how the Katipunan movement understood and fought their struggle for Philippine independence from Spain. Ileto suggests that the Katipunan had a fundamentally different appreciation of their role and the freedom they fought for than the elite nationalists, the so-called *illustrados* famously represented by the national hero José Rizal, an elite that ended up winning the struggle for independence. The conflict between the elite nationalists and the Katipunan ended with the execution of the leader of the latter, Andres Bonifacio. At stake in the conflict between the two sides seemed to be questions of social hierarchies. Where the Katipunan struggled against not only Spanish control but also the abuses of important local families—the so-called *principalia*—the elite nationalists, deriving mostly from the indigenous landed elite, had no such issues. Social levelling, or equality, was simply not a concern for the elite—on the contrary, it could even be argued. Apart from focusing on equality, religious and millenarian symbols and practices were also central to the Katipunan. While he has been criticized for his analysis, Ileto clearly shows the millenarian elements in the discourse and practices of the Katipunan. It serves no purpose here to repeat his analysis; instead, we will dwell briefly on the rites of initiation that he describes as an illustration, not least because they are so closely mirrored by the rituals of the fraternities discussed later in the chapter.

Ileto (1979, 91–98) begins his analysis of the initiation rituals into the Katipunan by refuting the claim that they were Masonic, as Masonic rituals demand a high degree of literacy. Drawing on a prolific nationalist writer of the time, Isabelo de los Reyes, he suggests that the rites were simplified to allow and draw in men of the peasant and laborer classes. Hence, already from the beginning, equality was central, compared to the Masonic secret society, for instance, with its insistence on social hierarchies. Courage, love of the motherland, and willingness to sacrifice and endure violent suffering were more important. The ritual also comprises several references to religious texts and practices. Entering into the Katipunan happened through the Holy Gate; here the neophytes needed to confirm their commitment to the movement and their willingness to abandon family and home, even life itself. Echoing Tadiar (2009) and her notion of historical experience, Ileto (1979) speculates that the neophyte would have been familiar with this kind of ritual: "His experience of religious rituals would have facilitated his understanding of Philippine history as a 'fall' that would be followed by redemption" (93). This redemption would be a Philippines without the Spanish colonial masters, and one in which the injustices of the principalia would have been done away with.

Despite the initial successes of the Katipunan, the popular revolution ended in defeat and a bloody war with the Americans, who would not accept the Spanish defeat in the Philippines. Contrary to the popular nationalists in the Katipunan, the following years saw important gains for many elite nationalists, as the American administration saw it as their task to hand over autonomy to the Philippine elite. However, against this tale of evolving sovereignty and democracy, there was trouble brewing on the rural front as tenure relations between tenants and landowners became increasingly strained, with the landed elite pressing for tougher tenure conditions. Hence, in the late 1920s and early 1930s, peasant movements emerged in many parts of the country, especially in central Luzon, the main rice-growing area north of Manila. As the state and the police began to persecute the peasant movements, they became increasingly militant and its leadership had to exert more and more care as the agents of the landed elite targeted them and their families. In his study of the Huk Rebellion, Benjamin Kerkvliet (2002b) follows and explores the development of the peasant movement; how it radicalized as land reform stalled in the years up to the Second World War; how it transmogrified into the most important armed resistance to the Japanese occupation; and how in the new independent postwar nation, it developed into full rebellion against the landed elite, whose leaders had often col-laborated with the Japanese and who continued to persecute them. This story of the struggle for equality and justice is relatively well known. However, the kinds of religious passion that are not often associated with peasant movements can be discerned in a few places in Kerkvliet's impressive study. Again, this concerns the initiation rites, which in many ways seem to draw strength from similar as-pirations to the Katipunan as a specific historical experience that also produces new social and political conditions. Kerkvliet (2002b) quotes a peasant activist, Hilario Felipe, seemingly about the size of the movement. Felipe explains:

> We used to have a simple initiation ceremony for members. A new member would prick his finger, then sign his name in blood to sym-bolize fraternity and unity. But there were others who were KPMP [Kalipunang Pambansa ng mga Magsasaka sa Pilipinas—the peasant movement] in their hearts. KPMP had an insignia shaped like . . . the yoke of the carabao to pull the plow. Anyone could wear that insignia. Some tattooed it on their arm, others drew it on their shirt sleeve. I'd say that about 40 or maybe 50 percent of the peasants in Talavera wore the insignia, and they agreed to the purposes of the KPMP and joined KPMP actions. Yes, they were KPMP, too. (32)

In the quote, the real issue—what prompts Hilario's words—is the number of active peasants. However, we are also made aware of another historical hori-zon of initiation and fraternity, presented as an aside but which brings passion and rituals into the account. There is probably nothing surprising in identify-ing religious sentiments in peasant movements in the 1930s, but it does suggest other practices and understandings than simply the ones concerned with land reform and political campaigning, not least as these are increasingly militant and to different degrees entangled with the communist ideologies of the Par-tido Komunistas ng Pilipinas (PKP). It suggests intimate relations between pas-sion and a struggle for equality.

There were real fears within the Philippine elite and its American allies that the Huk Rebellion would threaten their interests and put the country on course for a communist takeover (Hedman and Sidel 2000; Constantino 1978). Through a violent counterinsurgency campaign, concessions to the peasant movements and other reform endeavors, the Huk Rebellion was finally defeated in the late 1950s and early 1960s. Peace did not last long, however, and already in 1968 the Maoist Communist Party of the Philippines—and later its military wing, the New People's Army—was founded under the leadership of José Maria Sison. It is be-yond the scope of this chapter to give a detailed account of the rise and fall of the Maoist insurgency.[1] Rather, we maintain the focus on the relationship between discourses and practices of equality and passion as historical experiences. To do so, let us return to Neferti Tadiar (2009) and her literary analysis of revolutionary subaltern subjectivities in the Philippines from 1960 to the 1990s. Through the lens of revolutionary literature, Tadiar illustrates the persistent presence of religious passion, even in the most committed ideologues whose goal was "a national, scientific and mass culture." By reading against the grain, in a sense, Tadiar discovers a messianic zeal in, for instance, Sison's poetry, in which the land and the masses "assume the ontological form and purpose of the Holy Mass" (265). But while the poetry of revolutionary ideologues such as Sison was replete with religious passion for land and the masses, they were still highly suspicious of those same masses. And with good reason: as Tadiar shows, atavistic consciousness seemed to course through what she terms peasant poetry, in which she finds a creative resurgence of tradition within revolutionary practices. Tadiar focuses purposefully on creativity, as she asserts that it was, in fact, these so-called atavistic practices that sustained the movement during the onslaught from the state, rather than the Maoist ideologies. She concludes: 'Outmoded and chiliastic spiritual practices continue to operate within, even as they exceed, the Messianic structure of experience of revolutionary struggle. Though diminished by party and Left criticism as semi-feudal habits, practices of spiritual mediumship and of cult values are shown in revolutionary literature to operate as affective technologies that make possible the everyday life of the movement" (15).

## Equality and Passion in the Fraternity

In the previous discussion, we attempted to illustrate the persistent presence and development of historical experiences structured around equality and passion in Philippine history, through tracing more than a century of resistance, revolt, and revolution. But the passion and the quest for equality have not been constant. As experiences were reactualized in new circumstances, they developed and reshaped the sociocultural context in which they existed. Nonetheless, we have tried to show how ideas of equality and passion persisted in these different forms of revolt. Let us now return to Bagong Silang and Bobs's fraternity, Tau Gamma Phi and explore the discourses found there to illustrate that discourses of equality have coexisted in a conflictual relation with ideas of social hierarchies. Locating the struggle for equality in the fraternities might at first hand seem odd, not least because they seldom express militant opposition to the Philippine regime. While this is correct, we are nonetheless able to identify comparable ambitions, historical experiences, and understandings of justice that animated groupings like the peasant movements.

Tau Gamma Phi was established in 1968 in the University of the Philippines by four young men in the social sciences during the tumultuous time leading up to the state of emergency that ensued as a response to the increasingly dictatorial ways of President Ferdinand Marcos. Greek-letter fraternities have been a staple of Philippine political culture and in the reproduction of the elite and were probably inspired by the American university fraternities that proliferated across the United States since the early nineteenth century (Syrett 2009). In its own narrative, Tau Gamma Phi was different from the truly elite fraternities such as Upsilon and Delta Phi, whose members have populated the court system and the offices of political power for most of Philippine independence. One of its founders, Rodrigo Alolor Confessor, asserts: "We knew what we wanted. We will build a new fraternity—an organization founded on a new set of ideals, democratic in practice, liberal in thinking, distinct but not elitist in its perspective, rich in diversity, and most of all open and tolerant in its views" (Tau Gamma Phi 2012a).

A central tenet was the notion that members should strive toward "excellence in [their] chosen field of endeavor" (Tau Gamma Phi 2012a). While the focus on excellence might not be surprising, it must be understood within the context of a distinctly unequal social structure in which meritocracy is not a given and where patrimonial relations are eternally reproduced. Hence, the fraternity welcomed "people who are not rich, of no political voice, people struggling in life but who want to excel. As long as a person is of good moral character and believes in the theory of excellence, you can be accepted to the Order of Triskelion." As a consequence, Tau Gamma Phi members started coming from the different walks of life and strata of society (Tau Gamma Phi 2012b).

As an illustration of this commitment to engage people based on egalitarian principles rather than elite reproduction, the Triskelion Youth Movement (TYM) was established as a community-based part of Tau Gamma Phi during the 1970s. Despite the ideology of equality, the two lines of Tau Gamma Phi existed parallel to each other, with little or no contact between them, and the community-based chapters were vilified and criticized by the "real" fraternity.

In recent years, university-based fraternities have weakened considerably, for a number of reasons. Their violent initiation rites and the fighting with other fraternities have been causes for concern (Zarco and Shoemaker 2000). In 1994, following a number of spectacular deaths during initiation and fraternity fights (called rumbles), parliament passed an Act Regulating Hazing and Other Forms of Initiation Rites in Fraternities, Sororities and Organizations and Providing Penalties Therefore (Republic Act 8049), which de facto outlawed initiation rites in the Philippines. It is only speculation, but it seems probable that initiation was explicitly banned because it began to affect the children of the middle class. Furthermore, as the elite had other means of reproducing itself, fraternities lost importance. Eventually, a number of private schools and universities outlawed fraternities on campus. Yet, no matter what caused the decline, Tau Gamma Phi in the universities began to "lay low" during the mid-1990s. Parallel to the decline, but probably also caused by it, fraternities in poor communities such as Bagong Silang began to grow in the late 1990s and early 2000s.

We have explored elsewhere how fraternities began to grow in the poor, urban fringes of Manila (Jensen 2015a). Here, we want to emphasize the discursive and ideological draw of Tau Gamma Phi's egalitarian narrative and its focus on excellence. Bagong Silang is far from the main flows of power and opportunity. In this place, discourses of equal opportunity and meritocracy resonate, as do notions of fraternity and unity. Hopes for the future are often dwarfed by social structures and young men are at risk from other peer groups of young men. Hence, the fraternity becomes a vehicle for affirmation and for security. This is evident in this account by Francis, an older member of the Tau Gamma Phi, of his initial doubts about joining the fraternity: "At first, they [other members] were asking me and I said I have not memorized the codes and tenets yet. Then they gave me *bagsak* [humiliated him]. Yes, they used to give me *bagsak* there before. I said, 'I apologize master, I did not memorize it yet.' Then Pitong [the head of the chapter] said, 'Brother, it's not that important, it is not important with us; what matters the most is our relationship.'"

The head of the chapter, Pitong, stresses the importance of values before scholarly knowledge or knowing the rules and regulations by heart. While in principle this would resonate with the egalitarian discourses of the fraternity, it is clearly not the case at the university-based chapters. The case of the Talisay community chapter in Phase 4 in Bagong Silang provided a good illustration of the tensions between the elitist, hierarchical, and egalitarian notions.

The Talisay chapter was founded by a former student of a technical college. In the same area, there lived another brod, Ken, who used to be involved in Tau Gamma Phi at Far Eastern University, and later on in community chapters in Novaliches, a district adjacent to Bagong Silang. Ken was adamant that if there was no endorsement from a university-based chapter, they would be *colorum* (fake). Everybody in the chapter was very proud to have these two university graduates as part of the chapter. On top of this, the four children of probably the oldest Triskelion in Bagong Silang also lived in Talisay and they had all agreed to join the chapter. Things looked even brighter for Talisay when the chapter at the technical college agreed to sponsor the community chapter. One of the leading members of the college chapter told me: "It was an exception because we know and trust the founder. He's a perfectly good frat man; we don't have a problem with his values." He was not impressed, however, with the entire concept of community chapters. His basic objection was that fraternities belong in universities. As he noted laconically, "How can you have an alma mater if you haven't been to school?" He stressed that without tertiary education people simply do not have the intellectual skills to grasp the deep meaning of fraternity. He illustrated this lack of skill by referring to one of the tenets: "Salute and address your brothers and sisters in a proper manner." A proper salute consists in a special handshake—but only if you are in a position to reveal your identity to the world. Thus, saluting fellow brothers and sisters relies on a deep knowledge of the fraternity that allows members to recognize each other, not paraphernalia like frat shirts or ostentatious exposure of fraternity affiliation. While the college chapter sponsored Talisay, it did so with little respect. The disavowal indicated that the importance of social hierarchies, rather than equality, was at the heart of the values of the university-based chapters, in much the same way that revolutionary ideologues lamented the existence of atavistic practices.

Although the university-based chapters' insistence on social hierarchies often dominated in the world of Bagong Silang, they were not hegemonic as the case of Ken illustrates. At the time of fieldwork, Ken was part of the pride of Talisay. As the owner of the proper knowledge, he would incessantly correct the behavior of the younger ones, sometimes in a violent way. Ken helped one of the brods, Vidal, to become an officer of the chapter, but went on to undermine him constantly. In one dramatic moment, Ken burned a banner that Vidal had designed and paid for out of a very meager salary, on the grounds it was too bloody and not dignified enough for the fraternity. Slowly, toward the end of our stay, the rest of the chapter began to resent Ken's "orientation," They began calling him "Bidaman" (a local fictional superhero) behind his back. In a series of conflicts with Vidal, he began to lose authority. Just before leaving, we asked Ken whether his orientation was working or whether the "tribes" (the youth groups organizing younger teenagers) were taking over the fraternities. He said, "Yes, it seems like the community is changing the fraternity and not the fraternity the community." This was also the case for Ken. During our acquaintance, he had always insisted that the burn scars from initiation (also called subjections or *zondos*) did not prove allegiance to the fraternity. These were practices of those (in the community) who did not know that the commitment to the fraternity was part of a deep mental process, not the physical scars from red-hot coins. Ken said of the people, including his own neighbors: "They are like fish in a fishbowl, swimming around killing each other without ever looking out to the rest of the world." He continued: "But I will have my *zondo* at the next anniversary." In other words he, the one fish that was looking out, had decided to turn his gaze inward into the fishbowl. A year later, Ken had been expelled because he and his wife had had a row in the house, during which she had accused him of lying about his credentials in the fraternity. He was, in other words, *colorum*, or fake.

Due to the intimate space of the path walk, everybody became privy to this information. In a sense, Ken had fallen victim to his own sense of superiority, to his insistence on social hierarchies.

What these ethnographic vignettes suggest is the ever-present focus on equality as a central ideological tenet or aspiration in the fraternity. However, it is infused by and entangled with social hierarchies as well as the constant presence of other, more passionate, or perhaps, in the eyes of ideologues like Ken, more irrational practices.

## Ritual Violence and Pain as Performance

Ritualized violence in the form of initiation, subjection, or disciplinary action (DA) occupied a central role in the life of the fraternity in Bagong Silang. Brods would discuss endlessly how different brods had fared in the initiation: the skill of different masters of initiation; the transgressions that lead to DA; mishaps and near-death experiences; the many rules that regulated how pain was inflicted and the ideology that legitimized it. This controlled violence—supported by ideological underpinnings of ritual, discipline, and sacrifice—was seen as opposed to the excessive forms of violence that were associated with the so-called tribes, or younger teenage groups. Hence, joining the fraternity was part of a maturing process in which managed violence and pain were central. To join the fraternity, the newcomers (or neophytes) needed what was referred to as orientation. Orientation would be about what the codes and tenets were, the proper understanding of history and the moral comportment expected of members, as well as about the right use of violence. Initiation was an important part of the orientation and was heavily ritualized. Let us return to the ordeal Bobs was going through.

### The Ritual

The initiation begins with collective singing of the national hymn and a prayer said in a read-and-reply style. After the prayer, two members of the fraternity hold the arms of the neophyte, who is blindfolded and turned to face a wall with his arms outstretched, as Bobs was in the vignette that opened this chapter. The master of initiation (the MI) then asks what the fraternity name of the neophyte will be. Taking turns, the other brods hit the neophyte across the upper thighs. At each stroke, the MI reads from the codes and tenets, beginning with the founding fathers: "I love lord high Vedastro 'Tito' Venida, November 17, 1949, A.B. Political Science. Accept?" The neophyte receives the blow while responding "Accept." This continues until the initiation is over. All the founding fathers must be accepted, along with the codes and tenets. There are strict rules governing the initiation, both in relation to the violence itself—which needs to be measured and ordered, rather than ruthless—and in relation to dress codes. After the initiation the new member is welcomed by his new brothers, who celebrate him while he recovers, and then the fraternity hosts a *tagay*, or drinking session.

To perform the initiation is about "giving" (in Tagalog, *bigayan*) whereas the initiate "receives" orientation, discipline, and fraternity, and ultimately is transformed by the initiation. Hence, giver and receiver enter into a relationship in which both access the transcendental world of the timeless fraternity. The initiation becomes the stage for the performance of masculinity for both those who give and those who receive, although in different ways. For those who give, it is about benevolent administration of violence, knowledge of the rules, discipline, and restraint. For those who receive, it is about being able to stomach the pain. However, the drama of initiation also draws on cultural-religious registers, which we referred to above as passion. In his book *Prey into Hunter*, Maurice Bloch (1991) explores rituals of initiation in a way that is useful for understanding Tau Gamma Phi's rites of initiation. Bloch suggests that the initiate is taken out of his normal context and ritually sacrificed in ways that endanger him physically. This is similar to Tau Gamma Phi's initiation, which can lead to life-threatening situations as the blood in the thighs can clot and prevent circulation. Although initiation runs smoothly most of the time, initiates do sometimes die, as almost happened in early 2010 in the Talisay chapter when an initiate was unconscious for several minutes. Hence, although initiation has been relaxed, it must include a level of danger. It is through the pain, which the initiate agrees to be subjected to, that transformation (accessing the transcendental) is achieved. This happens when the initiate "accepts" the next blow, which gains him access to another secret—another step into the transcendental. The fact that the initiate is blindfolded and not allowed to see the whip also suggests, in line with Bloch's theorization, that the initiate is barred from the transcendental and must be left in the "dark" until he is ready—that is, until the initiation is over.

In many ways, Maurice Bloch builds on predecessors such as Van Gennep (2004) and Victor Turner (1995) in arguing that the initiation entails three moves: the initial separation, the liminal phase, and the return. Where he differs from the earlier work is in what he calls the "rebounding violence." For Bloch, the initiate loses something of his past vitality in the liminal phase in return for bringing something back from the world of the transcendental, for instance the secrets, the discipline of the fraternity, and its codes and tenets. With the transcendental element, he can "dominate the here and now of which he previously was a part" (Bloch 1991, 5) and reclaim, in a new form, the vitality he lost in the liminal phase.

**FIGURE 12.** Screenshot of Tau Gamma Phi initiation in Bagong Silang. Photo by Steffen Jensen.

The return, armed with the vitality of the transcendental, is what constitutes the political moment of the ritual, where the ritual allows individuals to transcend the everyday life they come from. Entering the fraternity means entering a world of significance, sacrifice, and meaning, which, due to the secret nature of the fraternity, is inaccessible to anyone on the outside.

Considering the initiation through the eyes of Bloch, what the initiate loses in limbo is the problematic and excessive youth who drinks and uses drugs, engages in excessive violence, and lacks the maturity of an adult. Furthermore, following Bloch, the newly initiated brod will rebound and forcefully return to claim the vitality that was lost in limbo in a different way. In Bloch's analysis, the young men, half profane and half sublime, engage in the conquest of outside people. The question, then, is who is the victim of the rebounding violence in the case of the fraternity? One answer is that it is other fraternities. In equally ritualized ways—at least in discourse—frat wars, or rumbles, happen relatively frequently. While these frat wars are often the result of personal skirmishes, they are almost always framed within the narrative of the collective antagonism. In a rare inside description of frat wars, Raymund Narag (2009), who spent seven years in jail for a frat-related murder, lists the reasons for frat wars as ranging from affronts to personal dignity to troubles with women or affronts to the dignity of the fraternity. However, there may also be other victims of the rebounding violence. Dan Hirslund (2012) explored the rebounding violence of young Maoists in Nepal. Hirslund illustrates convincingly that the young cadres sacrifice their youth (Bloch's vitality lost in limbo), but through rituals of rebounding violence target other youth who had not chosen the Maoist path. These wayward youth—that is, similar to the cadres before their initiation—need to be disciplined and transformed through pain. In this way, the victims of rebounding violence are, in fact, the brods themselves, but in their untransformed incarnation—an incarnation that does not deserve to be recognized. If we continue this line of thought, initiation is a performance directed at the young men themselves; ways of disciplining themselves of the unruly elements. However, it seems likely that the ritualized forms of violence are also performed for other strands of the society—notably the Philippine elite and their representatives in the university-based fraternities, including Tau Gamma Phi. Hence, far from distancing themselves from society, the Tau Gamma Phi ritual aims to demonstrate and perform discipline and the capacity to sacrifice and suffer for a higher cause as compared to the dominant stereotypes, casting them as semicriminal, violent, and lumpen—the very incarnation of those who will be about to die in the war on drugs. This suggests a rather complex relationship with the discourses of equality. On the one hand, the ritual practices illustrate that the brods are worthy of recognition; on the other hand, calls for recognition and inclusion often seem to be directed at patrimonial structures of politics, money, and influence.

Let us explore some performances in relation to the fraternity, and follow this with a look at its relations to the broader elite. In relation to the fraternity, it is necessary to distinguish briefly between community chapters in Bagong Silang and the university chapters. In regard to the former, at the time of fieldwork in 2010, conflicts were brewing between different chapters and factions. While the conflicts were often about control over the sizable number of new chapters, they became discussions about who was true to the rules and regulations of the fraternity, who was more authentic, and, by contrast, who was colorum, or fake.

## The Authentic and the Fake

Central to the discussions about the authentic and the fake were the proper use of violence and knowledge about the fraternity's codes and tenets. In Bobs's initiation, a number of visitors were present to witness the act as well as participate in the initiation itself. Foremost among the visitors were a sizable delegation from the Kaunlaran Chapter, who had also brought the bloody banner that Bobs faced. Dennis, the founder of the Kaunlaran Chapter, was several times asked to "give," that is, to use the whip on Bobs. Every time, he refused. Afterward, he said that he had not been impressed with the initiation. It lacked the somber atmosphere. Those who were "giving" were not properly dressed; they wore jewelry and accessories. Finally, Bobs did not receive the standard initiation which consists of— and here the discussions begin. What is "standard" initiation? How many times must you "give"? In a competing chapter, they insist that they only give standard, and that is 68 (the year of the founding of Tau Gamma Phi at the University of the Philippines) full swings. Talisay concurs that 68 is standard, but that due to the anti-hazing law, they now give 45. Philrods Chapter puts initiation at 50 swings. However, in every initiation I recorded, there were reductions. Bobs received 24 swings, some of which were half-swings. Intoy, the son of one of the most famous members of Tau Gamma Phi, had negotiated down to 5 swings. The need to initiate new people into the fraternity drove the reductions, as they were among the selling points that chapters could use to attract young men to join. At the same time, allegations of the reductions were used to prove or disprove the authenticity of the individual chapters. In order to receive the transcendental elements, the initiate simply had to be subjected to standard initiation. This was used, together with the reductions, in the constant fighting about who was authentic and who was colorum.

However, it is not only about how many swings are "given." Equally important is the way one "gives." Note the following exchange from Bobs' initiation:

> GT: Who is the—?
> KUYA A: One! [first]
> KUYA J: That one! Come here Bobs! [calling the neophyte]
> KUYA J: I'll borrow your handkerchief.
> KUYA A: Tol! I'm not allowed to do the initiation.
> KUYA J: The MI [pointing to the Master of Initiation]
> GT: Here is the MI. You, Bunso—
> KUYA A: Don't you dare drop that, huh [talking about the whip]
> KUYA A: Don't you dare drop that [talking about the whip]
> GT: If you drop that you'll receive six, huh! [six lashes for disciplinary action]
> KUYA A: You'll receive six, huh!
> GT: You'll receive six even if you are still holding that [talking about the whip]
> The guys from the group: *Yari ka* Bunso. [Fear Bunso!]

From this short excerpt, it is possible to see some of the rules governing the violence of initiation. Kuya A is no longer a member but an adviser (alumnus), so he cannot partake in the initiation (although he does so later). Bunso, the MI, is not allowed to drop the whip and is threatened with disciplinary action (DA). Then there are all the rules about dress and accessories. Besides this, there is the way the violence is used, which must not be excessive. Starhouse, another chapter, had a reputation for ruthlessness in initiation, but their initiation was never excessive or meant to hurt for the sake of pain. Rather, inflicting—or "giving"—pain in initiations, as in frat wars, had to be measured and ordered. The moment violence turned into excessive cruelty (Balibar 1998), it was no longer within the parameters of the fraternity. In Bobs' initiation, the master of initiation was Bunso. Although he was a short, skinny youngster, he had a mean swing. When asked how he felt when he "gave," he said, "I just want them to go down. . . . When they see me, they think it will be light but it is different after they feel me." Aside from the evident homoeroticism, Bunso's use of violence was out of order and excessive. When confronted with Bunso's statement, Ken from Talisay responded, "He is an animal, that one." He contrasted Bunso with his own master of initiation, Bernie, who used violence in the "proper" way. Bernie confirmed, "It hurts me to hurt them. I just want to help them through the ordeal because I know how hard it is."

As the different chapters visit each other and take part in each other's initiations, there is a constant circulation of stories about the proper or improper use of violence and of initiation that is colorum. In this way, initiation and the use of violence become spectacles, where what is at stake is a chapter's status as either authentic or colorum. However, organizational recognition also matters to whether one is colorum or not. To see this, let us explore the performances in relation to the wider fraternity.

In May 2010, the community chapters were recognized by one of the four founding fathers of the chapter at the University of the Philippines. This unprecedented event had all the chapters rejoicing. As Ken said when he held the certificate signed by the founding father, "This is what we have been waiting for all these years. This is what makes it all worthwhile. I am so proud. One of the people that I respect most in the world actually signed this certificate." In this way, the community chapters had been "seen" from outside by the "real" fraternity at the university. The link between the brods in the community and the university fraternity, with its connection to power on the outside, had been confirmed. The question is, what did the latter actually see? We have already seen how the chapter at the technical college had little regard for Ken and the community brods, and how Ken was also inherently contemptuous of his fellow brods, which in turn did not go unnoticed. Here is what Aldin, a brod from another chapter, said after an encounter with Ken:

> They [those from university] think that they are more educated than we are because they are in school. Yet for me, if you memorized [the codes and tenets] by thought and not by heart it's useless. I am not admiring them that much. And because of looking at us that way, it only shows that they did not put the codes in their heart. It should be like this: "Capital T [one of the tenets]—treat others as what you want others

to treat you." If that's how they look at us then we'll look at them with the same opinion. . . . When they said that we are not that oriented, did they not know that it's up to the person to have orientation? For me, if my brother memorizes it and puts it in his heart, I will see it and feel it. That's the person I will salute.

Aldin stresses the principle of equality and distinguishes between those who adopt the rules with the head and those who do so with the heart—with passion, we might say. This resembles what Pitong told Francis: it is brotherhood that matters, not rules. In this way they assert the inherent immorality of the social hierarchies in the fraternity that is promoted by the university fraternity chapters. However, Aldin's position is highly ambivalent. At a presentation of the research at the University of the Philippines (UP), with several brods present, including Aldin, a professor rose and said in disgust: "I am a Triskelion here at UP, and I am shocked about the things you present." Afterward, she confided to me that the university chapter was investigating fraternity practices in the community "in order to put a stop to it." I asked Aldin what he thought about the professor's words. "I am so proud of her," he said, unfazed by the scathing criticism. The professor had seen the performances of the community chapters and had not been impressed. Aldin, meanwhile, had heard what she had to say and was impressed. Despite Aldin's insistence on equality, it is social hierarchies that are reproduced rather than egalitarian practices.

## Transcendence

The reproduction of social hierarchy over equality can also be witnessed in relation to the broader political elite. Philippine electoral politics are dominated by political machines (Sidel 1999; Abinales 2005; McCoy 1999). Politicians at every level try to assemble election-winning alliances. Both nationally and locally, Tau Gamma would be a prize for most politicians if the fraternity could be harnessed as a voting bloc or if its many members could be the foot soldiers— even possibly the goons—of an electoral campaign. In the 2010 presidential campaign, there were a number of politicians who promised the fraternity particular favors nationally. For instance, vice-presidential candidate Bayani Fernando gave P5,000 to the Bagong Silang fraternity to distribute flyers and put up posters. Also, at the recognition ceremony days before the national election, three politicians were allowed to address the fraternity. Two of them spoke about the general responsibility of the youth to engage in politics, study hard, and be well behaved. However, one candidate addressed them as the fraternity rather than as individuals: "We promise the proud fraternity of Tau Gamma that should we win the election, we will create an office that will deal with the concerns of the fraternity—to find jobs and to help projects. You will have the full support of [City] Mayor Recom."

The assembled brods (maybe a thousand) went wild with jubilation over such direct recognition from the politicos, especially someone as important as Mayor Recom. Along with the recognition from the founding fathers, this was the major topic of conversation as I met the brods for yet another drinking session the day after. For a while, at least, the fraternity—through its disciplining violence, its connection to power, and its timeless history—had opened a door to a world of significance beyond the temporal and spatial confines of Bagong Silang. However, the drabness of the yard we were sitting in, the heat, and the alcohol, along with the smell of the smoldering embers after cooking, added to what may best be described as the hangover of a partial inclusion. Elsewhere we have discussed the ensuing malaise as a looming sense that the present may be perpetuated endlessly into the future (Jensen 2014). As Aldin said: "I had so many dreams in life. I had dreams like I wanted to have a stable job, to continue my studies, to have my own family and to [be] able to help my parents. I also dreamt of being a painter or photographer. Also of being a call center agent, a teacher, psychologist and psychiatrist—I had so many dreams. I also dreamt of being a tourist, of being able to travel the world. Now, the only dream I have is to find a stable job."

Aldin was painfully aware of the limitations of his options, and just how far the society was from being egalitarian. Short of a revolution, the best hope for him and his fellow brods lay not in discourses of equality but in the patron-client relations of the patrimonial and hierarchical society of the politicos and the powerful. Mayor Recom won, but it was not necessarily the actual outcome that was most significant. That night in 2010, the mayor included the marginalized as politically important and authentic. Recom did not see the young men as marginalized; nor was he, that night, interested in their illegal activities and violence. He saw numbers and hierarchy.

## A World of Significance—or Death

This chapter has explored what the fraternity offered to young men and how this resonated with their historical experiences, both as memories and as tacit knowledge of the past and of their everyday life in Bagong Silang. The historical experience of the young brods in Bagong Silang cannot be divorced from a longer Philippine history of struggle between egalitarian and hierarchical political discourses and practices. Importantly, this struggle was not only infused with rational political discourses but exhibited strong elements of passion. As Neferti

**FIGURE 13.** Recognition ceremony of Tau Gamma Phi community chapters by one of the founding fathers. Photo by Steffen Jensen.

**FIGURE 14.** A chapter holding up their certificate of recognition. Photo by Steffen Jensen.

**FIGURE 15.**   March of Tau Gamma Phi. Photo by Steffen Jensen.

Tadiar (2009, 15) notes in her analysis of subaltern voices in revolutionary discourse and practice, these discourses and practices are not residues of an earlier atavistic past; rather, they are central elements that sustain and even enable revolutionary struggle for equality in the present. In the analysis of the fraternity in Bagong Silang, we identified and explored the production and understanding of equality in the discourses and rituals of the fraternity. However, clearly there was a deeply ambivalent and fraught relationship with social hierarchies and the socioeconomic conditions. These constantly reproduced hierarchies and removed the possibility of realizing an egalitarian society. While brods criticized the university fraternities for being arrogant, they reproduced the centrality of the latter in how the world should be. While they claimed equal worth, they also had to face an everyday reality dominated by marginalization and the vague promises of a political class structured around social hierarchies; and with the rather depressing realization of the force of social conditions never far from the minds of the brods, the painful rituals did not disappear but rather intensified. As much as the passionate plea for equality was systematically dwarfed, so the ritual practices of accepting suffering needed to be performed repeatedly—what Butler (1993, 15) talks of as reiterative performativity—not as ways of forgetting social realities but rather to enable a world of significance despite the social realities. In Bagong

Silang—at least for a while, around 2010—the fraternities provided that avenue for imagining a different world. This is what young men like Aldin sensed, and what drew them in flocks to the Triskelion Grand Fraternity. It did not last, of course. According to our interviews, the fraternities had already started to wane in 2011. The brods met at less regular intervals and no new chapters emerged. The fraternity was laying low.

The war on drugs fundamentally challenged the morality of the fraternity as there was a strong resemblance between the victims of the war and the members of the fraternity. While the war operated with the same moral distinctions between the disciplined and the worthless (Kusaka 2017a), the agents of the war refused to acknowledge that the brods were on the side of the worthy. The war did not target the fraternity; it targeted the kind of people who made up the fraternity. Again, this was not something that only became relevant in the war on drugs. In fact, already in 2010, residents—not least, worried families of members and authorities—intensely discussed the morality and the potential benevolence of fraternities. The Ponte family, whom we visited in an earlier chapter, were quite adamant about the immorality and violence of the fraternity and its members, after the eldest daughter and our best friend, Mariza, lost her husband in a fight with a member of the fraternity. Mariza blamed the fraternity for covering up for the murder. Others took the stance that the fraternity could sort out young people—instill the necessary *disiplina*. Some barangay officials already worked with the fraternities simply because of their impressive membership, and politicians also tapped into the fraternity as a cog in their political machines.

The fraternity argument was that the fraternity could help members attain discipline and order. Still, individual members were constantly harassed. In one conversation with young Michael on one of our first days inside the fraternity, he told of his troubles with purok leader Boy, who would beat him up regularly for curfew violations, for loitering, and for just being in the streets. Michael said, "On the inside of my closet at home, I have etched a list of all the people who have humiliated me. Purok Boy is at the top of the list." Michael's closet of skeletons was no exception. Almost all the young frat members we talked with had had serious and violent encounters with local authorities and the police. While our survey data does not allow us to conclude that frat members made up a significant part of the victims of violence documented in chapter 4, the interviews suggest that they often encountered this kind of disciplinary violence from the very same people that became the central implementers of the drug war, the purok leaders, and other barangay officials. For instance, in the so-called massacre of Phase 8 in December 2016 that we explored in chapter 2, three of the victims allegedly belonged to the fraternity. In conversations with officers of Tau Gamma Phi in the area after the event, one said, "We try to tell our members of the dangers of drugs," but it was to little avail as the perpetrators of violence did not recognize the moral standing of the frat members. In a replay of Michael's list, in a case we explored earlier, one of them predicted the premature death of Purok Tan because of his involvement in the production of the watch list. In this way, at least some frat members seem to have understood that the dangers of violent death were just the latest instantiation of the century-long struggle against equality and dignity—against poor, young men of the resettlement site. For a while, they put their bets on the fraternity to help them transcend their present life conditions characterized by stuckness and poverty. Tragically, this became another case of fraternity denied to the larger, national community.

7

# THE WAR ON DRUGS AND BEYOND
## Leaving Bagong Silang

This book is about one specific place during extraordinary times. Rather than being a book about the war on drugs as such or about Bagong Silang, we have aimed to understand the war on drugs from a position inside areas whose populations have endured the brunt of the violence. Based on our longitudinal work on policing, violence, and intimate, communal politics that spans almost ten years, this analysis has privileged the understanding of the impact and effect above the rationalities of the war—the "why" of the war. This longitudinal view from below has allowed us to explore the effects of the war on drugs as well as the ingrained historical forms of inequality and violence that allowed it in the first place. As we have argued throughout the book, while there is no doubt that the war came to Bagong Silang from the outside due to the machinations of President Duterte and his administration, its local implementation and effects were animated by historical structures much older than the war. The war on drugs was a critical event (Kapferer 2010) and represented an escalation of existing violent politics (Højer et al. 2018). It was embedded in larger social structures in Philippine society and in Bagong Silang itself, and it reconfigured boundaries of death and survival, structures of trust and sociality, and relations between residents and between residents and the state. In this way, the war could not have happened the way it did, had it not been for the embedded structures, but at the same time, the war also fundamentally reconfigured sociality in Bagong Silang.

Critics of the drug war suggest that the war on drugs in reality is a war on the poor.[1] There is little doubt that the majority of the victims have been young, indigent men from the poorest sections of Metro Manila. However, if it is a war

144

on the poor, it is a war where the poor, willingly or unwillingly, have been made complicit. While the onslaught may have emerged from the outside, it reverberated through the resettlement site, widening and recasting existing conflictual fault lines in devastating ways. As we know from the anthropology of violence (Das 2007; Bourgois 2003; Green 1994; Feldman 1991), this resonates with countless other cases of state violence around the world. In this way, it may be useful to think about the war on drugs in relation to other wars on—in the Philippines as well as globally. If we do that, we see that in many ways the 2016 war on drugs mirrors and echoes other violent state campaigns at other times and in other places. Seen this way, the war on drugs is not a one-off or isolated event but one that relates intimately to state formation and elite consolidation. Based on these observations, in this final chapter we want to achieve two objectives. First, by way of conclusion, we will briefly summarize the main points of the book and each of the chapters and how they contribute to embedding the war on drugs in historical structures as well as how the war on drugs has facilitated the production of new forms of sociality. Second, and on the basis of the summary, we situate the war on drugs temporally and spatially in relation to what we can call "wars on . . ."—in the Philippines and globally. Throughout the book, we have made references to other contexts as a way of better understanding the Philippine war on drugs. However, understanding the war on drugs in the Philippines also contributes to a wider debate about global violent politics that are framed as war on . . . something. There are uncanny resemblances between, for instance, the war on gangs in Cape Town that Steffen explored some decades ago (Jensen 2010) and the present war on drugs in the Philippines. At the same time, there are huge differences attributable to different political, social, and cultural contexts and histories. Hence, we need to understand both local and global histories of marginalization and how they relate to violent politics. We start with the local histories.

## Revisiting Intimacy and Violence

In order to explore the effects of the war on drugs as both continuity and transformation, we invoked the notion of communal intimacy as a way of theorizing from Bagong Silang. We aimed to understand how forms of affective and intimate relationality were embedded in urban space, what kind of violent politics emerged before and developed through the war on drugs, and how this politics has reconfigured urban space and the possibility for survival for residents in Bagong Silang. Along with Auyero and Berti (2016), we may say that the war on drugs folded itself into the intimate spheres of communal and family affective relationality. This made the effects of the war much more insidious. Communal intimacy—knowledge of each other, neighbors, and local state officials—had been central in surviving the harsh realities of life in the resettlement site. However, it was exactly this intimate knowledge of each other that put people at risk during the war. Intimacy was both a resource and a risk. Evoking Singh's (2011) concept of agonistic intimacy, we suggested that intimacy constantly had to be renegotiated and that the war on drugs reconfigured the parameters for getting along—in conflictual as well as convivial ways. This understanding of intimacy pointed to the importance of affective relationality and exchange relations within families, with neighbors and fellow community members, and also with state officials. Clearly, these exchange relations were never equal but rather articulated and actualized power relations. With the war on drugs, these unequal exchange relations attained a new level of deadliness as well as they became increasingly difficult and expensive to navigate. This renders intimacy paradoxical—compelled as well as compelling—in that intimate, affective relationalities are and have been central for survival but at the same time, it is the intimate knowledge of their neighbors—representatives of the state or otherwise—that puts people at ultimate risk.

While the killings and the social repercussions of the war affected Bagong Silang as an area, it is also clear that it affected people very differently as well as reproduced and deepened existing class, generational, and gendered fault lines. Older, respectable men, often in some kind of employ of the local state, filled out the watch lists that formed the basis for the war. While this constituted a new high in the violent complicity, older men had also used disciplinary violence against younger and poorer men before the war, as evidenced by surveys and interviews. As we illustrate through the book, these older, respectable men were often extremely supportive of the war on drugs. While it is not a representative sample, it might not be a surprise that the purok leaders we interviewed most ardently in favor of the war were all men, whereas those with some kind of misgivings or fears were younger, poorer, and often women. When that is said, the support for the war on drugs has remained high—also much higher than we, two middle-class, educated, and human rights–minded scholars are able to comprehend. Perception polls, the so-called Social Weather Stations, have registered up toward 80 percent support for the war. Throughout this book, we have explored support in more qualitative terms among community activists and our other friends and neighbors in ways that resonate with the analyses of Wataru Kusaka (2017a) and Nicole Curato (2016), which focus, respectively, on discipline and a latent anxiety of drugs. In many ways, even the fraternity work along similar constructions around worthy and unworthy youth and the need to employ violence to instill discipline.

There has, of course, been opposition to the war on drugs. Most direct opposition has come from human rights groups and parts of the media, which have often paid a high price for the opposition or simply raising critical points in terms of attempted reductions in state funding and legal procedures against journalists and media operations. The Catholic Church has also been vocal in opposition. In Bagong Silang, Palatino (2019) has documented diverse forms of protests, marches, and the formation, for instance, of victims' associations. Likewise, together with Balay we have addressed the effects of the war on drugs in the form of human rights interventions, support for families, and documentation of the effects of the war. However, as we note in a 2018 position paper coauthored by DIGNITY and Balay, the rather defeatist sense is that human rights as a language of protest is not very effective and that other languages of protest must be identified and employed. Our analysis points to some of these possible alternative languages. Popular support also became more ambivalent. One young man, a former member and officer of Tau Gamma Phi, said in May 2017, "I was very supportive of the president. Now it is *halo-halo* [Now I have mixed feelings]." We were sitting on the rooftop of his unfinished house as the sun was setting over the massive resettlement site, talking about the dangers of drugs, the effects of the war and the modifications they were making to the house: *halo-halo*.

We noted the same mixed feelings troubling Emilio, Lita, and Junior as well as purok leaders like Juancho. Juancho, for instance, invoked religious notions around his pro-life ideology as well as suggesting that the drug abuse in his area was not so bad that it warranted a violent response. Other potentially critical voices articulated fears that they or their families would somehow be entangled in the drug war. Hence, the 80 percent support of the war was matched by an equal percentage of people fearful for their life (Social Weather Stations 2017). Finally, throughout the book we have identified and explored the perpetual conflict between (revolutionary) calls for equality and equal worth and social hierarchies of patron-client relations, patrimonialism, and patriarchy as different models for society and different forms of inclusion into a national community. We have showed, especially in the three chapters on moral community, community activism, and fraternities, how this perpetual struggle most often seem to end in a defeat or compromise of the egalitarian calls at the expense of reproduced, hierarchical relations—be that in relation to pakikisama, activism, or fraternity. The war on drugs did not necessarily work on hierarchical notions. Arguably, it constructed potential equal worth between all those who refrained from drugs as part of a national, moral community, regardless of who they were and their social standing. However, as we illustrate in different ways in the analytical chapters, the war, for instance, reproduced the territorial stigmatization of Bagong Silang on the metropolitan level and gerontocratic hierarchies enabled the watch lists. In this way, the war denied equal value outside certain class, gender, and generational structures. Furthermore, as survival often relied on connections, hierarchies—knowing someone in power and in government—became imperative. Nonetheless, the calls for equality and equal worth have been so consistent throughout the history of Bagong Silang and the Philippines that this call continues to comprise the strongest political language for expressing resistance to the war on drugs.

We explored these points in different ways over five empirical chapters. In chapters 2 and 3, we explored two aspects of policing that are central to how people in Bagong Silang experience policing—intimacy and exchange relations—before and during the war on drugs. As they explore policing, these two chapters most directly relate to the war on drugs in Bagong Silang. In the three remaining, empirical chapters (chapters 4–6), we took a step back and explored how displacement produced Bagong Silang as a social and moral space that enabled the war on drugs and what kind of political culture emerged there. Following communal, intimate relations in the path walk, among activists, and in fraternities, we illustrate the extent to which violence and struggles between equality and hierarchy shaped Bagong Silang by and how they have informed support or opposition to Duterte's war. Furthermore, the three chapters allow us to understand the external and internal differentiations that animated the implementation of the war, the activists who took a political stance against domination, and the young men who finally ended up as victims of the war.

In chapters 2 and 3, we directly explored policing structures and practices in Bagong Silang before and going into the drug war. In chapter 2, we focused on the relationship between order making, politics, and intimacy, whereas we focused on exchange relations, money, and survival in chapter 3. Chapter 2 traced policing practices and how they are inextricably entangled with local politics and intimate communal relationality. The chapter traced the emergence and practices of machine politics, that is, the transformation of electoral politics into politics of specific (personalized) interests, as well as how intimate communal relations informed the practices of policing. With the war on drugs, policing acquired an even more important role. Increasingly, policing the war on drugs began to work on and transform the very societal relations in which it was practiced. This led to a fundamental reconfiguration and destabilization of culturally intimate state-resident relations as well as relations between residents and neighbors. For instance, while the national police force was the lead agency in carrying out the war, it relied heavily on local support and active participation from Barangay authorities and residents in the neighborhoods. Worries about drugs had existed in Bagong Silang as "latent anxieties" (Curato 2016) that the discourse of the drug war articulated in new and public ways among people in Bagong Silang, indeed even among some of those using drugs (Kusaka 2017a). Local Barangay officials and residents became the main implementers of the war on drugs, not least because of their intimate knowledge of their neighbors. Some of these officials embraced the war wholeheartedly—and some of them paid a price—while others desperately tried to navigate the murky social waters of intimate and affective relationality. In this way, the chapter illustrated what happens when state violence folds itself into intimate communal relations.

Chapter 3 continued this line of inquiry but shifted the focus slightly. While we examined police violence prior to and during the drug war as in the previous chapter, we homed in on the moral justifications regulating police violence and illustrated how before the onset of the war people managed their relationship with the police through interpersonal networks, cunning, and money. In the second part of the chapter on the drug war, we described its impact in Bagong Silang and how exchange relationships between the police and the policed were reconfigured, not least in relation to what has been known as Tokhang for Ransom, that is, how police have been cashing in on the war on drugs. By focusing on money and violence, we were able to understand how the war on drugs could not be reduced to sovereign acts of violence but had to be understood also as part of old, embedded structures of exchange and entanglement between authority and population. These constituted the best option people had for survival and they were often couched in mutually beneficial ways, as when the police offered to "help" people in trouble—help (*tulong*) that was also solicited by those in need. The war on drugs made this much more unpredictable and expensive, as when Stella, a local drug merchant, first paid a sizable sum to be released from prison and then another sizable sum to get police assistance to escape other police units that were hot on her heels. While this form of murderous enterprise (Coronel 2017) or exchange relations clearly works on extremely unequal terms, they are often people's best option to escape violence or get out of prison. While the president and the police management tried to cleanse the war of such corrupt practices, for instance by circulating police personnel between Manila and Mindanao, police as well as residents attempted to reestablish them on the go. As Mariza, an old acquaintance put it, "They [police and residents] are not strangers for long."

In chapters 4, 5, and 6, we explored the different conditions that allowed the war on drugs to take the specific form it took, as well as to understand the political culture that in some ways resisted but also allowed the war on drugs to remain in a constant tension between calls for equality and social hierarchies. Chapter 4 explored the production of Bagong Silang as a territorially stigmatized space on the edge of the urban political economy where particular forms of social, gendered, and generational moralities emerged. In the second part of the chapter, we homed in on the community and the moral economy of violence. The chapter built on quantitative and qualitative surveys, interviews, and observations in Bagong Silang over a decade. One conclusion from the survey carried out in 2010 was that contrary to popular perceptions, violence was more likely to be perpetrated by older men against younger men than the opposite. The perceptions and the experiences explain each other. As young men were perceived to be the main perpetrators of violence, they must be in need of discipline. This suggested the existence of a gerontocratic and patriarchal system of authority in Bagong Silang. This, again, goes a long way to explain why many older people who were recruited into the war on drugs took such pride in participation. This was not a break from previous political practices of violence; rather, it echoed and drew on the moral economy of violence that had existed long before the introduction of the war on drugs. A second conclusion from the chapter revolves around emic notions of neighborliness and community. Again, we illustrated the gendered notions of community as well as showing how the sense of community has been transformed as state violence has folded itself into communal affairs. People like our friend Maricel, who used to be seen as very good at doing *pakikisama* and a shrewd political navigator, suddenly ended on the wrong side of new, moral divides.

Chapter 5 explored community activists and their decade-long struggle for equality and dignity. The chapter illustrated how these struggles have transformed over the years in Bagong Silang. Many of the activists came to Bagong Silang fighting. They were often affiliated directly or indirectly to the revolutionary left and saw the struggles in Bagong Silang as a direct continuation and as embedded in larger, political struggles to topple the dictatorship and for a more just Philippine society. Increasingly, however, the parameters of politics changed. It was professionalized and projectified, subjected not least to foreign funding requirements. While the community activists were often involved in the work of national human rights and development NGOs, they were not able to pursue their agenda in the same way. Demands were different; languages were different; motivations were different. Partially as a response to the professionalization, many activists left activism and focused on *ekonomiya*, or survival. Others struck deals with trapos, that is, traditional politicians or strong, local political families where they used their political capital to promote the interests of their patrons and themselves. While some activists nourished strong moral objections to jumping "into the pigsty" with politicians, most understood the rationalities and necessities of such alliances. When the war on drugs was initiated, many of the activists joined—or were made to join—the war because they had specific and privileged knowledge about their communities and because their present political patrons were part of the implementation. This was true for those involved in the political and electoral system. Others who had been affiliated with human rights organizations often went the other way. However, in many cases like that of Emilio, this was no simple choice. He knew about the damages of drugs from his everyday life; he was affiliated with a human rights organization; he still preferred a much more radical, revolutionary language. In this way, Emilio embodied many of the paradoxes of the war on drugs locally between hierarchy and equality.

In chapter 6, we focused on a male peer group organization, a fraternity, which had up to as many as six thousand members in Bagong Silang in 2010. The chapter explored the young male members' attempt to break from the spatial and temporal confinement of the resettlement site by engaging in violent and ritualistic practices. As we illustrated in the chapter, through disciplining the body and the mind to overcome the chaotic and unregulated violence of other, younger youth groups, the fraternities allowed their members to grow up, to become adult, and mature members of the community. Furthermore, they allowed the young men to imagine a world of equality and transcendence in which they were connected to networks outside the area and in another time. While the analysis focuses on the year 2010, well before the onset of the war on drugs, it is still relevant for our understanding of the war on drugs in Bagong Silang. Echoing the analysis of Wataru Kusaka (2017a), the fraternities bought into a distinction between those who were good people and those who constituted trouble. This was, as Kusaka shows, exactly the same distinction that animated the war on drugs. However, tragically, the young men failed to convince those around them, both locally and nationally, that this was indeed the case, and they became the typical victims of the war on drugs. The war did not target the fraternity as such. Rather, the brods simply resembled the typical victim—young, indigent, male and marginalized. Gone were notions of transcendental love of country, discipline, and adult aspirations. Reduced to pure body form, many of them perished in the war, including some of the brods present at the initiation that we described in detail.

## War on . . . : Politics and Policing

In this book, we have focused on a longitudinal analysis from Bagong Silang of the war on drugs. We have done so because, to our mind, such an analysis has been lacking in scholarly accounts focusing either on Duterte or on rationalities of the war. However, our approach carries several dangers. While we locate our analysis in larger and longer-term structures of marginalization, we risk rendering Bagong Silang unique. Similarly, exploring the effects of the war—a before and an after—risks reducing the war to a singular, extraordinary and critical event or escalation. This would be a serious error of analysis and of politics. It would suggest that merely ending the war in its present form would solve the problem of state violence, much like the illusion that getting rid of Marcos signaled the end to injustice and the violence of politics in the Philippines in the period after the dictatorship. While we needed the longitudinal view from below, one avenue to escape this necessary impasse is to relate the analysis to perspectives outside Bagong Silang. Hence, in the remainder of the chapter, we try to answer two questions—first, about the war on drugs itself as a global phenomenon and what kind of politics the war it represents, and second, what form of policing we are looking at.

## Security and Differentiated Citizenship

Discussions of the phenomenon of drug wars and their legitimacy often translate into whether they worked. A cursory review of this question of legitimacy and efficiency in combating drugs will reveal that the answers often depend on where specific observers stand on the continuum between a (conservative) belief in the power of punishment and deterrence and a (liberal) conviction that crime and drug abuse are functions of social marginalization. There are clearly all kinds of positions in between these two general points. However, there seems to have been a general move among political elites (back) to a law-and-order position, believing in the power of punishment and deterrence. While many academics, especially within sociology, legal studies, cultural studies, and anthropology, have produced compelling evidence for the problem of the punitive approach (Bourgois 2015; Wacquant 2008a), this seems to have less and less impact on policy (Simon 2007). We will not go into detail about the problems of the punitive trend. Others have done so more competently. Suffice to say that the problems in the United States alone include exceedingly high levels of incarceration for especially people of color (Alexander 2011; Wacquant 2009); health crises (Bourgois 2003, 2004); the erosion of the power of the judiciary at the expense of the executive (Simon 2007); and massive costs to restrict the illegal drug supply, often involving interventions into foreign countries and ensuing human rights abuses (Bourgois 2015); to mention but a few. Since the official introduction of the war on drugs in the early 1970s by Richard Nixon, these massive costs have not led to any significant decrease in the consumption of drugs. Rather, it has led, for example, to the emergence of entire nation-states in the throes of drug-dealing cartels and exceedingly complex and entrenched gang and drug-dealing structures to cope with and profit from the state's drug war practices. Similar in other countries around the world, wars on drugs have had massive consequences but few results measured in decreased drug abuse.[2] In many ways, we can see the contours of these issues as well in the Philippines where one could even legitimately ask if the Philippines had a real drug problem with below global average addiction rates (UNODC 2016). Hence, it is clearly relevant to ask questions about the war on drugs as an appropriate policy response to perceived or real drug epidemics.

Another way to ask questions about the wars on drugs is to explore what kind of politics they represent. Asking this question moves attention away from drugs as a substantive problem into questions about political languages. There is little doubt that law-and-order agendas have worked well at the polls. Any politician in the United States who is seen as soft on crime will likely lose elections. Furthermore, as a host of commentators in the Philippines argues (Kusaka 2017a; Curato 2016; Reyes 2016; Thompson 2016), Duterte won the 2016 presidential election on his antidrug campaign. Nathan Quimpo (2017), in his contribution to the *Duterte Reader* (Curato 2017a), usefully evokes the concept of securitization (Buzan, Wæver, and De Welde 1998). Securitization theory has produced a rich literature of security as a political language. The basic tenet in the theory is that security is a speech act by which means a politician or persons in power move a particular issue into a new kind of politics structured by "us versus them" and engage in an existential conflict over the survival of the polity. As it is a question of survival, any—or many more—steps are legitimate in order to block the threat. Securitization is about the ability of enunciating a given threat as existential. Like other political leaders evoking the war on crime, terror, drugs, and gangs worldwide, this is exactly what Duterte was able to do. The Philippines was a nation under threat and radical action was necessary. In this way, the war on drugs constituted a move into another kind of politics that legitimized extraordinary measures to protect it against onslaught to secure the survival of the nation. The war worked as what William Walters (2008) called an anti-policy defined as the assembly of "discourses, measures and policies whose stated objective is to combat or prevent bad things" (277). Anti-policy relies on what Walters terms the subject-perpetrator, who is the ultimate evil to be eradicated at all costs. This leaves the fighters of the bad thing to assume a position of moral authority, and even the right to rule. The subject-perpetrator in the Philippines, the drug personality, is contrasted with real citizens, who in the logic of the war can be talked about as citizens cum (potential) victims of crime (Simon 2007, 8). Hence, citizenship is no longer a function of legal claims to a state to provide meaningful inclusion but a function of securitized notions of danger.

It is useful to think about the political effects of such constructions through James Holston's influential 2009 study on what he calls "differentiated citizenship." Based on his analysis of urban forms of marginalization in Brazil, Holston asks the basic question of how states can maintain the idea of universal inclusion of citizens with the coexistence of massive inequality. In Brazil, citizenship is no guarantee of inclusion. Holston (2009, 7) suggests that the simultaneous presence of universal inclusion and inequality is negotiated through differenti-ated citizenship, that is, a citizenship that is qualified by a range of socioeco-nomic, political, racial and cultural markers. These markers constitute the means through which to include people in the polity as for instance voters while main-taining their exclusion from substantive rights. As we have seen throughout this book, people in Bagong Silang were denied even the most basic rights purport-edly extended to citizens. Rather than seeing the war on drugs as a radical de-parture from an inclusive past, we need to think of the securitized war on drugs as yet another moment of violently differentiated citizenship that leaves many residents in Bagong Silang devoid of rights even to life and many other residents scrambling to be on the right side of the new divide—with some succeeding, others not. In this light, this book has detailed the struggles of people in Bagong Silang to deal with this new form of securitized politics. Furthermore, while dif-ferentiated citizenship before the war on drugs was caused by exclusion of the poor by callous elites and sometimes incompetent and corrupt state practices, the war placed the blame of exclusion on the excluded themselves in their ca-pacity as subject-perpetrators. In this way, the Philippine case illustrates that se-curitization represents a depoliticization of marginalization and exclusion that serves to preserve elite privilege. "Wars on" do not represent a societal transfor-mation; they preserve a conservative status quo and leave the poor with the blame for their own suppression.

## Policing as Counterinsurgency

We are able to understand the ramifications of this form of politics globally by asking what kind of policing the war on drugs has called forth. Perhaps slightly controversially we argue that policing practices during the war on drugs in many ways resembled counterinsurgency practices.[3] To analyze the war on drugs as counterinsurgency is useful for both conceptual and empirical reasons, and it potentially provides us with new ways of engaging the consequences of the war. Beginning with the conceptual resonances between the war on drugs and coun-terinsurgency, we do not argue that they are the same or alike. Rather, we may think of their similarities with Wittgenstein's concept of family resemblance. Wittgenstein (1953) attempted—unsuccessfully—to formulate a theory of simi-larities in language. Instead, he opted for the term family resemblances as a use-ful way of comparing phenomena. He said, "We see a complicated network of similarities overlapping and crisscrossing: sometimes overall similarities, some-times similarities of detail. I can think of no better expression to characterize these similarities than 'family resemblances' for the various resemblances be-tween members of a family" (31–32). Adopting counterinsurgency concepts, then, may tell us something new about the war on drugs. First, counterinsurgency and wars on drugs both work as anti-policies with clearly marked subject-perpetrators threatening the survival of the nation. The most important difference in that sense is who embodies the subject-perpetrator position—political insurgents or drug personalities—not what governments can do to them. Second, the war on drugs is a far more holistic and all-encompassing form of policing than reacting to singular events of crime because it works at the level of entire populations. One influential counterinsurgency theorist, John McCuen, wrote in 1966 in relation to the U.S. war effort in Vietnam that counterinsurgency is a "psycho-politico-military process" (327). Hence, counterinsurgency merges development, security, and warfare in the most direct manner, with developmental strategies being deployed in the pursuit of state security. Third, counterinsurgency violence is being deployed preventatively in order to reclaim territory supposedly lost to insurgents rather than wait for the insurgents to strike. As McCuen (1966) stresses, it is imperative that states act decisively and preemptively. Jennifer Schirmer (1998, 35), working in Guatemala, quotes generals behind the counterinsurgency campaign that cost more than 80,000 people their lives in 1982, that it is necessary to use both bullets and beans but that in the beginning it was only bullets. Again, this mirrors how the war was fought in Bagong Silang. While there were promises of rehabilitation of drug users, the violence has dominated state practices. Finally, counterinsurgency cannot rely only on the police but needs to work through local partnerships. The underlying idea is that only by establishing local partnerships can the state win decisively. This clearly echoes the reliance on local partners and people willing or forced into collaboration in the policing of Bagong Silang.

While these resemblances do not prove that the war in fact constituted counterinsurgency, the examples clearly illustrate that policing was not only about identifying criminal elements and bringing them to justice. Rather, both counterinsurgency and the war on drugs relate to the fundamental problem of how to maintain order in a deeply divided and unequal society. Furthermore, while there are important, conceptual (family) resemblances between counterinsurgency and the war on drugs, this relation emerges even more clearly if we consider the simple empirical and historical insight that it is often the same people in the Philippine National Police that fight the war on drugs in Bagong Silang and the insurgents in rural Philippines and Mindanao.

Firstly, observers have noted that to understand the war on drugs as it has been fought, notably in the poorer sections of Manila, directly relates to Duterte's violent antidrug drives in Davao on the island Mindanao (Altez and Caday 2017; Curato 2017a, 2017b).[4] Duterte's alleged success of ridding Davao of drugs played a major part in his electoral win. However, Mindanao is also important for other reasons. While the political culture of the Philippines is animated by violence, poverty, and corruption (McCoy 2009; Sidel 1999), what sets Mindanao apart is the widespread warfare, the rogue military, and police counterinsurgency strategies (Tidwell 2016). For many people in Manila, Mindanao is perceived as incarnating danger and violence, and as a place where human rights are translated into particular notions of honor and revenge (Rafael 2016). Duterte brought this mentality of warfare along with him to the presidency. To operationalize the drug war, he brought in key police officials from Mindanao. Ronald "Bato" Dela Rosa, for instance, who served as a close ally and former police chief under Duterte in Davao, was appointed chief of the Philippine National Police at the inception of the drug war. Together, Duterte and Dela Rosa brought in other trusted officers from Mindanao to form the core of the anti-drug units with the responsibility to implement the war on drugs. These units have been referred to as the "Davao Boys" (Baldwin and Marshall 2017). Personnel also went the other way. The successive corruption scandals and failures of the Philippine National Police that have marred the war on drugs did not result in major reforms. Instead of sacking corrupt police officers, the administration's attempt to cleanse the police took the form of publicly scolding so-called *skalawags* (corrupt police officials) and sending them to Mindanao as a form of punishment and disciplining. The redeployment of policing strategies and police personnel from Davao and Mindanao meant stricter regulations in the city, and it signaled the targeting of drug personalities as legitimate nationwide (Reyes 2016, 125). In the State of the Barangay Address (SOBA) in 2017, the then station commander in Bagong Silang, himself straight from Mindanao, stressed to the crowd that if the Barangay personnel refused to collaborate with the police in the war, "I will bring the hell of Mindanao here." In this way, the wars of Mindanao produce hard men who have returned to undisciplined Manila to haunt the city's unruly underbelly.

While it is tempting to conclude that the war on drugs emanated out of Davao, we suggest that in fact the war drew on the experiences and practice-based analysis of counterinsurgency wars. Indeed, it may be that also the Davao death squad was influenced by this longer history of policing. As Al McCoy (2009) illustrates, Philippine policing cannot be divorced from histories of policing insurgencies. At least since the establishment of the Philippine Constabulary in the early American period, the Philippine police have, in different guises, fought internal insurgencies. This history spans the fight against Philippine nationalists, oppressing rural revolts of Marxist and Maoist ilk, Moro nationalists, and Islamic insurgencies. The history spanning more than a century of almost perpetual war provides the cultural and practical backdrop for how to police challenges to the state. The Philippines is often explored as a weak state (Abinales

2005; Quimpo 2009), and it is if we think of state capacity in a particular reading of Weberian legitimacy. However, it has been remarkably successful in maintaining control and crushing insurgencies through a combination of savvy political maneuverings, development, and divide and rule combined with sheer, brutal force, which bears the signature imprint of counterinsurgency strategies.[5] In interviews we conducted with police officers in Bagong Silang, this history is a source of true pride. In their words, they have salvaged the nation against attacks. It is no coincidence that police killings are still referred to as salvaging. Looking carefully at the war on drugs, we can identify at least five (family) resemblances of the imaginaries and practices of the counterinsurgency wars and the drug war as it played out in Bagong Silang—the spatialization of violence, modalities of violence, militarization, civil-police partnerships, and infiltration.

First, counterinsurgency strategies rely crucially on spatialized notions of threat where areas are divided into fragile, threatened, or stable areas in which different strategies are deployed. While many counterinsurgency strategists insist that it is imperative to win the hearts and minds of the people (Kilcullen 2010), many scholars argue that violence plays a crucial part in pacifying dangerous areas. In Jennifer Schirmer's excellent 1998 account of the counterinsurgency war in Guatemala that claimed as many as eighty thousand lives in 1982 (56), she reports that the generals insisted that while "beans" (food and development) were imperative, it was all about bullets to pacify the dangerous areas in the beginning. Areas like Bagong Silang have not been labelled in the same way explicitly. However, policing practices, notably the killings, have de facto marked these areas as in need of specific violent intervention. This was the case from its birth during the Maoist incursion into Metro Manila. Police officers have continued to describe the neighborhood as a notorious place permeated by high rates of crime, violence, and a widespread use of drugs. Its remoteness from central economic and political networks has also set it apart as a zone of the dispossessed and disposable (Tadiar 2013). Hence, when the war on drugs began, it was zones like this, separate and marginalized, that bore the brunt of the violence. The existence of such zones of exclusion structured the war on drugs and the violence itself perpetuated the borders separating them from polite society.

Second, regarding modalities of violence, it was during former President Marcos's presidency that extrajudicial killings of opponents became a certified state practice. As we explore in chapter 3 especially, the emic concept for this practice was salvaging, performed by the police and recognized by residents, at least in Bagong Silang.[6] According to interviews with police, salvaging should be understood as the salvation of the nation through killings of people in opposition to the state. Hence, salvaging was a thing of which to be proud. Salvaging claimed tens of thousands of lives in a social cleansing of society during the dictatorship (Quimpo 2008, 28–33). As a fragile democracy replaced martial law with extensive corruption, poverty and continued insurgency, the killings continued. Especially in the insurgency wars against the New People's Army (NPA), salvaging was a constant element, targeting not only insurgents but also union leaders, land rights organizers, and human rights groups (AHRC 2006, 2007). These latter killings were often carried out by masked assailants in drive-by shootings on motorcycles, "riding in tandem." These motorcycle-riding assassinations have become the hallmark of the drug-related killings in Bagong Silang. Arguably, the violent practices of Duterte's war on drugs were made possible exactly through this history of excessive violence and the recognizable, performative logic of killing.

Third, the police are willing and ready participants in the drug war, which has seen the increased militarization of the police. Arguably, one of the main reasons for this is because the form of policing introduced in the war on drugs allowed the police to engage in the violence they deem necessary without being hampered by local politics and human rights. This is a welcome break from the post-Marcos era, where the Philippine National Police underwent a process of demilitarization, decentralizing, and democratizing. As they had been prior to the Marcos regime, the police again became subordinate to local politics and strong political families (McCoy 2009, 435; Sidel 1999). Under Duterte, the police has reclaimed its autonomy and role of salvaging the nation. In this way, the war on drugs became a promise of remilitarization and depoliticization with a drug policy allowing the discretionary power of the police to expand the law with violent forms of order making. Indeed, one officer in Bagong Silang proudly exclaimed that the core of the police organization had been strengthened: "We now have a strong top." Apart from the rediscovered pride in belonging to a strong organization, militarization directly relates to the frequent redeployment of police personnel, especially between Manila and Mindanao. Intended to address the high levels of corruption by severing ties between the population and the police, the police have been confined to something akin to barrack life, where their entanglements with local residents are intentionally kept at a minimum. This has significantly reconfigured how residents can negotiate with police about the price of their survival as we have seen, and it has alienated the police from the people they must police, who now are seen purely as the subject-perpetrator.

Fourth, civil-military partnerships play a central role in counterinsurgency theories (Kilcullen 2010; McCuen 1966) and Philippine practice (Adam et al 2014; Banlaoi 2010). Civilians are drawn in (or forced) to participate in the war on the side of the state. Only by enrolling local people in the counterinsurgency, voluntarily or with a gun to their heads, can the state hope to win, the argument

goes (Kilcullen 2010; McCuen 1966). One example of a civilian-military partnership as central in counterinsurgency was the Citizens Armed Forces Geo-
graphical Unit (CAFGUs), which became particularly important in Corazon
Aquino's total war on communism starting in 1987 (Hedman and Sidel 2000,
64). While formally under army command, it quickly developed into private
armies of strong political families. They were legitimized by perceived threats
from insurgencies and given free reins to fight any challenge to local (state) power.
In counterinsurgency drives in Mindanao, CAFGUs worked side by side with
Civilian Volunteer Organizations (CVOs). Outside war zones, CVOs are, in fact,
simply part of the Barangay Justice System. However, in counterinsurgency
drives these peace officers appear to become almost weaponized and receive new
roles in the fight against insurgents (Banlaoi 2010). This is, of course, remarkably similar to the fate of the Barangay Justice System in Bagong Silang, where
the peace officers, sometimes against their will, became implicated in the war
on drugs (Palatino 2019).

A final resemblance that we would like to point to is the importance of what is
referred to as infiltration or collaboration. In war zones, collaboration and infiltration are often associated with treason (Thiranagama and Kelly 2010). While sometimes an explicit strategy, it always generates fear. One example from the state war
against the NPA is the so-called Deep Penetration Agents (DPAs). During one of
the more intense periods of struggle in the early 1990s, about a thousand NPA
soldiers were accused of being DPA. Many were killed, and these purges were ac-
credited with a fundamental and crippling weakening of the NPA. In his 2001
book, *To Suffer Thy Comrades*, former NPA soldier and survivor of the purges
Robert Garcia tells the harrowing story of the fear of infiltration and the lack of
trust in everybody. Garcia speculates that perhaps the regime did not send out the
DPAs but that fear itself did most of the work. Something similar was produced
during the war on drugs as we have shown in the book. The existence of lists, secret networks, and vigilante groups along with unknown assailants and secret in-
formers produced a level of fear that transformed sociality and trust, and indeed
the constitution of urban space itself (Warburg and Jensen 2020b).

# Conclusion

We began thinking about writing this book in 2015, one year before the war on
drugs began. The question we asked ourselves back then was why such a book
would be a necessary and important contribution. When the war on drugs broke
out, the answer to the question became obvious. In fact, it was a matter of urgency. At the time of writing, nearly four years into the drug war, thousands had

perished, families had been left struggling, and communities are reeling from fear and mistrust. Despite the horrific consequences of the war, public support has not wavered. In this book, we have explored how the war on drugs came to Bagong Silang and situated this new form of state violence in wider historical and social structures. While it represents an escalation of previous state violence, we have argued that it is in no way an isolated or onetime event. This suggests that the killings of *adiks* and perhaps those deemed part of disposable populations will not end. This, in many ways, is a tragic prognosis of what lies ahead for Filipinos, especially for those who are in the margins. Through its attempt to situate the war on drugs in larger and longer structures of displacement, dispossession, and violence, the book has aimed to render the violence of politics visible. Violence embodied by the war on drugs is a function of deep social divisions, histories of displacement and counterinsurgency, and localized attempts to deal with and make sense of it through the employment of various political languages and strategies. In this way, we hope that it facilitates a degree of criticality by looking at the campaign beyond the figureheads, statistics, and official discourses. Drawing from much of the book's theme, it is an invitation to look beneath and beyond the bloody campaign and to unearth the intimate, insidious, and at times deadly politics that has rendered Philippine society bifurcated and bloodied.

While the book focuses on a very Philippine history, we believe that this study of the intimate violence of politics of the drug war in Bagong Silang and the Philippines helps us understand "wars on" elsewhere. The book contributes to global discussions on the implementation and consequences of these wars declared to keep a part of the population safe by identifying existential threats in the other part of the population that governments need to deal with urgently. First, it is clear that the war on drugs in the Philippines was inspired by other wars on drugs elsewhere, not only in discourses of security but also in practice as our discussion of counterinsurgency suggests. Templates for best practices for fighting these wars on drugs, crime, gangs, or terror circulate among police agencies, military, intelligence, welfare offices from country to country and city to city (Rodgers and Jensen 2015). These are anti-policy networks (Walters 2008) many times stronger than the human rights networks that try to alleviate the consequences of the wars and make governments accountable. So while the Philippine drug war drew inspiration, both directly and indirectly, it now functions as an inspiration for others. Hence, the Indonesian President Jokowi has expressed admiration and encouragement for the Philippine war (Mutiarin, Tomaro, and Almarez, 2019), as has, not surprisingly, Donald Trump (Bach 2018). Hence, it is no far off idea that one day, Philippine police officers will give presentations and write manuals for how to conduct a war on drugs in a democratic state. As the historically high support for Duterte illustrates, democracy is no guarantee of fairness or justice for the poor and the marginalized (Curato 2016). Jennifer Schirmer's 1998 analysis, *The Guatemalan Military Project*, points to this, given that she subtitled her book, *A Violence Called Democracy*. The Philippine case actualizes this potential link between democracy and violence in important ways. So, the question we are left with is what kind of politics or political responses can stem the tide of this kind of war?

# Notes

## 1. INTRODUCING INTIMACY, VIOLENCE, AND SUBALTERN POLITICS

1. This is what sociologist Randy David (2016) calls "Dutertismo." In the time just after the beginning of the drug war, and surprisingly quickly for the academic world, a number of lucid accounts emerged, not least Nicole Curato's *A Duterte Reader* (2017a) and Mark Thompson, in a special issue of the *Journal of Current Southeast Asian Affairs* on the Duterte presidency (2016). While these contributions expanded on and explained how the drug war was possible, most of the explanations naturally centered on Duterte and his past political trajectory as a major source for understanding the drug war.

2. Of course, Tadiar's analysis echoes other postcolonial studies. One example of such an approach is Ann Laura Stoler, who, in her 2013 work on postcolonial subjectivity in Indonesia, on archives and ruins, and her 2016 work on what she calls "duress," has developed postcolonial studies. Other examples include Comaroff and Comaroff 2008 and Mbembe 2001.

3. See, for instance, analyses of what became referred to as factional politics (Hollnsteiner 1963; Landé 1965; Lynch 1962) focusing on the cultural reproduction of hierarchy in relatively benevolent paternalistic forms. Later, this was critiqued by a host of scholars focusing on what became known as the elite's approach to democracy (Pinches 1997), which was pioneered by Alfred McCoy (1994), John Sidel (1999), and not least, Benedict Anderson (1998). Contrary to the former approach, the elite democracy thesis highlighted the existence of negative and violent politics. Despite their differences, the two approaches take as their point of departure the perspective of the elite, whereas the actions of the poor or dependents are reduced to functions of elite politics.

4. See, for example, Kerkvliet 1995, 2002a, as well as Ileto 2001, Berner 1997, 2000, and Pinches 1997. More recent work attempts to explore politics from below—or at least the consequences of politics for the urban poor; see, for instance, Garrido 2019, Arcilla 2018, and Ortega 2016.

5. See, for instance, Thompson 2016, Curato 2017a, Adam, Ariate, and Cruz 2019, and Johnson and Fernquest 2018, Warburg and Jensen 2020, Jensen and Hapal 2018.

6. According to the Dangerous Drugs Board (2015), a policymaking and strategy-formulating body on drug prevention and control serving under the president, the number of drug users in the Philippines two years before this study, according to a nationwide survey, was close to 1.8 million—less than half the 4 million that Duterte claimed. In May 2017 Duterte fired the DDB head, Benjamin Reyes, for publicly contradicting his figures (Punongbayan 2017) and announced a new estimate of 4.7 million drug users via the Philippine Drug Enforcement Agency and the Philippine National Police (Philstar 2017). This estimate is based on the total number of "surrenders"—self-confessed users or dealers who hand themselves over to the authorities—and the number of households visited in antidrug operations. Other numbers calling the existence of a drug problem into question are drug-prevalence rates. Based on the DDB's 2015 survey, the drug-prevalence rate in the Philippines is around 2.3 percent of the population. This is less than half the global average, which is estimated at 5.3 percent (UNODC 2017). In comparison to the global average of drug prevalence, the Philippines arguably does not appear to be facing any kind of drug crisis or to be at risk of turning into a narco-state.

7. As we were rewriting this book in mid-2020, a similar or parallel process of securitization could be observed in the regime's handling of the COVID-19 crisis with large-scale security operations, detaining thousands of largely poor people who are seen to be in contravention of the lockdowns. For further analysis, see Hapal forthcoming.

8. This analysis taps into a more theoretical debate that draws important inspiration from a Foucauldian analytics of biopolitics and violence (Foucault 1978). See, for instance, Das 2007, Agamben 1998, Hindess 2001, and Povinelli 2011.

9. See, for instance, Chester Arcilla's 2018 work on socialized housing and Marco Garrido's 2019 work on what he calls the patchwork city. While these studies foreground the drivers of urban marginalization, they also explore how people reacted to the displacement.

10. We are clearly not the first to understand intimacy as interpersonal. See for instance Reis and Shaver 1988.

11. We return to this incidence in chapter 6.

12. This separation between the private and the public has, of course, animated much social and political analysis. As it often corresponds to a binary gender separation, feminists were among the first to question this distinction. Not surprisingly, much of the literature on intimacy emerges from a strong feminist critique. See, for example, Haraway 1994 and Povinelli 2011.

13. Auyero and Berti (2016, 10) use the example of how a mother beats her son to a pulp to protect him against worse dangers on the outside in the form of gang membership and police brutality. During fieldwork in Cape Town our interlocutors tell of similar practices as mothers "burn out" their sons' gang tattoos by putting their arm on the stove or by stabbing them.

14. See, for instance, Lynch 1962, Enriquez 1993, and Pe-Pua and Protacio-Marcelino 2000.

15. In this sense, *pakikisama* resembles what Ernesto Laclau (1996a, 1996b) has called an empty signifier.

16. Quezon City is the city adjacent to Caloocan, where Bagong Silang is located. It is the largest of the nineteen cities making up Metro Manila and has long been the administrative and educational center of region.

17. For an account of social capital measurements, see de Silva et al. 2006.

18. Barangay is loosely translated into "village." It is the lowest tier of government in the Philippines. Barangays used to be small entities, but with demographic changes, some of the Barangays have become huge administrative entities, like Bagong Silang, which has about 250,000 inhabitants. We will define the contemporary usage of barangays later in this book, not least the barangay justice system.

19. In collaboration with DIGNITY—Danish Institute against Torture and Balay Rehabilitation Center, in 2018 we published a short position paper finding answers to "Seven Essential Questions to Ask about the Philippine War on Drugs."

20. The work has been reported in Warburg 2017, Warburg and Jensen 2020a, Warburg and Jensen 2020b, Jensen and Hapal 2018, Hapal and Jensen 2017, and Jensen, Hapal, and Quijano 2020.

## 2. INTIMACY, POLICING, AND VIOLENT POLITICS IN BAGONG SILANG

A part of this chapter is adapted from Jensen, S., and K. Hapal, 2015, "Policing Bagong Silang: Intimacy and Politics in the Philippines," in *Policing and the Politics of Order-Making*, edited by P. Albrecht and H. Kyed, 24–39 (New York: Routledge).

1. We use the term "policing" to indicate that policing is a practice rather than only an institution and that more institutions are engaged in the act of policing than just the national police (Albrecht and Kyed 2015).

2. This approach draws on what Hansen and Stepputat (2001) have called the "ethnography of the state."

3. PHP50 equals approximately USD1.

4. Parallel to the Barangay Justice System, in 2007 the barangay captain in Bagong Silang also instituted the task force to be a rapid response team to assist purok leaders in cases of violence. The task force consists of twenty members who also perform adjudication as well as enforce by-laws on traffic and hawking.

5. See also chapter 4 for further elaboration on these emic concepts.

6. All policing structures must in some way pay tribute to the political masters. The PNP differs from the Barangay Justice System in that they have two masters to serve. Their salary comes from the national government through the Department of the Interior and Local Government (DILG). However, local governments are also able to "command" them. This happens through the right of the local government to hire and place police officers at will and to give them support in terms of vehicles; that is, their daily working lives are influenced by local political patrons.

7. As it happened, Echiverri did not manage to get his son elected. Rumor has it that he made peace with his family's main rival, Oca Malapitan. In the election in 2013, Oca became mayor whereas Recom took Oca's place in the Congress as representative for the Caloocan First District.

8. Later, in 2012, Erice also tried to topple Echiverri through the court system. He warned an official bureau investigating corruption that Echiverri had stolen pension money due to be paid to a fund. Echiverri was suspended for three months pending an investigation. However, the allegation backfired as Echiverri was exonerated and Erice had to abandon his ambitions. He was not even a contender in the 2013 election.

9. See https://drugarchive.ph/page/40-about-the-project for the Ateneo-led initiative and https://dahas.upd.edu.ph/ for the University of the Philippines initiative.

10. As one of a very few scholars, Anna Warburg managed to conduct fieldwork among the police in Bagong Silang. Her findings are revealing of the support enjoyed by the police of the war on drugs, something we return to in the next chapter. See Warburg 2017 as well as Warburg and Jensen 2020a and 2020b.

11. Riding in tandem is the emic description of many of the killings in which two, masked people on a motorbike carry out the killing. As the Melo report suggests, this has been a template for executions in the Philippines of land activists, unionists, and other protesting against domination (Asian Human Rights Commission 2006).

12. This account is pieced together from interviews conducted by Mong Palatino (2019), Anna Warburg, and Steffen Jensen, as well as police and media reports.

13. The fraternity mentioned in the reports is Scouts Royale Brotherhood (SEB), a subdivision of Alpha Phi Omega (APO) which traditionally has recruited especially from high schools and the less prestigious colleges. The other fraternity might have been the Triskelion Grand Fraternity, which we describe in chapter 6. At least, when we returned to Phase 8 in May, Triskelion were present in large numbers. As chapter 6 will illustrate, we cannot think of the fraternities as drug gangs; rather individual members of the fraternities in Bagong Silang may have problems with drugs. It is in the very core of fraternity ideology to combat drugs and discipline addicts. As one brod explained about the fraternal version of Tokhang: "Of course we discuss in meetings about the Tokhang. We go chapter by chapter by chapter and try to identify who might be in trouble with drugs. We talk to them and we maybe also talk to the purok and we try to find out about what should be done." This shows why we should critically engage with the discourse of "gang-related drug dealing."

14. This way of exorcizing guilt can also be found in many gang-related conflicts. For instance, in Cape Town, mothers would insist that their sons were not involved in gangs

and that gang violence emanated from the outside by noting that "our boys just sit on the steps" (Jensen 2008).

15. Personal communication with Anna Warburg during supervision and field report meetings, February 2017.

16. Methodologically, and facilitated by Balay, Anna came to the field through formal channels in the Barangay and the police, whereas Steffen followed networks established a decade earlier and consisting in no small measure by people with links to the fraternities and neighbors in the area in which he lived. In this way, Anna was probably more exposed to people who supported the war whereas the opposite might be true for Steffen's contacts.

17. The tricycle is one of the major modes of public transportation in the Philippines. It is built by attaching a motorcycle to a sidecar. Tricycles are partly regulated by local governments in coordination with the tricycle operators and drivers association (TODA).

## 3. POLICE VIOLENCE AND CORRUPTION IN THE WAR ON DRUGS AND BEFORE

This chapter is a revised version of Jensen, S., and K. Hapal, 2018, "Police Violence and Corruption in the Philippines: Violent Exchange and the War on Drugs," *Journal of Current Southeast Asian Affairs* 37 (2): 39–62.

1. Graeber (2011) writes, "It is only by the threat of sticks, ropes, spears and guns that one can tear people out of those endlessly complicated webs of relationship with others (sisters, friends, rivals . . .) that render them unique, and thus reduce them to something that can be traded" (208).

2. This is, of course, similar to what Loïc Wacquant (2008a) describes as "territorial stigmatization."

3. We are grateful to the anonymous reviewer for pointing this out to us.

4. Years later we asked Karl about the event. At first, he couldn't remember it. Then his face lit up: "Yeah, now I remember. But that's just the way it is," he concluded.

5. A haunting illustration of this process can be followed in Brilliante Mendoza's 2016 film *Ma'Rosa*.

6. This goes against the conclusions from the victimization survey we conducted in 2010 (Jensen, Hapal, and Modvig 2013), in which people indicated that it was not ok for the police to beat up suspects. We tend to think that respondents in the survey probably thought it was the right thing to oppose police violence rather than speak their minds regarding the victimizability of robbers. Hence, one woman noted in conversation, "It's ok they are beaten up. They are bad people." This reading is also supported by Curato (2016) and Kusaka (2017a).

7. This is due to a Republic Act (RA 9344), also called the Juvenile Justice Act of 2006, that stipulates that minors under the age of eighteen cannot be detained in jail but rather must be put into youth shelters. However, as the shelters are mostly full, the youngsters are often released.

8. This echoes police complaints about human rights across the world. People in every country use almost identical words to describe their opposition to human rights. For South Africa, see Marks 2005 and Hornberger 2011.

9. The idea of the thin blue line is shared in many policing organizations across the world, as is the notion that violence is necessary to carry out what they see as their duty (Hornberger 2011; Steinberg 2008; Jensen 2008).

10. See reports by Human Rights Watch (2017) and reports from the UN Special Rapporteur for Extra-Judicial Killings Agnes Callamard (Gamil 2017). While our own analysis from Bagong Silang backs up the reports, the government might be correct in

suggesting that the UN and international organizations have been narrow-minded in identifying the police as the ultimate perpetrators. Our material suggests that there is great uncertainty about the identity of the perpetrators. Hence, it cannot be ruled out that other violent networks are involved, taking advantage of the war on drugs to settle other scores.

11. The fieldwork took place during the siege of the city of Marawi, the stronghold of the Maute brothers, who had affiliated themselves with IS (Banlaoi 2019). This initiated another round of hostility against Muslims among most of our informants in Bagong Silang.

12. Elsewhere we have explored how the war on drugs and gangs in Cape Town produced constant attempts to "read" the social terrain (Jensen 1999). Helene Risør (2010), working in Bolivia, shows how people constantly look for clues to be able to protect themselves from the next criminal activity. Even potential signs like white cars on the road or stones in particular patterns might be indications of criminal intent that people try to assess to stay safe.

## 4. THE VIOLENT PRODUCTION OF URBAN DIVIDES

1. This chapter draws on and adapts some of the analyses previously published in Jensen, Hapal, and Modvig 2013 and Jensen, Hapal, and Quijano 2020.

2. Shabu (Crystal Meth) is said to stave off hunger and fight fatigue during long working days of up to seventeen hours for a jeepney driver, for instance.

3. This claim is corroborated by a study conducted by PhilRights, which profiled victims of the war on drugs (Philippine Human Rights Information Center 2018).

4. Elsewhere, we describe Emilio's case and others in more detail (Jensen, Hapal, and Quijano 2020).

5. Much has been written about urban development and displacement in Manila. However, as we are primarily concerned with the production of Bagong Silang, we will not engage this discussion in much detail. For more recent discussions, see Berner 1997, 2000; Ortega 2012, 2016; Arcilla 2018; and especially Garrido 2019. See also Jensen, Hapal and Quijano (2020) for an account that situates Bagong Silang displacement and resettlement within the greater framework of Manila urban politics.

6. Needless to say, this did not end evictions or squatting. As Berner 2000 shows, Manila grew annually at around 5 percent. Constant battles between squatters and government and private landholders have been the norm in Manila for decades (Ortega 2012; Berner 1997; Garrido 2019; Jensen, Hapal, and Quijano 2020).

7. The provision of "thin shell houses" was the initial housing and site development model used in Bagong Silang. This model entailed the provision of pit privies (i.e., toilets) and core housing structures to the relocatees. The building materials given by the local NHA, however, were insufficient. Due to its disastrous implementation, the provision of thin shell houses was largely abandoned by 1989. Consequently, the NHA introduced the Mortgage Take-Out (MTO) Program, in which the government partnered with a private contractor to provide low-cost housing and financing options to the relocatees. The ensuing partnership with private developers proved to be anomalous and poorly executed, leaving residents with substandard or unfinished houses. Subsequent site development projects, particularly at the outskirts of the Bagong Silang Resettlement Project, included the building of medium-rise condominiums. By 1995, through RA 7999, 50 hectares of land reserved for the NHC and 70 hectares of the 130 hectares reserved for the leprosarium (for a total of 120 hectares) was declared as alienable and disposable land for housing and sites. This prompted another wave of demolition, resettlement, and building of houses. By 2000, through Proclamation 366, the 50 hectares out of the

remaining 60 hectares reserved for the leprosarium was declared by then President Estrada as alienable and disposable land for housing sites.

8. In her book *In the Wake,* Christina Sharpe (2016) discusses how we can think of historical processes and their importance for contemporary politics by looking at transatlantic slavery. She argues that even centuries after, many African Americans are still confined in "the hold of the ship" (14). As such, there are no necessary expiry dates of historical processes. It depends whether we can still identify processes that relate directly to the historical process.

9. See also Jefferson, Turner, and Jensen 2019 for an analysis of stuckness across sites of detention, camps, and ghettos.

10. We draw inspiration to the concept of backyarders from our work in South African resettlement sites or townships. Backyarders are those, opposed to frontyarders, who cannot claim privileged access to plots or houses but who have to move from place to place. Struggle emerges around access to sanitation, sleeping quarters, entrances, or just the noise children of backyarders might make.

11. This process of consecutive displacement and resettlement is not a unique Manila phenomenon. The same process can be followed in Sudhir Venkatesh's seminal 2009 study *American Project: The Rise and Fall of the American Ghetto,* which studied how the Robert Taylor homes emerged as a result of a resettlement on the South Side of Chicago only for their inhabitants to be displaced again when the ghetto "failed" and the land on which it stood became too valuable for poor people to stay there.

12. Carey critiques the use of trust as an indicator of real communal life, which often finds its way into literature on, for instance, social capital and also inspired the wording and questions in our survey in Bagong Silang.

13. This clearly reminds us of Janet Roitman's 2006 analysis of what she calls the "ethics of illegality."

14. In cases where the offence is punishable by more than one-year imprisonment or fines exceeding P5,000, the police must take over. Even in such cases, the complainant must have a letter from the purok leader to report the matter to the police.

15. Offences concerning children under the age of eighteen are dealt with by the Barangay Council for the Protection of Children (BCPC).

16. The following two cases are selected from among the sixteen thousand cases reported to the purok leaders.

17. Vergilio Enriquez (1977) writes that his exploration into indigenous philosophy "has led to the identification of the value pakikipagkapwa [being with others] which is surely more important than pakikisama. The barkada (peer group) would not be happy with the walang pakisama but the Philippine society at large cannot accept the walang kapwa tao. Pakikipagkapwa is both a paninindigan (conviction) and a value.... Pakikisama is a form of pakikipagkapwa but not the other way around" (6–7). Our intention here is not to dispute the analysis by Enriquez, but simply to say that pakikipagkapwa is not used on the streets of Bagong Silang whereas pakikisama is.

18. Theoretically, this is called an empty signifier (Laclau, 1996a, 1996b) within discourse analysis. It denotes that particular signifiers do not exist in a one-to-one relationship to the signified, that is, the object that it describes. The concept, like, for instance, the concept of community or national identity, is contested to the degree where it loses its self-evident meaning. Hence, there is a constant struggle in order to fill the concept with particular meaning.

19. For a similar analysis on the concept of community in South Africa and India, see Jensen 2004 and Agraval 2003, respectively.

20. In an insightful review of Matthew Carey's (2017) theory of mistrust, Maya Mayblin (2019) suggests that in fact what Carey is describing is how the sociality of mistrust

cannot be separated from mistrust among men, and hence Carey, Mayblin asserts, is actually describing structures of patriarchy. In many ways, this resembles Bagong Silang, where the dominance of patriarchal gerontocracy does not spell less conflict. Rather, conflicts and mistrust are structures organized around a patriarchal sociality.

21. Arguably, at the time of writing Covid-19 policing has inspired a new round of violent disregard for poor people.

22. Maricel illustrated that women can also be "good at pakikisama." However, she often assumed male forms of comportment, not least constantly occupying public spaces. Furthermore, her husband, while running the cockfights in the block, was able as well to ensure her position in the path walk. In this way, it makes sense to think about dominant forms of masculinity as part of a hierarchy of masculinity where, as Connell (1995) asserts, dominant masculinity is the form that allows patriarchy to perpetuate itself. Arguably, Maricel was part of ensuring the continuation of patriarchy in the path walk.

## 5. COMMUNITY ACTIVISM

1. By 1987, an all-out war against so-called communist insurgents and their allies was launched (Hedman and Sidel 2000). This crackdown led to 6,130 cases of human rights violations with 20,591 individual victims (Task Force Detainees of the Philippines 2006).

2. The most important split was between what are referred to as the affirmists and the rejectionists. In 1992, José Maria Sison issued what he called an affirmation of basic strategy, which was an affirmation of Maoist dogma about waging war from the countryside. Together with the NPA's decision not to partake in electoral politics, the split weakened fundamentally the support not least in the urban centers. For elaboration, see Abinales 1996, 2005.

3. This is the point of view of a range of prominent observers like Benedict Anderson (1998) and John Sidel (1999), who argue that the post-Marcos government, for all its promises, in practice reinstated patronage elite politics.

4. Bibingka is a type of rice cake in the Philippines. It is cooked in a terra-cotta pot exposed to heat from both the top and the bottom.

## 6. FRATERNITY DENIED

This is a reworked version of Jensen, S., (2018). "A World of Significance: Equality, Ritual and Violence in a Manila Fraternity," in *Sporadically Radical: Ethnographies of Organized Violence and Militant Mobilization*, edited by S. Jensen and H. Vigh, 147–165 (Copenhagen: Museum Tusculanum).

1. See, for instance, Abinales 1996; Rutten 2008; Caouette 2004.

## 7. THE WAR ON DRUGS AND BEYOND

1. See, for instance, Amnesty International 2017.

2. For Latin America, see, for instance, Rodgers 2009; Hume 2007; Feltran 2010. For South Africa, see Standing 2006; Jensen 2010.

3. See Jensen 2010 for an analysis of the war on gangs as counterinsurgency in South Africa.

4. This section draws on and is detailed further in Warburg and Jensen 2020b.

5. See Roitman 2004 for a similar analysis of putatively "weak states" in Africa.

6. Steffen first learned about salvaging in a survey where around half of the seventy-five participants in the pilot survey independently noted "salvaging' when asked what was the worst crime in their area. Hence, police killings were present in the minds of people long before the war on drugs. In the actual survey, we changed the question to a public health–relevant inquiry about the crime perceived to have the greatest frequency.

# References

Abinales, Patricio. 1996. *The Revolution Falters: The Left in Philippine Politics after 1986.* Ithaca: Cornell University Press.

Abinales, Patricio. 2005. *State and Society in the Philippines.* Oxford: Rowman and Littlefield Publishers.

Adam, Jeroen, Joel Ariate Jr., and Elinor May Cruz. 2019. "Violence, Human Rights, and Democracy in the Philippines." *Kasarinlan: Philippine Journal of Third World Studies* 34, nos. 1–14.

Adam, Jeroen, Boris Verbrugge, and Dorien van den Boer. 2014. "Hybrid Systems of Conflict Management and Community-Level Efforts to Improve Local Security in Mindanao." *Justice and Security Research Programme Paper* 13.

Agamben, Giorgio. 1998. *Homo Sacer: Sovereign Power and Bare Life.* Stanford, CA: Stanford University Press.

Agrawal, Arun. 2003. "State Formation in Community Spaces? Decentralization of Control over Forests in the Kumaon Himalaya, India." *Journal of Asian Studies* 60: 1–32.

Albrecht, Pete, and Helene Maria Kyed. 2015. "Introduction: Policing and the Politics of Order-Making on the Urban Margins." In *Policing and the Politics of Order-Making*, edited by Peter Albrecht and Helene Kyed, 1–23. London: Routledge.

Alexander, Michelle. 2011. "The New Jim Crow." *Ohio State Journal of Criminal Law* 9, no. 1: 7–26.

Alinsky, Saul. 1971. *Rules for Radicals: A Practical Primer for Realistic Radicals.* New York: Vintage Books.

Altez, Jesus, and Kloyde Caday. 2017. "The Mindanaoan President." In *A Duterte Reader: Critical Essays on Rodrigo Duterte's Early Presidency*, edited by Nicole Curato, 111–26. Quezon City: Ateneo de Manila University Press.

American Academy of Allergy, Asthma, and Immunology. 2020. "Autoimmune Disease Definition." https://www.aaaai.org/conditions-and-treatments/conditions -dictionary/autoimmune-disease.

Amnesty International. 2017. "'If You Are Poor, You Are Killed': Extrajudicial Executions in the Philippines' 'War on Drugs.'" Report. Amnesty International, London.

Amoore, Louise, and Marieke de Goede. 2008. "Transactions after 9/11: The Banale Face of the Preemptive Strike." *Transactions of the Institute of British Geographers* 33: 173–85.

Anderson, Benedict. 1998. "Cacique Democracy in the Philippines." In *The Spectre of Comparison: Nationalism. Southeast Asia and the World*, edited by Benedict Anderson, 192–226. London: Verso.

Anderson, Benedict. 2006. *Imagined Communities: Reflections on the Origins and Spread of Nationalism.* 6th edition, London: Verso.

Arcilla, Chester. 2018. "Producing Empty Socialized Housing: Privatizing Gains, Socializing Costs, and Dispossessing the Filipino Poor." *Social Transformations: Journal of the Global South* 6, no. 1: 77–105.

Arias, Enrique Desmond. 2006. "The Dynamics of Criminal Governance: Networks and Social Order in Rio de Janeiro." *Journal of Latin American Studies* 38, no. 2: 293–325.

Asian Development Bank. 2009. "Background Notes on the Philippine Justice System." Asian Development Bank, Mandalyong City.

Asian Human Rights Commission (AHRC). 2006. "Appendix 2: The Melo Report." http://www.humanrights.asia/resources/journals-magazines/article2/0601-2 /appendix-ii-the-melo-commission-report.

Asian Human Rights Commission (AHRC). 2007. "The Criminal Justice System of the Philippines Is Rotten." http://alrc.asia/article2/2007/02/the-criminal-justice-system -of-the-philippinesis-rotten.

Austin, Timothy. 1999. *Banana Justice: Field Notes on Philippine Crime and Custom.* Westport, CT: Praeger Publishers.

Auyero, Javier, and Fernanda Berti. 2016. *In Harm's Way: The Dynamics of Urban Violence.* Princeton: Princeton University Press.

Bach, Natasha. 2018. "Trump's Reported Stance on Executing Drug Dealers Is His Latest Nod to the Philippines' Authoritarian Leader." *Fortune,* February 26. https:// fortune.com/2018/02/26/trump-death-penalty-capital-punishment-drug -dealers-duterte/.

Balay Rehabilitation Center and DIGNITY—Danish Institute against Torture. 2018. "Seven Essential Questions to Ask about the Philippine War on Drugs—Answers from Bagong Silang, Metro Manila." https://www.dignity.dk/wp-content/uploads /SEVEN-ESSENTIAL-QUESTIONS-TO-ASK-ABOUT-THE-PHILIPPINE-WAR -ON-DRUGS_digital.pdf.

Baldwin, Clare, and Andrew R. C. Marshall. 2017. "How a Secretive Police Squad Racked Up Kills in Duterte's Drug War." Reuters, December 19. https://www .reuters.com/investigates/special-report/philippines-drugs-squad/.

Balibar, Etienne. 1998. "Ideality, Violence and Cruelty." *New Formations* 35: 7–18.

Balibar, Etienne. 2001. "Outlines of a Topography of Cruelty: Citizenship and Civility in the Era of Global Violence." *Constellations* 8, no. 1: 15–29.

Bankoff, Greg. 1996. *Crime, Society, and the State in the Nineteenth-Century Philippines.* Quezon City: Ateneo University Press.

Banlaoi, Rommel. 2010. "CAFGUs, CVOs and the Maguindanao Massacre." *Autonomy and Peace Review* 6, no. 1: 61–78.

Banlaoi, Rommel. 2019. *The Marawi Siege and Its Aftermath: The Continuing Terrorist Threat.* Cambridge: Cambridge Scholars Publishing.

Barber, Pauline. 2000. "Agency in Philippine Women's Labour Migration and Provisional Diaspora." *Women's Studies International Forum* 23, no. 4: 399–411.

Benjamin, Walter. 2018. *Critique de la violence.* Paris: Éditions Payot.

Berlant, Laurent. 1998. "Intimacy: A Special Issue." *Critical Inquiry* 24, no. 2: 281–88.

Berner, Erhard. 1997. *Defending a Place in the City: Localities and the Struggle for Urban Land in Metro Manila.* Quezon City: Ateneo de Manila University Press.

Berner, Erhard. 2000. "Poverty Alleviation and the Eviction of the Poorest: Towards Urban Land Reform in the Philippines." *International Journal of Urban and Regional Research* 24, no. 3: 554–66.

Bloch, Maurice. 1991. *Prey into Hunter: The Politics of Religious Experience.* Cambridge: Cambridge University Press.

Böhme, Gernot. 2016. *The Aesthetics of Atmospheres.* London: Routledge.

Borras, Saturnino. 1998. *The Bibingka Strategy to Land Reform and Implementation: Autonomous Peasant Mobilizations and State Reformists in the Philippines.* The Hague: Institute of Social Studies.

Bourgois, Philippe. 2003. *In Search of Respect: Selling Crack in El Barrio*. Cambridge: Cambridge University Press.

Bourgois, Philippe. 2004. "US Inner City Apartheid and the War on Drugs: Crack among Homeless Heroin Addicts." In *Unhealthy Health Policy: A Critical Anthropological Examination*. Edited by Arachu Castro and Merill Singer, 303–13. Lanham, MD: Altamira Press.

Bourgois, Philippe. 2015. "Insecurity, the War on Drugs, and Crimes of the State: Symbolic Violence in the Americas." In *Violence at the Urban Margins*, edited by Javcier Auyero, Philippe Bourgois, and Nancy Schepers-Hughes, 305–21. Oxford: Oxford University Press.

Butler, Judith. 1993. *Bodies That Matter: On the Discursive Limits of Sex*. New York: Routledge.

Butler, Judith. 2004. *Precarious Life: The Powers of Mourning and Violence*. New York: Verso.

Buur, Lars, and Steffen Jensen. 2004. "Introduction: Vigilantism and the Policing of Everyday Life in South Africa." *African Studies* 63, no. 2: 139–52.

Buzan, Barry, Ole Wæver, and Jaap De Wilde. 1998. *Security: A New Framework for Analysis*. Boulder, CO: Lynne Rienner Publishers.

Cannell, Fanella. 1999. *Power and Intimacy in the Christian Philippines*. Cambridge: Cambridge University Press.

Caouette, Dominique. 2004. "Persevering Revolutionaries: Armed Struggle in the 21st Century: Exploring the Revolution of the Communist Party of the Philippines." Ph.D dissertation, Cornell University.

Carey, Matthew. 2017. *Mistrust: An Ethnographic Theory*. London: Hau Books.

Caroll, John. 1998. "Philippine NGOs Confront Urban Poverty." In *Organizing for Democracy: NGOs, Civil Society and the Philippine State*, edited by Sydney Silliman and Lela Noble, 113–37. Honolulu: University of Hawai'i Press.

Cayabyab, Marc Jayson. 2017. "CHR Asks Ombudsman to Probe Tondo Secret Detention Cell." *Philippine Daily Inquirer*, May 10. https://newsinfo.inquirer.net/895871/chr-asks-ombudsman-to-probe-tondo-secret-detention-cell.

Choudhury, Zahid, Steffen Jensen, and Toby Kelly. 2018. "Counting Torture: Towards the Translation of Robust, Useful, and Inclusive Human Rights Indicators." *Nordic Journal of Human Rights* 36, no 2: 132–50.

Comaroff, Jean, and John Comaroff. 2008. *Of Revelation and Revolution*. Vol. 1, *Christianity, Colonialism and Consciousness in South Africa*. Chicago: University of Chicago Press.

Cone, Allen. 2017. "Duterte Resumes Police's War on Drugs in the Philippines." *UPI*, February 28. https://www.upi.com/Top_News/World-News/2017/02/28/Duterte-resumes-polices-war-on-drugs-in-Philippines/5181488297974.

Connell, Robert W. 1995. *Masculinities*. Berkeley: University of California Press.

Constantino, Renato. 1978. *The Philippines: The Continuing Past*. Manila: Foundation for Nationalist Studies.

Coronel, Sheila. 2017. "Murder as Enterprise: Police Profiteering in Duterte's War on Drugs." In *A Duterte Reader: Critical Essays on Rodrigo Duterte's Early Presidency*, edited by Nicole Curato, 167–98. Ithaca: Cornell University Press.

Crenshaw, Karen. 1990. "Mapping the Margins: Intersectionality, Identity Politics and Violence Against Women of Color." *Stanford Law Review* 43: 1241–1299.

Curato, Nicole. 2016. "Politics of Anxiety, Politics of Hope: Penal Populism and Duterte's Rise to Power." *Journal of Current Southeast Asian Affairs* 35, no. 3: 91–109.

Curato, Nicole. 2017a. *A Duterte Reader: Critical Essays on Rodrigo Duterte's Early Presidency*. Ithaca: Cornell University Press.

Curato, Nicole. 2017b. "Flirting with Authoritarian Fantasies? Rodrigo Duterte and the New Terms of Philippine Populism." *Journal of Contemporary Asia* 47, no. 1: 142–53.

Dangerous Drugs Board. 2015. "2015 Nationwide Survey on the Nature and Extent of Drug Abuse in the Philippines." Republic of the Philippines.

Das, Veena. 2007. *Life and Words: Violence and the Descent into the Ordinary.* Berkeley: University of California Press.

Das, Veena, and Deborah Poole. 2004. "State and Its Margins: Comparative Ethnographies." In *Anthropology in the Margins of the State*, edited by Veena Das and Deborah Poole, 3–33. New Delhi: Oxford University Press.

David, Randy. 1988. "The Role of International Development Agencies." *Kasarinlan: Philippine Journal of Third World Studies* 8, no. 2: 21–24.

David, Randy. 2016. "Dutertismo." *Philippine Daily Inquirer,* May 1. https://opinion.inquirer.net/94530/dutertismo.

de Campos, Cicero. 1983. "The Role of the Police in the Philippines: A Study from the Third World." Ph.D. dissertation, Michigan State University.

Derrida, Jacques. 2003. *Rogues: Two Essays on Reason.* Translated by Pascale Anne-Brault and Michael Nas. Stanford, CA: Stanford University Press.

de Sardan, Jean Pierre Olivier. 1999. "A Moral Economy of Corruption in Africa?" *Journal of Modern African Studies* 37, no. 1: 25–52.

de Sardan, Jean Pierre Olivier. 2005. *Anthropology and Development: Understanding Contemporary Social Change.* London: Zed Books.

De Silva, Mary, Trudy Harpham, Tran Tuan, Rosario Bartolini, Mary Penny, and Sharon Huttly. 2006. "Psychometric and Cognitive Validation of a Social Capital Measurement Tool in Peru and Vietnam." *Social Science and Medicine* 62, no. 4: 941–53.

Doherty, John. 1985. "The Philippine Urban Poor." *Occasional Papers* 8, University of Hawai'i, Philippine Studies Program.

Elias, Norbert. 1994. *The Civilizing Process: The History of Manners and State Formation and Civilization.* Translated by Edmund Jephcott. Oxford: Blackwell.

Enriquez, Virgilio. 1977. "Filipino Psychology in the Third World." *Philippine Journal of Psychology* 10, no. 1: 3–16.

Enriquez, Virgilio. 1993. "Developing a Filipino Psychology." In *Indigenous Psychologies: Research and Experience in Cultural Context*, edited by Uichol Kim and John Berry, 152–69. Newbury Park, CA: Sage Publications.

Feldman, Alan. 1991. *Formations of Violence: The Narrative of the Body and Political Terror in Northern Ireland.* Chicago: University of Chicago Press.

Feltran, Gabriel de Santis. 2010. "The Management of Violence on the São Paulo Periphery: The Repertoire of Normative Apparatus in the PCC Era." *VIBRANT—Vibrant Virtual Brazilian Anthropology* 7, no. 2: 109–34.

Foucault, Michel. 2012. *Discipline and Punish: The Birth of the Prison.* London: Vintage, 2012.

Freire, Paolo. 1984. *Pedagogy of the Oppressed.* Translated by Myra Bergman-Ramos. New York: Continuum.

Fuller, Ken. 2007. *The Lost Vision: The Philippine Left 1986–2010.* Quezon City: University of the Philippines Press.

Galupo, Rey. 2016. "Cops Eyed in Caloocan Barangay Chairman's Slay." *Philippine Star,* June 27. https://www.philstar.com/metro/2016/06/27/1596966/cops-eyed-caloocan-barangay-chairmans-slay.

Gamil, Jaymee. 2017. "Callamard: War on Drugs Doesn't Work in Any Country." *Philippine Daily Inquirer,* May 6. https://globalnation.inquirer.net/156149/callamard-war-drugs-doesnt-work-country.

Garcia, Robert. 2001. *To Suffer Thy Comrades: How the Revolution Decimated Its Own.* Manila: Anvil Publishing.

Garrido, Marco Z. 2019. *The Patchwork City: Class, Space, and Politics in Metro Manila.* Chicago: University of Chicago Press.

Gavilan, Jodezs. 2018. "Seeking Justice for Kian delos Santos." *The Rappler.* https://www.rappler.com/newsbreak/iq/timeline-justice-trial-kian-delos-santos.

Goodfellow, Aron, and Sameena Mulla. 2008. "Compelling Intimacies: Domesticity, Sexuality, and Agency." *Home Cultures* 5, no 3: 257–69.

Graeber, David. 2011. *Debt: The First 5,000 Years.* London: Penguin UK.

Green, Linda. 1994. *Fear as a Way of Life: Mayan Widows in Rural Guatemala.* New York: Columbia University Press.

Guerrero, Amado. 1972. *Philippine Society and Revolution.* Quezon City: Bandilang Pula Publications.

Gutang, Robert. 1991. *Pulisya: The Inside Story of the Demilitarization of Law Enforcement in the Philippines.* Quezon City: Daraga Press.

Hansen, Thomas, and Finn Stepputat. 2001. *States of Imagination: Ethnographic Explorations of the Postcolonial State.* Durham, NC: Duke University Press.

Hapal, Karl. 2017. "Interrogating Community Organizing in an Urban Poor Community: The Case of Bagong Silang, Caloocan City." Master's dissertation, University of the Philippines, Diliman.

Hapal, Karl. 2019. "Engaging the Trolls: Reactions of 'Netizen' and Philippine Human Rights Organizations on Extrajudicial Killings." In *Exploring the Nexus between Technologies and Human Rights: Opportunities and Challenges in Southeast Asia,* edited by Ying Hooi and Deasy Simandjuntak. Bangkok: Strengthening Human Rights and Peace Research/Education in ASEAN–Southeast Asia Programme (SHAPE-SEA): 185–209.

Hapal, Karl. 2021. "The Philippines' COVID-19 Response: Securitising the Pandemic and Disciplining the Pasaway." *Journal of Current Southeast Asian Affairs* (2021): 1868103421994261.

Hapal, Karl, and Steffen Jensen. 2017. "The Morality of Corruption: A View from the Police in the Philippines." In *Corruption and Torture: Violent Exchange and the Everyday Policing of the Poor,* edited by Steffen Jensen and Morten Andersen. Aalborg, Denmark: Aalborg University Press: 39–68.

Haraway, Donna. "A manifesto for cyborgs: Science, technology, and socialist feminism in the 1980s." *Australian Feminist Studies* 2, no. 4 (1987): 1–42.

Hedman, Eva-Lotta, and John Sidel. 2000. *Philippine Politics and Society in the Twentieth Century: Colonial Legacies, Post-Colonial Trajectories.* London: Routledge.

Herzfeld, Michael. 2014. *Cultural Intimacy: Social Poetics in the Nation-State.* New York: Routledge.

Hindess, Barry. 2001. "The Liberal Government of Unfreedom." *Alternatives* 26, no. 2: 93–111.

Hirslund, Dan. 2012. "Sacrificing Youth: Maoist Cadres and Political Activism in Post-War Nepal." PhD dissertation, University of Copenhagen.

Højer, Lars, Anja Kublitz, Stine S. Puri, and Andreas Bandak. 2018. "Escalations: Theorizing Sudden Accelerating Change." *Anthropological Theory* 18, no. 1: 36–58.

Hollnsteiner, Mary Racelis. 1963. *The Dynamics of Power in a Philippine Municipality (No. 7).* University of the Philippines, Community Development Research Council.

Holston, John. 2009. *Insurgent Citizenship: Disjunctions of Democracy and Modernity in Brazil.* Princeton: Princeton University press.

Honculada, Jurgette. 1985. "Case Study: ZOTO and the Twice-Told Story of Philippine Community Organizing." *Kasarinlan* 1, no. 2: 13–24.

Hornberger, Julia. 2011. *Policing and Human Rights: The Meaning of Violence and Justice in the Everyday Policing of Johannesburg.* London: Routledge.

Human Rights Watch. 2017. "'License to Kill': Philippine Police Killings in Duterte's 'War on Drugs.'" Report. Human Rights Watch, New York.

Hume, Mo. 2007. "Mano Dura: El Salvador Responds to Gangs." *Development in Practice* 17, no. 6: 739–51.

Hutchcroft, Paul. 1998. *Booty Capitalism: The Politics of Banking in the Philippines.* Ithaca: Cornell University Press.

Hutchcroft, Paul, and Joel Rocamora. 2003. "Strong Demands, Weak Institutions: The Origins and Evolution of the Democratic Deficit in the Philippines." *Journal of East Asian Studies* 3: 259–292.

Ileto, Reynaldo Clemeña. 1997. *Pasyon and Revolution: Popular Movements in the Philippines, 1840–1910.* Honolulu: University of Hawaii Press.

Ileto, Reynaldo Clemeña. 2001. "Orientalism and the Study of Philippine Politics." *Philippine Political Science Journal* 22: 1–32.

Jefferson, Andrew, Simon Turner, and Steffen Jensen. 2019. "Introduction: On Stuckness and Sites of Confinement." *Ethnos* 84, no. 1: 1–13.

Jensen, Steffen. 1999. "Discourses of Violence: Coping with Violence on the Cape Flats." *Social Dynamics* 25, no. 2: 75–97.

Jensen, Steffen. 2004. "Claiming Community: Local Politics on the Cape Flats, South Africa." *Critique of Anthropology* 24, no. 2: 179–207.

Jensen, Steffen. 2008. *Gangs, Politics and Dignity in Cape Town.* Oxford: James Currey.

Jensen, Steffen. 2010. "The Security and Development Nexus in Cape Town: War on Gangs, Counterinsurgency and Citizenship." *Security Dialogue* 41, no. 1: 77–97.

Jensen, Steffen. 2012. "Shosholoza: Political Culture in South Africa between the Secular and the Occult." *Journal of Southern African Studies* 38, no. 1: 91–106.

Jensen, Steffen. 2014. "Stunted Future: Buryong among Young Men in Manila." In *Ethnographies of Youth and Temporality*, edited by Anne Line Dalsgard, Martin Frederiksen, Susanne Hojlund and Lotte Meinert. Philadelphia: Temple University Press.

Jensen, Steffen. 2015a. "Between Illegality and Recognition: Exploring Sacrificial Violence in a Manila Brotherhood." *Critique of Anthropology* 35, no. 1: 64–77.

Jensen, Steffen. 2015b. "Corporealities of Violence: Rape and the Shimmering of Embodied and Material Categories in South Africa." *Critical African Studies* 7, no. 2: 99–117.

Jensen, Steffen. 2018. "A World of Significance." In *Sporadically Radical: Ethnographies of Organized Violence and Militant Mobilization*, edited by Steffen Jensen and Henrik Vigh. Copenhagen: Museum Tusculanum.

Jensen, Steffen, Morten Andersen, Kari Larsen, and Line Hansen. 2017. "Introduction: Towards Violent Exchange." In *Corruption and Torture: Violent Exchange and the Everyday Policing of the Poor,* edited by Steffen Jensen and Morten Andersen, 5–38. Aalborg, Denmark: Aalborg University Press.

Jensen, Steffen, and Karl Hapal. 2015. "Policing Bagong Silang: Intimacy and Politics in the Philippines." In *Policing and the Politics of Order-Making*, edited by Peter Albrecht and Helene Kyed, 24–39. New York: Routledge.

Jensen, Steffen, and Karl Hapal. 2018. "Police Violence and Corruption in the Philippines: Violent Exchange and the War on Drugs." *Journal of Current Southeast Asian Affairs* 37, no. 2: 39–62.

Jensen, Steffen, Karl Hapal, and Jens Modvig. 2013. "Violence in Bagong Silang." Report. DIGNITY, International Series on Torture and Organized Violence, Copenhagen.

Jensen, Steffen, Karl Hapal, and Salome Quijano. 2020. "Reconfiguring Manila: Displacement, Resettlement, and the Productivity of Urban Divides." *Urban Forum* 31, no. 3: 389–407.

Jensen, Steffen, and Henrik Ronsbo. 2014. *Histories of Victimhood*. Philadelphia: University of Pennsylvania Press.

Jensen, Steffen, and Henrik Vigh. 2018. *Sporadically Radical: Ethnographies of Organized Violence and Militant Mobilization*. Copenhagen: Museum Tusculanum.

Jocano, F. Landa. 1976. *Slum as a Way of Life: A Study of Coping Behavior in an Urban Environment*. Quezon City: University of the Philippines Press.

Johnson, David, and Jon Fernquest. 2018. "Governing through Killing: The War on Drugs in the Philippines." *Asian Journal of Law and Society* 5, no. 2: 359–90.

Kapferer, Bruce. 2010. "Introduction: In the Event—Toward an Anthropology of Generic Moments." *Social Analysis* 54, no. 3: 1–27.

Karaos, Anne Marie. 1993. "Manila's Squatter Movement: A Struggle for Place and Identity." *Philippine Sociological Review* 41, no. 1: 71–91.

Kerkvliet, Benjamin. 1995. "Towards a More Comprehensive Analysis of Philippine Politics: Beyond the Patron-Client, Factional Framework." *Journal of Southeast Asian Studies* 26, no. 2: 401–19.

Kerkvliet, Benjamin. 2002a. *Everyday Politics in the Philippines: Class and Status Relations in a Central Luzon Village*. Lanham, MD: Rowman and Littlefield.

Kerkvliet, Benjamin. 2002b. *The Huk Rebellion: A Study of Peasant Revolt in the Philippines*. Lanham, MD: Rowman and Littlefield.

Kilcullen David. 2010. *Counterinsurgency*. Oxford: Oxford University Press.

Kusaka, Wataru. 2017a. "Bandit Grabbed the State: Duterte's Moral Politics." *Philippine Sociological Review* 65: 49–75.

Kusaka, Wataru. 2017b. *Moral Politics in the Philippines: Inequality, Democracy and the Urban Poor*. Singapore: NUS Press.

Laclau, Ernesto. 1996a. "The Death and Resurrection of the Theory of Ideology." *Journal of Political Ideologies* 1, no. 3: 201–20.

Laclau, Ernesto. 1996b. *Emancipation(s)*. London: Verso.

Lamchek, Jason. 2017. "A Mandate for Mass Killings? Public Support for Duterte's War on Drugs." In *A Duterte Reader: Critical Essays on Rodrigo Duterte's Early Presidency*, edited by Nicole Curato, 199–218. Quezon City: Ateneo University Press.

Landé, Carl. 1965. *Leaders, Factions, and Parties: The Structure of Philippine Politics*. New Haven: Yale University Press.

Lopa, Consuela. 2003. *The Rise of Philippine NGOs in Managing Development Assistance*. New York: Synergos Institute.

Lund, Christian. 2006. "Twilight Institutions: Public Authority and Local Politics in Africa." *Development and Change* 37, no. 4: 685–705.

Lynch, Frank. 1962. "Philippine Values II: Social Acceptance." *Philippine Studies* 10, no. 1: 82–99.

Malakunas, Karl. 2017. "'You Are Corrupt to the Core,' Duterte Tells Cops." ABS-CBN News, January 30. https://news.abs-cbn.com/focus/01/30/17/you-are-corrupt-to-the-core-duterte-tells-cops.

Marks, Monique. 2005. *Transforming the Robocops: Changing Police in South Africa*. Durban: University of KwaZulu-Natal Press.

Mauss, Marcel. 1966. *The Gift: The Form and Functions of Exchange in Archaic Societies*. London: Cohen and West.

Mayblin, Maya. 2019. "The Anarchic Institution." *Anthropology of this Century* 24. http://aotcpress.com/articles/anarchic-institution.

Mbembe, Achille. 1992. "Provisional Notes on the Postcolony." *Africa* 62, no. 1: 3–37.

Mbembe, Achille. 2001. *On the Postcolony*. Berkeley: University of California Press.

Mbembé, Achille, and Libby Meintjes. 2003. "Necropolitics." *Public Culture* 15, no. 1: 11–40.

McCarthy, Niall. 2018. "The World's Most Overcrowded Prison Systems." *Forbes*, January 26. https://www.forbes.com/sites/niallmccarthy/2018/01/26/the-worlds-most-overcrowded-prison-systems-infographic/#7b1eeff11372.

McCoy, Alfred. 1994. *An Anarchy of Families: State and Society in the Philippines*. Madison: University of Wisconsin Press.

McCoy, Alfred. 2009. *Policing America's Empire: The United States, the Philippines, and the Rise of the Surveillance State*. Madison: University of Wisconsin Press.

McCuen, John. 1966. *The Art of Counter-Revolutionary War*. London: Faber and Faber.

Mercado, Eliseo. 2010. "The Maguindanao Massacre and the Making of the Warlords." *Autonomy and Peace Review* 6, no. 1: 11–32.

Mosse, David. 2004. *Cultivating Development: An Ethnography of Aid Policy and Practice*. London: Pluto Press.

Mutiarin, Daya, Queenie Tomaro, and David Almarez. 2019. "The War on Drugs of the Philippines and Indonesia: A Literature Review." *Southeast Asia* 9, no. 1: 41–59.

Narag, Raymond, 2009. "Inside the Brotherhood." December 10. http://raymundnarag. wordpress.com/category/social-advocacy/fraternity-violence-social-advocacy/.

Ortega, Arnisson. 2012. "Spatialities of Population Change, Mega-urbanization and Neoliberal Urbanism: The Case of Metro Cebu." *Philippine Population Review* 11, no. 1: 41–71.

Ortega, Arnisson. 2016. *Neoliberalizing Spaces in the Philippines: Suburbanization, Transnational Migration, and Dispossession*. Quezon City: Ateneo de Manila Press.

Oswin, Natalie. 2010. "Governing Intimacy." *Environment and Planning D: Society and Space* 28: 60–67.

Palatino, Mong. 2019. "Tokhang in North Caloocan: Weaponizing Local Governance, Social Disarticulation, and Community Resistance." *Kasarinlan: Philippine Journal of Third World Studies* 34, nos. 1–2: 15–41.

Pe-Pua, Rogelia, and Elizabeth Protacio-Marcelino. 2000. "Sikolohiyang Pilipino (Filipino Psychology): A Legacy of Virgilio G. Enriquez." *Asian Journal of Social Psychology* 3, no. 1: 49–71.

Philippine Human Rights Information Center. 2010. "Without a Roof above Their Heads." Quezon City: Philippine Human Rights Information Center.

Philippine Human Rights Information Center. 2018. "The War on the Poor: Extrajudicial Killings and their Effects on Urban Poor Families and Communities." https://www.philrights.org/the-war-on-the-poor-extrajudicial-killings-and-their-effects-on-urban-poor-families-and-communities.

Philippine National Police (PNP). 2018. "Towards a Drug-Cleared Philippines: #RealNumbersPH Year 2—From July 1, 2016 to August 31, 2018." http://www.pnp.gov.ph/images/News/2018/RealNumbers/rn_83118.pdf.

Philippine Human Rights Information Center (PhilRights). 2019. "The Killing State: The Unrelenting War against Human Rights in the Philippines. https://www.philrights.org/the-killing-state-the-unrelenting-war-against-human-rights/.

Philstar. 2017. "PDEA: Philippines has 4.7 M drug users." Published May 4, 2017. http://www.philstar. com/headlines/2017/05/04/1696547/pdea-philippines-has-4.7-m-drug-users.

Pinches, Michael. 1991. "The Working Class Experience of Shame, Inequality, and People Power in Tatalon, Manila." In *From Marcos to Aquino: Local Perspectives* on *Political Transition in the Philippines*, edited by Ben Kerkvliet and Resil Majores, 311–24. Quezon City: Ateneo de Manila University Press.

Pinches, Michael. 1997. "Elite Democracy, Development and People Power: Contending Ideologies and Changing Practices in Philippine Politics." *Asian Studies Review* 21, nos. 2–3: 104–20.

Porio, Emma. 2016. "Citizen Participation and Decentralization in the Philippines." In *Citizenship and Democratization in Southeast Asia*, edited Ward Berenschot, Henk Nordholt, and Laurens Bakker, 31–50. Leiden: Brill Open.

Povinelli, Elizabeth. 2011. *Economies of Abandonment: Social Belonging and Endurance in Late Liberalism*. Durham, NC: Duke University Press.

Pratt, Geraldine, Caleb Johnston, and Vanessa Banta. 2017. "Filipino Migrant Stories and Trauma in the Transnational Field." *Emotion, Space and Society* 24: 83–92.

Punongbayan, C. 2017. "Why Duterte's '4 Million Drug Users' Is Statistically Improbable." https:// www.rappler.com/thought-leaders/170975-duterte-drug-users-statistically-improbable.

Quimpo, Nathan. 2008. *Contested Democracy and the Left in the Philippines after Marcos*. Quezon City: Ateneo de Manila University Press.

Quimpo, Nathan. 2009. The Philippine Predatory Regime, Growing Authoritarian Features, *The Pacific Review*, 22 (3), pp. 335–353.

Quimpo, Nathan. 2017. "Duterte's War on Drugs." In *A Duterte Reader: Critical Essays on Rodrigo Duterte's Early Presidency*, edited by Nicole Curato, 111–26. Quezon City: Ateneo de Manila University Press.

Racelis, Mary, Anne-Marie Karaos, and Skilty Labastilla. 2016. "Identifying Options for an Urban Community-Driven Development Program in the Philippines." Department of Social Welfare and Development website: https://ncddp.dswd.gov.ph/Media/uploads/2016_Racelis_et_al_Identifying_Options_for_Urban_CDD.pdf.

Rafael, Vicente. 2000. *White Love and Other Events in Filipino History*. Durham, NC: Duke University Press.

Rafael, Vicente. 2016. "Duterte's Hobbesian World." *Philippine Daily Inquirer*, June 13 Https://opinion.inquirer.net/dutertes-hobbesian-world.

Ramirez, Robertzon. 2016. "Caloocan Barangay Chief Gunned Down." *Philippine Star*, June 26. https://www.philstar.com/metro/2016/06/26/1596704/caloocan-barangay-chief-gunned-down.

Reis, Harry, and Philip Shaver. 1988. "Intimacy as an Interpersonal Process." In *Handbook of Personal Relationships: Theory, Research and Interventions*, edited by Steve Duck, Dale Hay, Stevan Hobfoll, William Ickes, and Barbara Montgomery, 367–89. Hoboken, NJ: John Wiley and Sons.

Reyes, Danilo Andres. 2016. "The Spectacle of Violence in Duterte's 'War on Drugs.'" *Journal of Current Southeast Asian Affairs* 35, no. 3: 111–37.

Risør, Helene. 2010. "Twenty Hanging Dolls and a Lynching: Defacing Dangerousness and Enacting Citizenship in El Alto, Bolivia." *Public Culture* 22, no. 3: 465–85.

Roces, Mina. 2000. "Kinship politics in Post-War Philippines: The Lopez family, 1945–1989." *Modern Asian Studies* 34, no. 1: 181–221.

Rodgers, Dennis. 2009. "Slum Wars of the 21st Century: Gangs, Mano Dura and the New Urban Geography of Conflict in Central America." *Development and Change* 40, no. 5: 949–76.

Rodgers, Dennis, and Steffen Jensen. 2015. "The Problem with Templates: Learning from Organic Gang-Related Violence Reduction." *Stability: International Journal of Security and Development* 4, no. 1: 1–16.

Roitman, Janet. 2004. "Productivity in the Margins." In *Anthropology in the Margins of the State*, edited by Veena Das and Deborah Poole, 191–224. Oxford: James Currey.

Roitman, Janet. 2006. "The Ethics of Illegality in the Chad Basin." In *Law and Order in the Postcolony*, edited by Jean Comaroff and John Comaroff, 247–72. Chicago: University of Chicago Press: Chicago.

Romero, Alexis. 2020. "Hold Me Responsible for Drug War Deaths—Duterte." Philippine Star, Oct. 21. https://www.philstar.com/headlines/2020/10/21/2051155/hold-me-re sponsible-drug-war-deaths-duterte?utm_campaign=677a3a08ff-Arangkada _News%E2%80%A6%00%00.

Roxas, Joseph. 2018. "PNP Official Sacked over Kian Slay Returns as HPG chief." *GMA News*, June 4. https://www.gmanetwork.com/news/news/nation/655650/pnp-official-sacked-over-kian-slay-returns-as-hpg-chief/story.

Rutten, Rosanne. 2008. *Brokering a Revolution: Cadres in a Philippine Insurgency*. Quezon City: Ateneo de Manila University Press.

Santos, Paz. 2010. "The Communist Front: Protracted People's War and Counter-insurgency in the Philippines (Overview)." In *Primed and Purposeful: Armed Groups and Human Security Efforts in the Philippines*, edited by Diana Rodriguez, 17–42. Geneva: Small Arms Survey.

Santos, Tina. 2018. "25,000 Trees for 25,000 Dead in Homicides, War on Drugs." *Philippine Daily Inquirer*, August 25. https://newsinfo.inquirer.net/1021371/25000-tree s-for-25000-dead-in-homicides-war-on-drugs.

Schirmer, Jennifer. 1998. *The Guatemalan Military Project: A Violence Called Democracy*. Philadelphia: University of Pennsylvania Press.

Scott, James. 1985. *Weapons of the Weak*. Yale University Press, 2008.

Scott, Walther. 1994. *Barangay: Sixteenth-Century Philippine Culture and Society*. Quezon City: Ateneo University Press.

Serrano Cornelio, Jayeel. 2017. "Religion and Civic Engagement: The Case of Iglesia Ni Cristo in the Philippines." *Religion, State and Society* 45, no. 1: 23–38.

Sharpe, Christina. 2016. *In the Wake: On Blackness and Being*. Durham, NC: Duke University Press.

Shatkin, Gavin. 2007. *Collective Action and Urban Poverty Alleviation: Community Organizations and the Struggle Struggle*. Aldershot, UK: Ashgate Publishing.

Sidel, John. 1999. *Capital, Coercion and Crime: Bossism in the Philippines*. Stanford, CA: Stanford University Press.

Silliman, Sidney, and Lela Noble. 1998. Introduction. In *Organizing for Democracy: NGOs, Civil Society and the Philippine State*, edited by Sydney Silliman and Lela Noble, 3–25. Quezon City: Ateneo de Manila University Press.

Simon, Jonathan. 2007. *Governing through Crime: How the War on Crime Transformed American Democracy and Created a Culture of Fear*. Oxford: Oxford University Press.

Singh, Bhrigupati. 2011. "Agonistic Intimacy and Moral Aspiration in Popular Hinduism: A Study in the Political Theology of the Neighbor." *American Ethnologist* 38, no. 3: 430–50.

Social Weather Stations. 2017. "90% Say It Is Important That Drug Suspects Be Captured Alive." https://www.sws.org.ph/swsmain/artcldisppage/?artcsyscode=ART-20 171005100742.

Social Weather Stations. 2019. "Second Quarter 2019 Social Weather Survey: Net Satisfaction With Anti-Illegal Drugs Campaign at "Excellent" +70." Sept. 22. https://www.sws.org.ph/swsmain/artcldisppage/?artcsyscode=ART-20190922154614.

Soon, Chuan Yean. 2012. "Hidden Transcripts from 'Below' in Rural Politics of the Philippines: Interpreting the Janus-facedness of Patron-Client Ties and Tulong (Help)." *Southeast Asian Studies* 1, no. 2: 273–99.

Spivak, Gayatri Chakravorty. 1988. Can the Subaltern Speak? In C. Nelson & L. Grossberg (Eds.), *Marxism and Interpretation of Culture*. Urbana: University of Illinois Press, 271–315.

Standing, André. 2006. *Organised Crime: A Study from the Cape Flats*. Pretoria, South Africa: Institute for Security Studies.

Steinberg, Jonny. 2008. *Thin Blue: The Unwritten Rules of South African Policing*. Johannesburg, SA: Jonathan Ball.

Stoler, Ann Laura. 2013. *Along the Archival Grain: Epistemic Anxieties and Colonial Common Sense*. Princeton: Princeton University Press.

Stoler, Ann Laura. 2016. *Duress: Imperial Durabilities in Our Times*. Durham, NC: Duke University Press.

Strathern, Marilyn. 1988. *The Gender of the Gift: Problems with Women and Problems with Society in Melanesia*. Berkeley: University of California Press.

Strathern, Marilyn. 1992. "Qualified Value: The Perspective of Gift Exchange." In *Barter, Exchange and Value: An Anthropological Approach*, edited by Humphrey, Caroline and Stephen Hugh-Jones, 169–91. Cambridge: Cambridge University Press.

Syrett, Nicholas. 2009. *The Company He Keeps: A History of White College Fraternities*. Chapel Hill: University of North Carolina Press.

Tadiar, Neferti. 2004. *Fantasy Production: Sexual Economies and Other Philippine Consequences for the New World Order*. Hong Kong: Hong Kong University Press.

Tadiar, Neferti. 2007. Metropolitan Life and Uncivil Death. *PMLA* 122, no. 1: 316–20.

Tadiar, Neferti. 2009. *Things Fall Away: Philippine Historical Experience and the Makings of Globalization*. Durham, NC: Duke University Press.

Tadiar, Neferti. 2013. "Life-Times of Disposability within Global Neoliberalism." *Social Text* 31, no. 2: 19–48.

Tau Gamma Phi, 2012a. "About the Tau Gamma Phi Fraternity and Tau Gamma Sigma Sorority." http://www.taugamma.info/about-the-tau-gamma-phi-fraternity.html.

Tau Gamma Phi. 2012b. "History of Fraternities in the Philippines." http://www.taugamma.info/The-History-of-Philippine-Fraternities-in-the-Philippines.html.

Teehankee, Julio. 2001. "Emerging Dynasties in the Post-Marcos House of Representatives." *Philippine Political Science Journal* 22: 55–78.

Thiranagama, Sharika, and Toby Kelly. 2010. *Traitors: Suspicion, Intimacy and the Ethics of State-Building*. Philadelphia: University of Pennsylvania Press.

Thiranagama, Sharika, Toby Kelly, and Carlos Forment. 2018. "Introduction: Whose Civility?" *Anthropological Theory* 18. nos. 2–3: 153–74.

Thompson, Mark. 2016. "Bloodied Democracy: Duterte and the Death of Liberal Reformism in the Philippines." *Journal of Current Southeast Asian Affairs* 35, no. 3: 39–68.

Tidwell, Alan. 2016. "Duterte, Mindanao, and Political Culture." *Asia Pacific Bulletin*, no. 362. https://www.eastwestcenter.org/publications/duterte-mindanao-and-political-culture.

Turner, Victor. 1995. *The Ritual Process: Structure and Anti-Structure*. New York: Aldine de Gruyter.

United Nations Office on Drugs and Crime (UNODC). 2017. "World Drug Report 2017." New York: United Nations.

Valente, Catherine. 2017. "PNP Stops 'Tokhang,' Starts Cleanup." *Manila Times*, January 31. https://www.manilatimes.net/2017/01/31/news/top-stories/pnp-stops-tokhang-starts-cleanup/309811/.

Van Gennep, Arnold. 2004. *The Rites of Passage*. London: Routledge.

Van Naerssen, Ton. 1993. "Squatter Access to Land in Metro Manila." *Philippine Studies,* 40 (1): 3–20.

Varona, Glenn. 2010. "Politics and Policing in the Philippines: Challenges to Police Reform." *The Flinders Journal of History and Politics* 26: 102–25.

Venkatesh, Sudhir. 2009. *American Project: The Rise and Fall of a Modern Ghetto*. Cambridge, MA: Harvard University Press.

Vigh, Henrik. 2009. "Motion Squared: A Second Look at the Concept of Social Navigation." *Anthropological Theory* 9, no. 4: 419–38.

VOA News. 2017. "Jails, Justice System Strained as Philippine Drug War Intensifies." https://www.voanews.com/east-asia-pacific/jails-justice-system-strained-philippine-drug-war-intensifies.

Wacquant, Löic. 1998. "'Inside the "Zone": The Social Art of the Hustler in the American Ghetto.'" *Theory, Culture and Society* 15, no. 2: 1–36.

Wacquant, Löic. 2008a. "Territorial Stigmatization in the Age of Advanced Marginality." In *Symbolic Power in Cultural Contexts: Uncovering Social Reality*, edited by Jarmo Houtsonen and Ari Antikainen, 43–52. Leiden: Brill Sense.

Wacquant, Löic. 2008b. *Urban Outcasts: A Comparative Sociology of Advanced Marginality*. London: Polity.

Wacquant, Löic. 2009. *Punishing the Poor: The Neoliberal Government of Social Insecurity*. Durham, NC: Duke University Press.

Walters, Willam. 2008. "Editor's Introduction: Anti-Policy and Anti-Politics: Critical Reflections on Certain Schemes to Govern Bad Things." *European Journal of Cultural Studies* 11, no. 3: 267–88.

Warburg, Anna. 2017. "Policing in the Philippine 'War on Drugs': (In)Security, Morality and Order in Bagong Silang." Master's dissertation, Aarhus University, Denmark.

Warburg, Anna, and Steffen Jensen. 2020a. "Ambiguous Fear in the War on Drugs: A Reconfiguration of Social and Moral Orders in the Philippines." *Journal of Southeast Asian Studies* 51, nos. 1–2: 5–24.

Warburg, Anna, and Steffen Jensen. 2020b. "Policing the War on Drugs and the Transformation of Urban Space in Manila." *Environment and Planning D: Society and Space* 38, no. 3: 399–416.

Weiner, Anette. 1992. *Inalienable Possessions: The Paradox of Keeping-While-Giving*. Berkeley: University of California Press.

Wittgenstein, Ludwig. 1953. *Philosophical Investigations*. Oxford: Blackwell Publishing.

Zarco, Ricardo, and Donal Shoemaker. 2000. "Report on Student Organization Conflicts, University of the Philippines. Diliman, 1991–1998." Quezon City: University of the Philippines.

# Index

Figures are indicated by f.